Beginning Spring Boot 3

Build Dynamic Cloud-Native Java Applications and Microservices

Second Edition

K. Siva Prasad Reddy
Sai Upadhyayula

Apress®

Beginning Spring Boot 3: Build Dynamic Cloud-Native Java Applications and Microservices

K. Siva Prasad Reddy
Hyderabad, India

Sai Upadhyayula
Rotterdam, The Netherlands

ISBN-13 (pbk): 978-1-4842-8791-0
https://doi.org/10.1007/978-1-4842-8792-7

ISBN-13 (electronic): 978-1-4842-8792-7

Managing Director, Apress Media LLC: Welmoed Spahr
Acquisitions Editor: Steve Anglin
Development Editor: Laura Berendson
Coordinating Editor: Gryffin Winkler
Copy Editor: Mary Behr

Cover designed by eStudio Calamar

Cover image designed by Freepik (www.freepik.com)

Distributed to the book trade worldwide by Apress Media, LLC, 1 New York Plaza, New York, NY 10004, U.S.A. Phone 1-800-SPRINGER, fax (201) 348-4505, e-mail orders-ny@springer-sbm.com, or visit www.springeronline.com. Apress Media, LLC is a California LLC and the sole member (owner) is Springer Science + Business Media Finance Inc (SSBM Finance Inc). SSBM Finance Inc is a **Delaware** corporation.

For information on translations, please e-mail booktranslations@springernature.com; for reprint, paperback, or audio rights, please e-mail bookpermissions@springernature.com.

Apress titles may be purchased in bulk for academic, corporate, or promotional use. eBook versions and licenses are also available for most titles. For more information, reference our Print and eBook Bulk Sales web page at www.apress.com/bulk-sales.

Any source code or other supplementary material referenced by the author in this book is available to readers on GitHub (github.com/apress). For more detailed information, please visit www.apress.com/source-code.

Printed on acid-free paper

Table of Contents

About the Authors

Siva Prasad Reddy Katamareddy is a software architect with 16 years of experience in building scalable distributed enterprise applications. He has worked in banking and e-commerce domains using Java, Kotlin, GoLang, Spring Boot, JPA/Hibernate, microservices, REST APIs, SQL, and NoSQL databases. His current technical focus is on modern architectures, including microservices, CI/CD, and DevOps, as well as infrastructure automation using Jenkins, Terraform, AWS CDK, and Pulumi.

Sai Subramanyam Upadhyayula is a passionate software engineer who likes to share his knowledge about Java and Spring Boot through his blog and YouTube Channel, "Programming Techie." He has experience working with a variety of technologies including Java, Kotlin, Typescript, Spring Boot, JPA/Hibernate, MongoDB, Angular, and Golang. He also dabbles with DevOps-related activities by working with Jenkins and AWS.

About the Technical Reviewer

Preethi Vasudev earned an MS in Computer Information Systems and Cyber Security from Auburn University, Alabama. She is an Oracle-certified Java 8 programmer with more than 15 years of industry experience in investment banking, healthcare, and other areas. She is interested in Java and related technologies and enjoys participating in coding competitions.

Acknowledgments

I would like to thank my wife, Neha Jain, and my family members for their continuous support all the days I spent writing this book.

I would like to express my gratitude to the Apress team, specifically to Steve Anglin and Mark Powers, for their continuous support throughout the journey. I would also like to thank the reviewers for providing valuable feedback that helped improve the quality of the content.

Siva Prasad Reddy Katamareddy

I would like to thank and dedicate this to my lovely wife, Sowmya, for her continuous support and my father, Phani Kumar, my mother, Malliswari, and my sister, Anusha.

I would like to also thank Mark Powers and Shonmirin for their continuous support and patience throughout the journey. Special thanks also to the reviewers for the valuable feedback.

Sai Subramanyam Upadhyayula

Introduction

Spring is the most popular Java-based framework for building enterprise applications. The Spring Framework provides a rich ecosystem of projects to address modern application needs, like security, simplified access to relational and NoSQL datastores, batch processing, integration with social networking sites, and large volumes of data streams processing. As Spring is a very flexible and customizable framework, there are usually multiple ways to configure an application. Although it is a good thing to have multiple options, it can be overwhelming for beginners. Spring Boot addresses this "Spring applications need complex configuration" problem by using its powerful autoconfiguration mechanism.

Spring Boot is an opinionated framework following the "convention over configuration" approach, which helps build Spring-based applications quickly and easily. The main goal of Spring Boot is to help you quickly create Spring-based applications without requiring you to write the same boilerplate configuration again and again.

In recent years, the microservices architecture has become the preferred architecture style for building complex enterprise applications. Spring Boot is a great choice for building microservices-based applications using various Spring Cloud modules.

This book will help you understand what Spring Boot is, how Spring Boot helps you build Spring-based applications quickly and easily, and the inner workings of Spring Boot using easy-to-follow examples.

What This Book Covers

This book covers the following topics:

- What is Spring Boot and how does it improve developer productivity?
- How does Spring Boot autoconfiguration work behind the scenes?
- How do you create custom Spring Boot starters?

- Working with databases using JdbcTemplate, MyBatis, JOOQ, and Spring Data JPA

- Working with the MongoDB NoSQL database

- Developing web applications using Spring Boot and Thymeleaf

- Developing reactive web applications using Spring WebFlux and R2DBC

- Developing REST APIs using Spring Boot

- Developing a GraphQL API using Spring Boot

- Securing web applications using SpringSecurity and OAuth2

- Monitoring Spring Boot applications with Spring Boot Actuator

- Testing Spring Boot applications

- Developing Spring Boot applications in Groovy, Scala, and Kotlin

- Running Spring Boot applications in the Docker container

- Running Spring Boot applications natively using Spring Native

What You Need for This Book

To follow the examples in this book, you must have the following software installed:

- JDK 17

- Your favorite IDE

  - Spring Tool Suite

  - IntelliJ IDEA

  - NetBeans IDE

- Build tools

  - Maven

  - Gradle

- Database server
  - MySQL
  - PostgreSQL

Source Code

All source code used in this book can be downloaded from `github.com/apress/`
`beginning-spring-boot-3`.

## CHAPTER 1

Introduction to Spring Boot

The Spring Framework is a popular and widely used Java framework for building web and enterprise applications. Spring, at its core, is a dependency injection container that provides flexibility to configure beans in multiple ways, such as XML, Annotations, and JavaConfig. Over the years, the Spring Framework has grown exponentially by addressing the needs of modern business applications like security, support for NoSQL datastores, handling big data, batch processing, integration with other systems, and more. Along with its subprojects, Spring has become a viable platform for building enterprise applications.

The Spring Framework is very flexible and provides multiple ways of configuring application components. With rich features combined with various configuration options, configuring Spring applications becomes complex and error prone. The Spring team created Spring Boot to address configuration complexity through its powerful AutoConfiguration mechanism.

This chapter takes a quick look at the Spring Framework. You'll develop a web application using Spring MVC and JPA the traditional way (without Spring Boot). Then you will look at the pain points of the conventional way and see how to develop the same application using Spring Boot.

Overview of the Spring Framework

If you are a Java developer, there is a good chance that you have heard about the Spring Framework and have used it in your projects. The Spring Framework was created primarily as a dependency injection container, but it is much more than that. Spring is famous for several reasons:

1

K. S. P. Reddy and S. Upadhyayula, *Beginning Spring Boot 3*, https://doi.org/10.1007/978-1-4842-8792-7_1

- Spring's dependency injection approach encourages writing testable code.

- Easy-to-use and powerful database transaction management capabilities

- Spring simplifies integration with other Java frameworks, like the JPA/ Hibernate ORM and JooQ.

- State-of-the-art Web MVC framework for building web applications

Along with the Spring Framework, many other Spring subprojects help build applications that address modern business needs:

- **Spring Data:** Simplifies data access from relational and NoSQL datastores

- **Spring Batch:** Provides a powerful batch-processing framework

- **Spring Security:** Robust security framework to secure applications

- **Spring Cloud:** Provides a set of tools for developers to implement common distributed system patterns like Service Discovery, Configuration Management, Circuit Breaker, and more

- **Spring Integration:** An implementation of enterprise integration patterns to facilitate integration with other enterprise applications using lightweight messaging and declarative adapters

There are many other interesting projects addressing various other modern application development needs. For more information, take a look at `https://spring.io/projects`.

Spring Configuration Styles

Spring initially provided an XML-based approach for configuring beans. Later, Spring introduced XML-based DSLs, Annotations, and JavaConfig-based approaches for configuring beans. Listings 1-1 through 1-3 show each of those configuration styles.

Listing 1-1. Example of an XML-Based Configuration

```xml
<bean id="userService" class="com.apress.myapp.service.UserService">
    <property name="userDao" ref="userDao"/>
</bean>
<bean id="userDao" class="com.apress.myapp.dao.JdbcUserDao">
    <property name="dataSource" ref="dataSource"/>
</bean>
<bean id="dataSource" class="org.apache.commons.dbcp.BasicDataSource"
destroy-method="close">
    <property name="driverClassName" value="com.mysql.jdbc.Driver"/>
    <property name="url" value="jdbc:mysql://localhost:3306/test"/>
    <property name="username" value="root"/>
    <property name="password" value="secret"/>
</bean>

<!-- DSL based configuration  -->
<beans>
    <jee:jndi-lookup id="entityManagerFactory" jndi-name="persistence/
    defaultPU"/>
</beans>
```

Listing 1-2. Example of an Annotation-Based Configuration

```java
@Service
public class UserService
{
    private final UserDao userDao;
    public UserService(UserDao dao){
        this.userDao = dao;
    }
    ...
    ...
}
@Repository
public class JdbcUserDao
{
    private final DataSource dataSource;
```

```
    public JdbcUserDao(DataSource dataSource){
        this.dataSource = dataSource;
    }
    ...
    ...
}
```

Listing 1-3. Example of a JavaConfig-Based Configuration

```
@Configuration
public class AppConfig
{
    @Bean
    public UserService userService(UserDao dao){
        return new UserService(dao);
    }
    @Bean
    public UserDao userDao(DataSource dataSource){
        return new JdbcUserDao(dataSource);
    }
    @Bean
    public DataSource dataSource(){
        BasicDataSource dataSource = new BasicDataSource();
        dataSource.setDriverClassName("com.mysql.jdbc.Driver");
        dataSource.setUrl("jdbc:mysql://localhost:3306/test");
        dataSource.setUsername("root");
        dataSource.setPassword("secret");
        return dataSource;
    }
}
```

Spring provides multiple approaches for configuring application components. You can use JavaConfig- and Annotation-based configuration styles in the same application. That is a lot of flexibility, which is good and bad. People new to the Spring Framework may get confused about which approach to follow.

The Spring community suggests you follow the JavaConfig-based approach, as it gives you more flexibility. But there is no one-size-fits-all kind of solution. You have to choose the approach based on your own application needs.

Now that you've had a glimpse of how various styles of Spring Bean configurations look, you'll take a quick look at the configuration of a typical SpringMVC and JPA/Hibernate-based web application.

Developing a Web Application Using SpringMVC and JPA

Before getting to know Spring Boot and learning about its features, let's look at a typical Spring web application configuration and learn about the pain points. Then, you will see how Spring Boot addresses those problems.

The first thing to do is create a Maven project called **springmvc-jpa-demo** and configure all the dependencies required in the pom.xml file, as shown in Listing 1-4.

Listing 1-4. The pom.xml File

```
<?xml version="1.0" encoding="UTF-8"?>
<project xmlns="http://maven.apache.org/POM/4.0.0"
  xmlns:xsi="http://www.w3.org/2001/XMLSchema-instance"
  xsi:schemaLocation="http://maven.apache.org/POM/4.0.0
                http://maven.apache.org/maven-v4_0_0.xsd">
  <modelVersion>4.0.0</modelVersion>
  <groupId>com.apress</groupId>
  <artifactId>springmvc-jpa-demo</artifactId>
  <packaging>war</packaging>
  <version>1.0-SNAPSHOT</version>
  <name>springmvc-jpa-demo</name>

  <properties>
      <project.build.sourceEncoding>UTF-8</project.build.sourceEncoding>
      <maven.compiler.source>17</maven.compiler.source>
      <maven.compiler.target>17</maven.compiler.target>
      <failOnMissingWebXml>false</failOnMissingWebXml>
  </properties>
```

```
<build>
    <plugins>
        <plugin>
            <groupId>org.apache.maven.plugins</groupId>
            <artifactId>maven-war-plugin</artifactId>
            <version>3.3.2</version>
        </plugin>
        <plugin>
            <groupId>org.codehaus.cargo</groupId>
            <artifactId>cargo-maven3-plugin</artifactId>
            <version>1.9.13</version>
            <configuration>
                <container>
                    <containerId>tomcat10x</containerId>
                    <type>embedded</type>
                </container>
                <deployables>
                    <deployable>
                        <type>war</type>
                        <location>${project.build.directory}/${project.build.
                        finalName}.war</location>
                        <properties>
                            <context>/</context>
                        </properties>
                    </deployable>
                </deployables>
            </configuration>
        </plugin>
    </plugins>
</build>

<dependencies>
    <dependency>
        <groupId>org.springframework</groupId>
        <artifactId>spring-webmvc</artifactId>
        <version>5.3.21</version>
```

```xml
</dependency>
<dependency>
    <groupId>org.springframework.data</groupId>
    <artifactId>spring-data-jpa</artifactId>
    <version>2.7.1</version>
</dependency>
<dependency>
    <groupId>org.slf4j</groupId>
    <artifactId>jcl-over-slf4j</artifactId>
    <version>1.7.36</version>
</dependency>
<dependency>
    <groupId>org.slf4j</groupId>
    <artifactId>slf4j-api</artifactId>
    <version>1.7.36</version>
</dependency>
<dependency>
    <groupId>org.slf4j</groupId>
    <artifactId>slf4j-reload4j</artifactId>
    <version>1.7.36</version>
</dependency>
<dependency>
    <groupId>org.apache.logging.log4j</groupId>
    <artifactId>log4j-core</artifactId>
    <version>2.17.2</version>
</dependency>
<dependency>
    <groupId>com.h2database</groupId>
    <artifactId>h2</artifactId>
    <version>2.1.214</version>
</dependency>
<dependency>
    <groupId>org.apache.commons</groupId>
    <artifactId>commons-dbcp2</artifactId>
    <version>2.9.0</version>
</dependency>
```

```
<dependency>
    <groupId>mysql</groupId>
    <artifactId>mysql-connector-java</artifactId>
    <version>8.0.29</version>
</dependency>
<dependency>
    <groupId>org.hibernate</groupId>
    <artifactId>hibernate-entitymanager</artifactId>
    <version>5.6.10.Final</version>
</dependency>
<dependency>
    <groupId>javax.servlet</groupId>
    <artifactId>javax.servlet-api</artifactId>
    <version>3.1.0</version>
    <scope>provided</scope>
</dependency>
<dependency>
    <groupId>org.thymeleaf</groupId>
    <artifactId>thymeleaf-spring5</artifactId>
    <version>3.0.15.RELEASE</version>
</dependency>
    </dependencies>
</project>
```

All of the Spring MVC, Spring Data JPA, JPA/Hibernate, Thymeleaf, and Log4j dependencies are configured in the Maven pom.xml file. Also, it defines the maven-war-plugin and cargo-maven-plugin to run an embedded Tomcat container to save you the manual configuration of the Tomcat server to run your application.

Configure the service/DAO layer beans using JavaConfig, as shown in Listing 1-5.

Listing 1-5. The com.apress.demo.config.AppConfig.java File

```
package com.apress.demo.config;

import java.util.Properties;

import javax.persistence.EntityManagerFactory;
import javax.sql.DataSource;
```

8

```java
import org.apache.commons.dbcp2.BasicDataSource;
import org.springframework.beans.factory.annotation.Autowired;
import org.springframework.context.annotation.Bean;
import org.springframework.context.annotation.Configuration;
import org.springframework.context.annotation.PropertySource;
import org.springframework.context.support.
PropertySourcesPlaceholderConfigurer;
import org.springframework.core.env.Environment;
import org.springframework.core.io.ClassPathResource;
import org.springframework.data.jpa.repository.config.EnableJpaRepositories;
import org.springframework.instrument.classloading.
InstrumentationLoadTimeWeaver;
import org.springframework.jdbc.datasource.init.DataSourceInitializer;
import org.springframework.jdbc.datasource.init.ResourceDatabasePopulator;
import org.springframework.orm.hibernate5.HibernateExceptionTranslator;
import org.springframework.orm.jpa.JpaTransactionManager;
import org.springframework.orm.jpa.LocalContainerEntityManagerFactoryBean;
import org.springframework.orm.jpa.vendor.HibernateJpaVendorAdapter;
import org.springframework.transaction.PlatformTransactionManager;
import org.springframework.transaction.annotation.
EnableTransactionManagement;

@Configuration
@EnableTransactionManagement
@EnableJpaRepositories(basePackages="com.apress.demo.repositories")
@PropertySource(value = { "classpath:application.properties" })
public class AppConfig {

  @Autowired
  private Environment env;

  @Bean
  public static PropertySourcesPlaceholderConfigurer
  placeHolderConfigurer()
  {
      return new PropertySourcesPlaceholderConfigurer();
  }
```

```java
@Bean
public PlatformTransactionManager transactionManager()
{
    EntityManagerFactory factory = entityManagerFactory().getObject();
    return new JpaTransactionManager(factory);
}

@Bean
public LocalContainerEntityManagerFactoryBean entityManagerFactory()
{
    LocalContainerEntityManagerFactoryBean factory = new
    LocalContainerEntityManagerFactoryBean();

    HibernateJpaVendorAdapter vendorAdapter = new
    HibernateJpaVendorAdapter();
    vendorAdapter.setShowSql(Boolean.TRUE);

    factory.setDataSource(dataSource());
    factory.setJpaVendorAdapter(vendorAdapter);
    factory.setPackagesToScan(env.getProperty("packages-to-scan"));

    Properties jpaProperties = new Properties();
    jpaProperties.put("hibernate.hbm2ddl.auto", env.
    getProperty("hibernate.hbm2ddl.auto"));
    factory.setJpaProperties(jpaProperties);

    factory.afterPropertiesSet();
    factory.setLoadTimeWeaver(new InstrumentationLoadTimeWeaver());
    return factory;
}

@Bean
public HibernateExceptionTranslator hibernateExceptionTranslator()
{
    return new HibernateExceptionTranslator();
}
```

```
@Bean
public DataSource dataSource()
{
    BasicDataSource dataSource = new BasicDataSource();
    dataSource.setDriverClassName(env.getProperty("jdbc.driverClassName"));
    dataSource.setUrl(env.getProperty("jdbc.url"));
    dataSource.setUsername(env.getProperty("jdbc.username"));
    dataSource.setPassword(env.getProperty("jdbc.password"));
    return dataSource;
}

@Bean
public DataSourceInitializer dataSourceInitializer(DataSource dataSource)
{
    DataSourceInitializer dataSourceInitializer = new
    DataSourceInitializer();
    dataSourceInitializer.setDataSource(dataSource);
    ResourceDatabasePopulator databasePopulator = new
    ResourceDatabasePopulator();
    databasePopulator.addScript(new ClassPathResource(env.
    getProperty("init-scripts")));
    dataSourceInitializer.setDatabasePopulator(databasePopulator);
    dataSourceInitializer.setEnabled(Boolean.parseBoolean(env.
    getProperty("init-db", "false")));
    return dataSourceInitializer;
}
}
```

In the AppConfig.java configuration class, you do the following:

- Mark it as a Spring Configuration class using the @Configuration annotation.

- Enable annotation-based transaction management using @EnableTransactionManagement.

- Configure @EnableJpaRepositories to indicate where to look for Spring Data JPA repositories.

11

- Configure the PropertyPlaceHolder bean
  using the @PropertySource annotation and the
  PropertySourcesPlaceholderConfigurer bean definition, which
  loads properties from the application.properties file.

- Define beans for DataSource, JPA EntityManagerFactory, and
  JpaTransactionManager.

- Configure the DataSourceInitializer bean to initialize the database
  by executing the data.sql script on application start-up.

1. Now configure the property placeholder values in application.
   properties, as shown in Listing 1-6.

Listing 1-6. The src/main/resources/application.properties File

```
jdbc.driverClassName=com.mysql.jdbc.Driver
jdbc.url=jdbc:mysql://localhost:3306/test
jdbc.username=root
jdbc.password=admin
init-db=true
init-scripts=data.sql
hibernate.dialect=org.hibernate.dialect.MySQLDialect
hibernate.show_sql=true
hibernate.hbm2ddl.auto=update
packages-to-scan=com.apress.demo
```

2. Create a simple SQL script called data.sql to populate sample
   data into the USER table, as shown in Listing 1-7.

Listing 1-7. The src/main/resources/data.sql File

```
delete from user;
insert into user(id, name) values(1,'John');
insert into user(id, name) values(2,'Smith');
insert into user(id, name) values(3,'Siva');
```

3. Create the log4j.properties file with a basic configuration, as
   shown in Listing 1-8.

Listing 1-8. The src/main/resources/log4j.properties File

```
log4j.rootCategory=INFO, stdout
log4j.appender.stdout=org.apache.log4j.ConsoleAppender
log4j.appender.stdout.layout=org.apache.log4j.PatternLayout
log4j.appender.stdout.layout.ConversionPattern=%5p %t %c{2}:%L - %m%n
log4j.category.com.apress=DEBUG
log4j.category.org.springframework=INFO
```

4. Now configure the Spring MVC web layer beans such as
    ThymeleafViewResolver, static ResourceHandlers, and
    MessageSource for i18n, as shown in Listing 1-9.

Listing 1-9. The com.apress.demo.config.WebMvcConfig.java File

```
package com.apress.demo.config;

import org.springframework.context.MessageSource;
import org.springframework.context.annotation.Bean;
import org.springframework.context.annotation.ComponentScan;
import org.springframework.context.annotation.Configuration;
import org.springframework.context.support.
ReloadableResourceBundleMessageSource;
import org.springframework.web.servlet.config.annotation.
DefaultServletHandlerConfigurer;
import org.springframework.web.servlet.config.annotation.EnableWebMvc;
import org.springframework.web.servlet.config.annotation.
ResourceHandlerRegistry;
import org.springframework.web.servlet.config.annotation.WebMvcConfigurer;
import org.thymeleaf.spring5.SpringTemplateEngine;
import org.thymeleaf.spring5.templateresolver.
SpringResourceTemplateResolver;
import org.thymeleaf.spring5.view.ThymeleafViewResolver;

@Configuration
@ComponentScan(basePackages = {"com.apress.demo.web"})
@EnableWebMvc
public class WebMvcConfig implements WebMvcConfigurer {
```

```java
@Bean
public SpringResourceTemplateResolver templateResolver() {
    SpringResourceTemplateResolver templateResolver = new
    SpringResourceTemplateResolver();
    templateResolver.setPrefix("/WEB-INF/views/");
    templateResolver.setSuffix(".html");
    templateResolver.setTemplateMode("HTML5");
    templateResolver.setCacheable(false);
    return templateResolver;
}

@Bean
public SpringTemplateEngine templateEngine() {
    SpringTemplateEngine templateEngine = new SpringTemplateEngine();
    templateEngine.setTemplateResolver(templateResolver());
    return templateEngine;
}

@Bean
public ThymeleafViewResolver viewResolver() {
    ThymeleafViewResolver thymeleafViewResolver = new
    ThymeleafViewResolver();
    thymeleafViewResolver.setTemplateEngine(templateEngine());
    thymeleafViewResolver.setCharacterEncoding("UTF-8");
    return thymeleafViewResolver;
}

@Override
public void addResourceHandlers(ResourceHandlerRegistry registry) {
    registry.addResourceHandler("/resources/**").addResourceLocations
    ("/resources/");
}

@Override
public void configureDefaultServletHandling(DefaultServletHandlerConfigu
rer configurer) {
    configurer.enable();
}
```

```
@Bean(name = "messageSource")
public MessageSource messageSource() {
    ReloadableResourceBundleMessageSource messageSource = new
    ReloadableResourceBundleMessageSource();
    messageSource.setBasename("classpath:messages");
    messageSource.setCacheSeconds(5);
    messageSource.setDefaultEncoding("UTF-8");
    return messageSource;
}
}
```

In the WebMvcConfig.java configuration class, you do the following:

- Mark it as a Spring Configuration class using @Configuration annotation.

- Enable an annotation-based Spring MVC configuration using @EnableWebMvc.

- Configure ThymeleafViewResolver by registering the TemplateResolver, SpringTemplateEngine, and ThymeleafViewResolver beans.

- Register the ResourceHandlers bean to indicate requests for static resources. The URI /resources/** will be served from the /resources/ directory.

- Configure a MessageSource bean to load i18n messages from ResourceBundle messages_{country-code}.properties from the classpath.

5. Create the messages.properties file in the src/main/resources folder and add the following property:

   app.title=SpringMVC JPA Demo (Without SpringBoot)

6. Next, you register the Spring MVC FrontController servlet DispatcherServlet.

Note   Prior to the Servlet 3.x specification, you had to register servlets and filters in `web.xml`. Since the Servlet 3.x specification, you can register servlets and filters programmatically using `ServletContainerInitializer`. Spring MVC provides a convenient class called `AbstractAnnotationConfigDispatcherServletInitializer` to register `DispatcherServlet`.

Listing 1-10 shows how to configure the `SpringWebAppInitializer.java` class.

Listing 1-10.   The com.apress.demo.config.SpringWebAppInitializer.java File

```
package com.apress.demo.config;
import javax.servlet.Filter;
import org.springframework.orm.jpa.support.OpenEntityManagerInViewFilter;
import org.springframework.web.servlet.support.
AbstractAnnotationConfigDispatcherServletInitializer;
public class SpringWebAppInitializer extends
AbstractAnnotationConfigDispatcherServletInitializer
{
    @Override
    protected Class<?>[] getRootConfigClasses()
    {
        return new Class<?>[] { AppConfig.class};
    }
    @Override
    protected Class<?>[] getServletConfigClasses()
    {
        return new Class<?>[] { WebMvcConfig.class };
    }
    @Override
    protected String[] getServletMappings()
    {
        return new String[] { "/" };
    }
    @Override
```

```
protected Filter[] getServletFilters()
{
    return new Filter[]{ new OpenEntityManagerInViewFilter() };
}
}
```

In the `SpringWebAppInitializer.java` configuration class, you do the following:

- Configure `AppConfig.class` as `RootConfirationClasses`, which will become the parent `ApplicationContext` that contains bean definitions shared by all child (`DispatcherServlet`) contexts.

- Configure `WebMvcConfig.class` as `ServletConfigClasses`, which is the child `ApplicationContext` that contains `WebMvc` bean definitions.

- Configure `/` as `ServletMapping`, which means that all the requests will be handled by `DispatcherServlet`.

- Register `OpenEntityManagerInViewFilter` as a servlet filter so that you can lazy-load the JPA entity lazy collections while rendering the view.

7. Create a JPA entity user and its Spring Data JPA Repository interface `UserRepository`. Create a JPA entity called `User.java`, as shown in Listing 1-11, and a Spring Data JPA repository called `UserRepository.java`, as shown in Listing 1-12.

Listing 1-11. The com.apress.demo.domain.User.java File

```
package com.apress.demo.domain;
import jakarta.persistence.*;
@Entity
public class User
{
    @Id @GeneratedValue(strategy=GenerationType.AUTO)
    private Integer id;
    private String name;
    public User()
    {
    }
```

```
    public User(Integer id, String name)
    {
        this.id = id;
        this.name = name;
    }
    public Integer getId()
    {
        return id;
    }
    public void setId(Integer id)
    {
        this.id = id;
    }
    public String getName()
    {
        return name;
    }
    public void setName(String name)
    {
        this.name = name;
    }
}
```

Listing 1-12. The com.apress.demo.repositories.UserRepository.java File

```
package com.apress.demo.repositories;
import org.springframework.data.jpa.repository.JpaRepository;
import com.apress.demo.domain.User;
public interface UserRepository extends JpaRepository<User, Integer>
{
}
```

If you don't understand what `JpaRepository` is, don't worry. You will learn more about Spring Data JPA in future chapters.

8. Create a SpringMVC controller to handle URL /, which renders a list of users. See Listing 1-13.

Listing 1-13. The com.apress.demo.web.controllers.HomeController.java File

```java
package com.apress.demo.web.controllers;
import org.springframework.beans.factory.annotation.Autowired;
import org.springframework.stereotype.Controller;
import org.springframework.ui.Model;
import org.springframework.web.bind.annotation.RequestMapping;
import com.apress.demo.repositories.UserRepository;
@Controller
public class HomeController
{
    @Autowired
    private UserRepository userRepo;
    @RequestMapping("/")
    public String home(Model model)
    {
        model.addAttribute("users", userRepo.findAll());
        return "index";
    }
}
```

9. Create a Thymeleaf view called index.html in the /WEB-INF/ views/ folder to render a list of users, as shown in Listing 1-14.

Listing 1-14. The src/main/webapp/WEB-INF/views/index.html File

```html
<!DOCTYPE html>
<html xmlns="http://www.w3.org/1999/xhtml"
    xmlns:th="http://www.thymeleaf.org">
  <head>
      <meta charset="utf-8"/>
      <title>Home</title>
  </head>
  <body>
      <h2 th:text="#{app.title}">App Title</h2>
      <table>
          <thead>
```

```
                    <tr>
                        <th>Id</th>
                        <th>Name</th>
                    </tr>
                </thead>
                <tbody>
                    <tr th:each="user : ${users}">
                        <td th:text="${user.id}">Id</td>
                        <td th:text="${user.name}">Name</td>
                    </tr>
                </tbody>
            </table>
        </body>
</html>
```

You are all set now to run the application. Run the command `mvn cargo:run`. This command will start an embedded Tomcat container. Now point your browser to `http://localhost:8080/springmvcjpa-demo`. If you do, you should see the list of user details in a table, as shown in Figure 1-1.

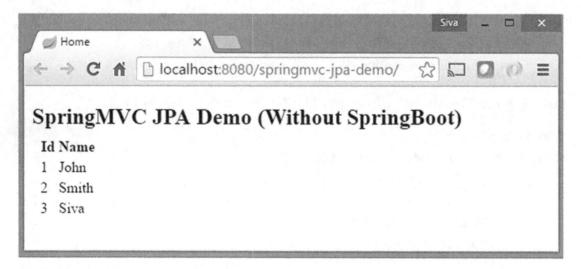

Figure 1-1. *Showing a list of users*

Yay, you did it. But wait, isn't this too much work to just show a list of user details pulled from a database table?

Let's be honest and fair. All this configuration is not just for this one use case. This configuration becomes the basis for the rest of the application. Again, this is too much work to do if you want to get up and running quickly. Another problem is assuming that you want to develop another SpringMVC application with a similar technical stack. You could copy and paste the configuration and tweak it. Right?

Remember one thing: if you have to do the same thing repeatedly, you should find an automated way to do it.

Apart from writing the same configuration again and again, do you see any other problems here? Let's take a look at the problems I see:

- You must search all the compatible libraries for the Spring version and configure them.

- Most of the time, you configure the `DataSource`, `EntitymanagerFactory`, `TransactionManager`, etc. beans the same way. Wouldn't it be great if Spring could do it for you automatically?

- Similarly, you configure the SpringMVC beans like `ViewResolver` and `MessageSource` the same way most of the time. If Spring can automatically do it for you, that would be awesome.

What if Spring is capable of configuring beans automatically? What if you can customize the automatic configuration using simple, customizable properties?

For example, instead of mapping the `DispatcherServlet url-pattern` to `/`, you want to map it to `/app/`. Instead of putting Thymeleaf views in the `/WEB-INF/views` folder, you want to place them in the `/WEB-INF/templates/` folder.

So basically, you want Spring to do things automatically yet provide the flexibility to override the default configuration more simply. You are about to enter the world of Spring Boot, where your dreams can come true!

A Quick Taste of Spring Boot

Welcome to Spring Boot! Spring Boot will configure application components automatically for you but allows you to override the defaults if you want to.

Instead of explaining this in theory, I prefer to explain it by example. In this section, you'll see how to implement the same application using Spring Boot.

1. Create a Maven-based Spring Boot project and configure the
    dependencies in the pom.xml file, as shown in Listing 1-15.

Listing 1-15. The pom.xml File

```xml
<?xml version="1.0" encoding="UTF-8"?>
<project xmlns="http://maven.apache.org/POM/4.0.0" xmlns:xsi="http://www.
w3.org/2001/XMLSchema-instance"
        xsi:schemaLocation="http://maven.apache.org/POM/4.0.0
                http://maven.apache.org/maven-v4_0_0.xsd">
    <modelVersion>4.0.0</modelVersion>
    <groupId>com.apress</groupId>
    <artifactId>hello-springboot</artifactId>
    <packaging>jar</packaging>
    <version>0.0.1-SNAPSHOT</version>
    <name>hello-springboot</name>

    <parent>
        <groupId>org.springframework.boot</groupId>
        <artifactId>spring-boot-starter-parent</artifactId>
        <version>3.0.0-SNAPSHOT</version>
    </parent>

    <properties>
        <project.build.sourceEncoding>UTF-8</project.build.sourceEncoding>
        <java.version>17</java.version>
    </properties>

    <dependencies>
        <dependency>
            <groupId>org.springframework.boot</groupId>
            <artifactId>spring-boot-starter-test</artifactId>
            <scope>test</scope>
        </dependency>
        <dependency>
            <groupId>org.springframework.boot</groupId>
            <artifactId>spring-boot-starter-data-jpa</artifactId>
        </dependency>
```

```xml
    <dependency>
        <groupId>org.springframework.boot</groupId>
        <artifactId>spring-boot-starter-web</artifactId>
    </dependency>
    <dependency>
        <groupId>org.springframework.boot</groupId>
        <artifactId>spring-boot-starter-thymeleaf</artifactId>
    </dependency>
    <dependency>
        <groupId>org.springframework.boot</groupId>
        <artifactId>spring-boot-devtools</artifactId>
        <optional>true</optional>
    </dependency>
    <dependency>
        <groupId>mysql</groupId>
        <artifactId>mysql-connector-java</artifactId>
    </dependency>
    <dependency>
        <groupId>com.h2database</groupId>
        <artifactId>h2</artifactId>
    </dependency>
</dependencies>

<build>
    <plugins>
        <plugin>
            <groupId>org.springframework.boot</groupId>
            <artifactId>spring-boot-maven-plugin</artifactId>
        </plugin>
    </plugins>
</build>
</project>
```

Wow, this pom.xml file suddenly became so small!

> **Note**   Don't worry if this configuration doesn't make sense at this point in time. You have plenty more to learn in the coming chapters.

If you want to use any of the MILESTONE or SNAPSHOT versions of Spring Boot, you need to configure the following milestone/snapshot repositories in pom.xml:

```xml
<parent>
    <groupId>org.springframework.boot</groupId>
    <artifactId>spring-boot-starter-parent</artifactId>
    <version>3.0.0--SNAPSHOT</version>
</parent>
<repositories>
    <repository>
        <id>spring-snapshots</id>
        <name>Spring Snapshots</name>
        <url>https://repo.spring.io/snapshot</url>
        <snapshots>
            <enabled>true</enabled>
        </snapshots>
    </repository>
    <repository>
        <id>spring-milestones</id>
        <name>Spring Milestones</name>
        <url>https://repo.spring.io/milestone</url>
        <snapshots>
            <enabled>false</enabled>
        </snapshots>
    </repository>
</repositories>
<pluginRepositories>
    <pluginRepository>
        <id>spring-snapshots</id>
        <name>Spring Snapshots</name>
        <url>https://repo.spring.io/snapshot</url>
        <snapshots>
```

```
        <enabled>true</enabled>
    </snapshots>
  </pluginRepository>
  <pluginRepository>
    <id>spring-milestones</id>
    <name>Spring Milestones</name>
    <url>https://repo.spring.io/milestone</url>
    <snapshots>
        <enabled>false</enabled>
    </snapshots>
  </pluginRepository>
</pluginRepositories>
```

2. Configure datasource/JPA properties in src/main/resources/ application.properties, as shown in Listing 1-16.

Listing 1-16. The src/main/resources/application.properties File

```
spring.datasource.driver-class-name=com.mysql.cj.jdbc.Driver
spring.datasource.url=jdbc:mysql://localhost:3306/test
spring.datasource.username=root
spring.datasource.password=admin
spring.sql.init.mode=always
spring.jpa.hibernate.ddl-auto=update
spring.jpa.show-sql=true
```

Copy the same data.sql file into the src/main/resources folder.

3. Create a JPA Entity called User.java, a Spring Data JPA Repository Interface called UserRepository.java, and a controller called HomeController.java, as shown in the previous springmvc-jpa-demo application.

4. Create a Thymeleaf view to show the list of users. You can copy / WEB-INF/views/index.html, which you created in the springmvc-jpa-demo application, into the src/main/resources/templates folder of this new project.

5. Create a Spring Boot EntryPointclass `Application.java` file with the main method, as shown in Listing 1-17.

Listing 1-17. The com.apress.demo.Application.java File

```
package com.apress.demo;
import org.springframework.boot.SpringApplication;
import org.springframework.boot.autoconfigure.SpringBootApplication;
@SpringBootApplication
public class Application
{
    public static void main(String[] args)
    {
        SpringApplication.run(Application.class, args);
    }
}
```

Now run `Application.java` as a Java application and point your browser to `http://localhost:8080/`. You should see the list of users in a table format.

By now, you might be scratching your head, thinking, "What is going on?" The next section explains what just happened.

Easy Dependency Management

The first thing to note is the use of the dependencies named `spring-boot-starter-*`. Remember that I said, "Most of the time, you use the same configuration." So, when you add the `springboot-starter-web` dependency, it will, by default, pull all the commonly used libraries while developing Spring MVC applications, such as `spring-webmvc`, `jackson-json`, `validation-api`, and `tomcat`.

You added the `spring-boot-starter-data-jpa` dependency. This pulls all the `spring-data-jpa` dependencies and adds Hibernate libraries because most applications use Hibernate as a JPA implementation.

Autoconfiguration

Not only does the `spring-boot-starter-web` add all these libraries but it also configures the commonly registered beans like `DispatcherServlet`, `ResourceHandlers`, `MessageSource`, etc. with sensible defaults.

You also added `spring-boot-starter-thymeleaf`, which not only adds the Thymeleaf library dependencies but also configures the `ThymeleafViewResolver` beans automatically.

You haven't defined any `DataSource`, `EntityManagerFactory`, or `TransactionManager` beans, but they are automatically created. How?

Suppose you have in-memory database drivers like H2 or HSQL in the classpath. In that case, Spring Boot will automatically create an in-memory data source and register the `EntityManagerFactory` and `TransactionManager` beans automatically with sensible defaults.

But you are using MySQL, so you need to provide MySQL connection details explicitly. You have configured those MySQL connection details in the `application.properties` file and Spring Boot creates a `DataSource` using those properties.

Embedded Servlet Container Support

The most important and surprising thing is that you created a simple Java class annotated with some magical annotation (`@SpringApplication`), which has a `main()` method. By running that `main()` method, you can run the application and access it at `http://localhost:8080/`. Where does the servlet container come from?

You added `spring-boot-starter-web`, which pulls `spring-boot-starter-tomcat` automatically. When you run the `main()` method, it starts Tomcat as an embedded container so that you don't have to deploy your application on any externally installed Tomcat server. What if you want to use a Jetty server instead of Tomcat? You simply exclude `spring-boot-starter-tomcat` from `spring-boot-starter-web` and include `spring-boot-starter-jetty`. That's it.

But this looks magical!. You may be thinking Spring Boot looks cool, and it's doing a lot of things for you. You still don't understand how it works behind the scenes.

I can understand. Watching a magic show is fun, but the mystery is not so fun with software development. Don't worry; we will be looking at each of these things and I will explain in detail what's happening behind the scenes. I don't want to overwhelm you by dumping everything on you in this first chapter.

Summary

This chapter was a quick overview of various Spring configuration styles. The goal was to show you the complexity of configuring Spring applications. Also, you had a quick look at Spring Boot by creating a simple web application.

The next chapter takes a more detailed look at Spring Boot and shows how you can create Spring Boot applications in different ways.

CHAPTER 2

Getting Started with Spring Boot

This chapter takes a more detailed look at Spring Boot and its features. Then this chapter looks at various options for creating a Spring Boot application, such as the Spring Initializr, Spring Tool Suite, and IntelliJ IDEA. Finally, this chapter explores the generated code and looks at how to run an application.

What Is Spring Boot?

Spring Boot is an opinionated framework that helps developers build Spring-based applications quickly and easily. The main goal of Spring Boot is to quickly create Spring-based applications without requiring developers to write the same boilerplate configuration again and again. Key Spring Boot features include

- Spring Boot starters

- Spring Boot autoconfiguration

- Elegant configuration management

- Spring Boot Actuator

- Easy-to-use embedded servlet container support

Spring Boot Starters

Spring Boot offers many starter modules to get started quickly with many of the commonly used technologies, like SpringMVC, JPA, MongoDB, Spring Batch, SpringSecurity, Solr, and ElasticSearch. These starters are preconfigured with the most

© K. Siva Prasad Reddy, Sai Upadhyayula 2023
K. S. P. Reddy and S. Upadhyayula, *Beginning Spring Boot 3*, https://doi.org/10.1007/978-1-4842-8792-7_2

widely used library dependencies, so you don't have to search for compatible library versions and configure them manually.

For example, the `spring-boot-starter-data-jpa` starter module includes all the dependencies required to use Spring Data JPA and Hibernate library dependencies, as Hibernate is the most commonly used JPA implementation.

Note   You can find a list of all the Spring Boot starters that come out of the box in the official documentation at `https://docs.spring.io/spring-boot/docs/ current/reference/htmlsingle/#using.build-systems.starters`.

Spring Boot Autoconfiguration

Spring Boot addresses the problem that Spring applications need complex configuration by eliminating the need to set up the boilerplate configuration manually.

Spring Boot takes an opinionated view of the application and configures various components automatically by registering beans based on multiple criteria. The criteria can be

- Availability of a particular class in a classpath

- Presence or absence of a Spring bean

- Presence of a system property

- Absence of a configuration file

For example, suppose you have the `spring-webmvc` dependency in your classpath. In this case, Spring Boot assumes you are trying to build a SpringMVC-based web application and automatically tries to register `DispatcherServlet` if it is not already registered.

If you have any embedded database drivers in the classpath, such as H2 or HSQL, and if you haven't configured a `DataSource` bean explicitly, Spring Boot will automatically register a `DataSource` bean using in-memory database settings. You will learn more about autoconfiguration in Chapter 3.

Elegant Configuration Management

Spring supports externalizing configurable properties using the `@PropertySource` configuration. Spring Boot takes it even further by using the sensible defaults and a powerful type-safe property binding to bean properties. Spring Boot supports having separate configuration files for different profiles without requiring many configurations.

Spring Boot Actuator

Getting the various details of an application running in production is crucial to many applications. The Spring Boot actuator provides a wide variety of production-ready features without requiring developers to write much code. Some of the Spring actuator features are

- Viewing the application bean configuration details

- Viewing the application URL mappings, environment details, and configuration parameter values

- Viewing the registered health check metrics

Easy-to-Use Embedded Servlet Container Support

Traditionally, while building web applications, you need to create WAR-type modules and then deploy them on external servers like Tomcat and WildFly. But by using Spring Boot, you can create a JAR-type module and embed the servlet container in the application very quickly to be a self-contained deployment unit. Also, during development, you can quickly run the Spring Boot JAR type module as a Java application from the IDE or the command line using a build tool like Maven or Gradle.

You will learn more about these features and how to use them effectively in the following chapters.

Your First Spring Boot Application

There are many ways to create a Spring Boot application. The simplest way is to use Spring Initializr at `https://start.spring.io/`, an online Spring Boot application generator. This section will show how to create a simple Spring Boot web application serving a simple HTML page and will explore various aspects of a typical Spring Boot application.

Using Spring Initializr

You can point your browser to `http://start.spring.io/` and follow the below steps.

1. Select Maven Project and a Spring Boot version (as of writing this book, the latest version is 3.0.0—SNAPSHOT).

2. Enter the Maven project details as follows:

   - Group: com.apress

   - Artifact: springboot-basic

   - Name: springboot-basic

   - Package Name: com.apress.demo

   - Packaging: JAR

   - Java version: 17

   - Language: Java

3. Click the Add Dependencies button. You can search for the starters if you are already familiar with their names. You'll see many starter modules organized into various categories, like Core, Web, and Data. Select the Web checkbox from the Web category.

4. Click the Generate Project button.

Now you can extract the downloaded ZIP file and import it into your favorite IDE.

Using the Spring Tool Suite

The Spring Tool Suite (STS: `https://spring.io/tools`) is an extension of widely used IDEs like Eclipse and Visual Studio Code, and there are lots of Spring framework-related plugins. You can easily create a Spring Boot application from the Eclipse variant of STS by selecting File ➤ New ➤ Other ➤ Spring Boot ➤ Spring Starter Project ➤ Next. You will see the wizard, which looks similar to the Spring Initializr (Figure 2-1).

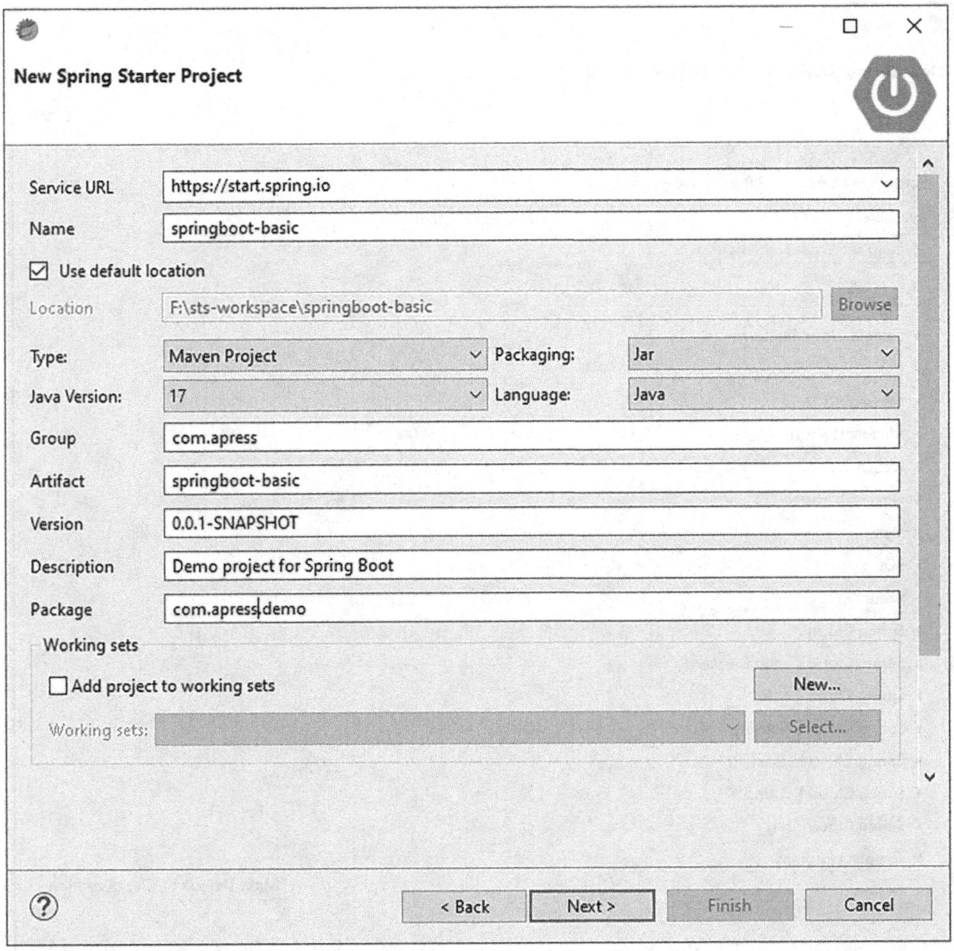

Figure 2-1. *STS New Spring Starter Project wizard*

Enter the project details and click Next. Then select the latest Spring Boot Version and Web starter (Figure 2-2) and click Finish.

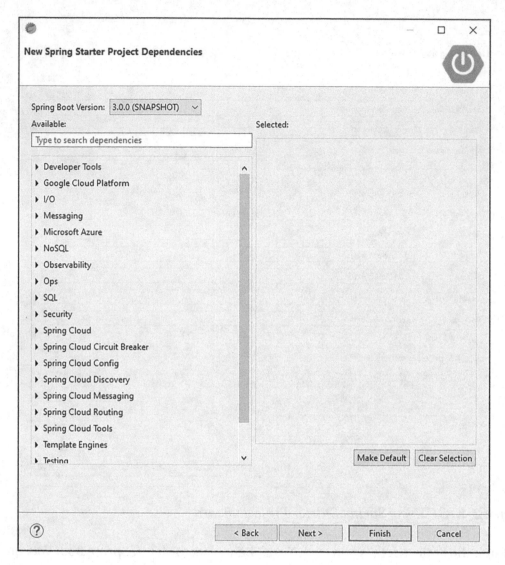

Figure 2-2. *STS Spring Starters selection wizard*

The Spring Boot project will be created and automatically imported into the STS IDE.

Using IntelliJ IDEA

Intellij IDEA is a powerful commercial IDE with great features, including support for Spring Boot. You can create a Spring Boot project from Intellij IDEA by selecting File ➤ New ➤ Project ➤ Spring Initializr ➤ Next. Enter the project details and click Next. Then select the starters and click Next. Finally, enter the project name and click Finish.

> **Note**   Spring Framework support comes only with the commercial Intellij IDEA Ultimate Edition, not the Free Community Edition. If you want to use the IntelliJ IDEA Community Edition, you can generate the project using Spring Initializr and import it into IntelliJ IDEA as a Maven/Gradle project.

Using NetBeans IDE

The NetBeans IDE is another popular IDE for developing Java applications. Currently, there is no out-of-the-box support for creating Spring Boot projects in NetBeans, but the community built the NB Spring Boot plugin (see `https://github.com/AlexFalappa/nb-springboot`), which supports creating Spring Boot applications directly from the IDE.

> **Note**   There are other options for quickly using Spring Boot by using Spring Boot CLI and SDKMAN. You can find more details at "Installing Spring Boot" at `https://docs.spring.io/spring-boot/docs/current/reference/htmlsingle/#getting-started.installing`.

Exploring the Project

Now that you have created a Spring Boot Maven-based project with the web starter, you're ready to explore what is in the generated application.

1. First, take a look at the pom.xml file, as shown in Listing 2-1.

Listing 2-1. The pom.xml File

```
<?xml version="1.0" encoding="UTF-8"?>
<project xmlns="http://maven.apache.org/POM/4.0.0"
        xmlns:xsi="http://www.w3.org/2001/XMLSchema-instance"
        xsi:schemaLocation="http://maven.apache.org/POM/4.0.0
    http://maven.apache.org/xsd/maven-4.0.0.xsd">
    <modelVersion>4.0.0</modelVersion>
    <groupId>com.apress</groupId>
```

```xml
<artifactId>springboot-basic</artifactId>
<version>0.0.1-SNAPSHOT</version>
<packaging>jar</packaging>
<name>springboot-basic</name>
<description>Demo project for Spring Boot</description>
<parent>
    <groupId>org.springframework.boot</groupId>
    <artifactId>spring-boot-starter-parent</artifactId>
    <version>3.0.0-SNAPSHOT</version>
    <relativePath/>
</parent>
<properties>
    <java.version>17</java.version>
</properties>
<dependencies>
    <dependency>
        <groupId>org.springframework.boot</groupId>
        <artifactId>spring-boot-starter-web</artifactId>
    </dependency>
    <dependency>
        <groupId>org.springframework.boot</groupId>
        <artifactId>spring-boot-starter-test</artifactId>
        <scope>test</scope>
    </dependency>
</dependencies>

<build>
    <plugins>
        <plugin>
            <groupId>org.springframework.boot</groupId>
            <artifactId>spring-boot-maven-plugin</artifactId>
        </plugin>
    </plugins>
</build>
<repositories>
    <repository>
```

```xml
            <id>spring-snapshots</id>
            <name>Spring Snapshots</name>
            <url>https://repo.spring.io/snapshot</url>
            <snapshots>
                <enabled>true</enabled>
            </snapshots>
        </repository>
        <repository>
            <id>spring-milestones</id>
            <name>Spring Milestones</name>
            <url>https://repo.spring.io/milestone</url>
            <snapshots>
                <enabled>false</enabled>
            </snapshots>
        </repository>
    </repositories>
    <pluginRepositories>
        <pluginRepository>
            <id>spring-snapshots</id>
            <name>Spring Snapshots</name>
            <url>https://repo.spring.io/snapshot</url>
            <snapshots>
                <enabled>true</enabled>
            </snapshots>
        </pluginRepository>
        <pluginRepository>
            <id>spring-milestones</id>
            <name>Spring Milestones</name>
            <url>https://repo.spring.io/milestone</url>
            <snapshots>
                <enabled>false</enabled>
            </snapshots>
        </pluginRepository>
    </pluginRepositories>
</project>
```

The first thing to note here is that the `springboot-basic` Maven module inherits from the `spring-boot-starter-parent` module. By inheriting from `spring-boot-starter-parent`, this new module will automatically have the following benefits:

- You only need to specify the Spring Boot version once in the parent module configuration. You don't need to specify the version for all the starter dependencies and other supporting libraries. To see the list of supporting libraries, check out the `pom.xml` file of the `org.springframework.boot:springboot-dependencies:{version}` Maven module.

- The parent module `spring-boot-starter-parent` already includes the most commonly used plugins, such as `maven-jar-plugin`, `maven-surefire-plugin`, `maven-war-plugin`, `exec-maven-plugin`, and `maven-resources-plugin`, with sensible defaults.

- In addition to the previously mentioned plugins, the `spring-boot-starter-parent` module also configures the `spring-boot-maven-plugin`, which is used to build fat JARs. I cover the `spring-boot-maven-plugin` in more detail later in this chapter.

This example selects only `web` starter, but `test` starter is also included by default. I selected 17 as the Java version, hence the property `<java.version>17</java.version>` is included. This `java.version` value will be used to configure the JDK version for the Maven compiler in the `spring-boot-starter-parent` module.

```
<maven.compiler.source>${java.version}</maven.compiler.source>
<maven.compiler.target>${java.version}</maven.compiler.target>
```

2. The generated Spring Boot JAR type module will have an application entry point Java class called `SpringbootBasicApplication.java` with the `public static void main(String[] args)` method, which you can run to start the application. See Listing 2-2.

Listing 2-2. com.apress.demo.SpringbootBasicApplication.java

```
package com.apress.demo;
import org.springframework.boot.SpringApplication;
```

```
import org.springframework.boot.autoconfigure.SpringBootApplication;
@SpringBootApplication
public class SpringbootBasicApplication
{
    public static void main(String[] args)
    {
        SpringApplication.run(SpringbootBasicApplication.class, args);
    }
}
```

Here, the SpringbootBasicApplication class is annotated with the @SpringBootApplication annotation, which is a composed annotation.

```
@Target(ElementType.TYPE)
@Retention(RetentionPolicy.RUNTIME)
@Documented
@Inherited
@SpringBootConfiguration
@EnableAutoConfiguration
@ComponentScan(excludeFilters = {
                @Filter(type = FilterType.CUSTOM, classes =
                TypeExcludeFilter.class),
                @Filter(type = FilterType.CUSTOM, classes =
                AutoConfigurationExcludeFilter.class) })
public @interface SpringBootApplication {
    ....
    ....
}
```

The @SpringBootConfiguration is another composed annotation with the @Configuration annotation.

```
@Target(ElementType.TYPE)
@Retention(RetentionPolicy.RUNTIME)
@Documented
@Configuration
public @interface SpringBootConfiguration {
}
```

Here are the meanings of these annotations:

- @Configuration indicates that this class is a Spring configuration class.

- @ComponentScan enables component scanning for Spring beans in the package defined by the current class.

- @EnableAutoConfiguration triggers Spring Boot's autoconfiguration mechanisms.

You are bootstrapping the application by calling SpringApplication. run(SpringbootBasicApplication.class, args) in the main() method. You can pass one or more Spring configuration classes inside the SpringApplication.run() method. But suppose you have your application entry point class in a root package. In that case, it is sufficient to pass the application entry class only, which takes care of scanning other Spring configuration classes in all the subpackages.

3. Now create a simple SpringMVC controller, called HomeController.java, as shown in Listing 2-3.

Listing 2-3. HomeController.java

```
package com.apress.demo;
import org.springframework.stereotype.Controller;
import org.springframework.ui.Model;
import org.springframework.web.bind.annotation.RequestMapping;
@Controller
public class HomeController
{
    @RequestMapping("/")
    public String home(Model model) {
        return "index.html";
    }
}
```

The above class is a simple SpringMVC controller with one request handler method for URL /, which returns the view named index.html.

4.   Create an HTML view called `index.html`.

Spring Boot serves the static content from the `src/main/resources/static/` directories. So, create `index.html` in `src/main/resources/static`, as shown in Listing 2-4.

Listing 2-4. index.html

```
<!DOCTYPE html>
<html>
<head>
<meta charset="utf-8"/>
<title>Home</title>
</head>
<body>
<h2>Hello World!!</h2>
</body>
</html>
```

Now, from your IDE, run the `SpringbootBasicApplication.main()` method as a standalone Java class that will start the embedded Tomcat server on port 8080 and point the browser to `http://localhost:8080/`. You should be able to see the response: `Hello World!!`

You can also run the Spring Boot application using `spring-boot-maven-plugin`, as follows:

```
mvn spring-boot:run
```

The Application Entry Point Class

Spring Boot applications should have an entry point class with the `public static void main(String[] args)` method, which is usually annotated with the `@SpringBootApplication` annotation and will be used to bootstrap the application (Listing 2-5).

Listing 2-5. Main Class com.mycompany.myproject.Application.java in the Root Package

```
package com.mycompany.myproject;
import org.springframework.boot.SpringApplication;
import org.springframework.boot.autoconfigure.SpringBootApplication;
@SpringBootApplication
public class Application
{
    public static void main(String[] args)
    {
        SpringApplication.run(Application.class, args);
    }
}
```

It is highly recommended that you put the main entry point class in the root package, say in com.mycompany.myproject, so that the @EnableAutoConfiguration and @ComponentScan annotations will scan for Spring beans, JPA entities, and such in the root and all of its subpackages automatically.

If you have an entry point class in a nested package, you might need to explicitly specify the basePackages to scan for Spring components (Listing 2-6).

Listing 2-6. Main Class com.mycompany.myproject.config.Application.java in a Non-Root Package

```
package com.mycompany.myproject.config;
@Configuration
@EnableAutoConfiguration
@ComponentScan(basePackages = "com.mycompany.myproject")
@EntityScan(basePackageClasses=Person.class)
public class Application
{
    public static void main(String[] args)
    {
        SpringApplication.run(Application.class, args);
    }
}
```

Here, the `Application.java` main class is in the `com.mycompany.myproject.config` package, which is not the root package. So, you need to specify `@ComponentScan(basePackages = "com.mycompany.myproject")` so that Spring Boot will scan `com.mycompany.myproject` and all of its subpackages for Spring components. Also, you specified `@EntityScan(basePackageClasses=Person.class)` so that Spring Boot will scan for JPA entities under the package where `Person.class` exists.

Fat JAR Using the Spring Boot Maven Plugin

You can run your application directly from the IDE or use Maven `spring-boot:run` during development, but ultimately you need to create a deployment unit that can run in the production environment without any IDE support. You can use `spring-boot-maven-plugin` to create a single deployment unit (a fat JAR) by executing the following Maven goals:

```
mvn clean package
```

There are two interesting files in the `target` directory: `springboot-basic-1.0-SNAPSHOT.jar` and `springboot-basic-1.0-SNAPSHOT.jar.original`. The `springboot-basic-1.0-SNAPSHOT.jar.original` file contains only the compiled classes and classpath resources.

But if you look at `springboot-basic-1.0-SNAPSHOT.jar`, you find the following:

- Compiled classes of your source code in `src/main/java` and static resources from `src/main/resources` will be in the `BOOT-INF/classes` directory

- All the dependent JARs in the `BOOT-INF/lib` directory

- Classes in the `org.springframework.boot.loader` package that does the Spring Boot magic of running the Spring Boot application

You can create self-contained deployment units for JAR-type modules using plugins like `maven-shade-plugin`, which packages all the dependent JAR classes into a single JAR file. But Spring Boot follows a different approach, and it allows you to nest JARs directly within your Spring Boot application JAR file. You can read more about it at `http://docs.spring.io/spring-boot/docs/current/reference/htmlsingle/#executable-jar`.

You can run the application using the following command:

```
java -jar springboot-basic-1.0-SNAPSHOT.jar
```

Spring Boot Using Gradle

Gradle is another popular build tool based on Groovy DSL. You can use Gradle instead of Maven to build Spring Boot applications. Gradle follows a similar project structure as Maven. For example, as the main Java source resides in `src/main/java`, the main resources reside in `src/main/resources`, and so on.

You can create a Gradle-based Spring Boot project by selecting Gradle as the build tool while creating the application through Spring Initializr or the IDEs. The generated `build.gradle` file will look like Listing 2-7.

Listing 2-7. build.gradle

```
buildscript {
    ext {
        springBootVersion = '3.0.0.BUILD-SNAPSHOT'
    }
    repositories {
        mavenCentral()
maven { url "https://repo.spring.io/snapshot" }
maven { url "https://repo.spring.io/milestone" }
    }
    dependencies {
        classpath("org.springframework.boot:spring-boot-gradle-
        plugin:${springBootVersion}")
    }
}
apply plugin: 'java'
apply plugin: 'eclipse'
apply plugin: 'org.springframework.boot'
version = '0.0.1-SNAPSHOT'
sourceCompatibility = 17
repositories {
    mavenCentral()
maven { url "https://repo.spring.io/snapshot" }
    maven { url "https://repo.spring.io/milestone" }
}
```

```
dependencies {
    compile('org.springframework.boot:spring-boot-starter-web')
    testCompile('org.springframework.boot:spring-boot-starter-test')
}
```

Now you can run the application by using the **gradle bootRun** command. You can also use the **gradle build** command, which generates the fat JAR in the build/libs directory.

Maven or Gradle?

Maven and Gradle are the two most popular build tools in the Java world. Maven was released in 2004 and is used widely by many developers. Gradle was released in 2012, and it's more powerful and easy to customize.

As Maven is still the most commonly used build tool, it is used throughout the book. However, you can find the Gradle build scripts in the book's sample code for each module. So, you can use Maven or Gradle. The choice is yours!

Summary

This chapter quickly covered Spring Boot's features and discussed different ways to create Spring Boot applications. Now that you know how to create a simple Spring Boot application and run it, you probably want to understand how Spring Boot's autoconfiguration works. But before that, you should know about Spring's @Conditional feature, on which Spring Boot's autoconfiguration depends.

The next chapter explores the power of the @Conditional annotation feature and looks at how Spring Boot autoconfiguration works.

## CHAPTER 3

Spring Boot Essentials

The primary goal of Spring Boot is to make it easy to develop Spring-based applications. Spring Boot provides several ways to implement commonly used features, such as logging and externalizing configuration properties. This chapter covers configuring logging, externalizing configuration properties, and configuring profile-specific properties. Then it explores how to use the Spring Boot developer tools to automatically restart the server on code changes, thereby improving developer productivity.

Logging

Logging is an essential part of any application and helps debug issues. Spring Boot, by default, includes `spring-boot-starter-logging` as a transitive dependency for the `spring-boot-starter` module. By default, Spring Boot includes SLF4J along with Logback implementations. Spring Boot has a `LoggingSystem` abstraction that automatically configures logging based on the logging configuration files available in the classpath.

If Logback is available, Spring Boot will choose it as the logging handler. You can easily configure logging levels within the `application.properties` file without having to create logging provider-specific configuration files such as `logback.xml` or `log4j.properties`.

```
logging.level.org.springframework.web=INFO
logging.level.org.hibernate=ERROR
logging.level.com.apress=DEBUG
```

If you want to log data into a file in addition to the console, specify the filename as follows:

```
logging.file.path=/var/logs/app.log
```

© K. Siva Prasad Reddy, Sai Upadhyayula 2023
K. S. P. Reddy and S. Upadhyayula, *Beginning Spring Boot 3*, https://doi.org/10.1007/978-1-4842-8792-7_3

or

```
logging.file.name=myapp.log
```

If you want more control over the logging configuration, create the logging provider-specific configuration files in their default locations, which Spring Boot will automatically use.

For example, if you place the logback.xml file in the root classpath, Spring Boot will automatically use it to configure the logging system. See Listing 3-1.

Listing 3-1. The logback.xml File

```
<configuration>
    <appender name="STDOUT" class="ch.qos.logback.core.ConsoleAppender">
        <encoder>
            <pattern>%d{HH:mm:ss.SSS} [%thread] %-5level %logger{36} -
            %msg%n</pattern>
        </encoder>
    </appender>
    <appender name="FILE" class="ch.qos.logback.core.FileAppender">
        <file>app.log</file>
        <encoder>
            <pattern>%date %level [%thread] %logger{10} [%file:%line]
            %msg%n </pattern>
        </encoder>
    </appender>
    <logger name="com.apress" level="DEBUG" additivity="false">
        <appender-ref ref="STDOUT" />
        <appender-ref ref="FILE" />
    </logger>
    <root level="INFO">
        <appender-ref ref="STDOUT" />
        <appender-ref ref="FILE" />
    </root>
</configuration>
```

If you want to use other logging libraries, such as Log4J or Log4j2, instead of Logback, you can exclude `spring-boot-starter-logging` and include the respective logging starter, as follows:

```
<dependency>
    <groupId>org.springframework.boot</groupId>
    <artifactId>spring-boot-starter</artifactId>
    <exclusions>
        <exclusion>
            <groupId>org.springframework.boot</groupId>
            <artifactId>spring-boot-starter-logging</artifactId>
        </exclusion>
    </exclusions>
</dependency>
<dependency>
    <groupId>org.springframework.boot</groupId>
    <artifactId>spring-boot-starter-log4j</artifactId>
</dependency>
```

Now you can add the `log4j.properties` file to the root classpath, which Spring Boot will automatically use for logging.

Externalizing Configuration Properties

Typically, you will want to externalize configuration parameters into separate properties or XML files instead of burying them inside code so that you can easily change them based on the application's environment. Spring provides the @PropertySource annotation to specify the list of configuration files.

Spring Boot takes it one step further by automatically registering a PropertyPlaceHolderConfigurer bean using the `application.properties` file in the root classpath by default. You can also create profile-specific configuration files using the filename as `application-{profile}.properties`.

For example, you can have `application.properties`, which contains the default properties values, `application-dev.properties`, which contains the dev profile configuration, and `application-prod.properties`, which contains the production profile configuration values. If you want to configure common properties for all the profiles, you can configure them in `application-default.properties`.

Note   You can also use YAML (`.yml`) files as an alternative to `.properties`. See the "Using YAML Instead of Properties" section of the Spring Boot reference documentation at `https://docs.spring.io/spring-boot/docs/current/reference/htmlsingle/#boot-features-external-config-yaml`.

Type-Safe Configuration Properties

Spring provides the `@Value` annotation to bind any property value to a bean property. Suppose you have the following `application.properties` file:

```
jdbc.driver=com.mysql.jdbc.Driver
jdbc.url=jdbc:mysql://localhost:3306/test
jdbc.username=root
jdbc.password=secret
```

You can bind these property values into bean properties using `@Value` as follows:

```
@Configuration
public class AppConfig
{
    @Value("${jdbc.driver}")
    private String driver;
    @Value("${jdbc.url}")
    private String url;
    @Value("${jdbc.username}")
    private String username;
    @Value("${jdbc.password}")
    private String password;
    ...
    ...
}
```

But binding each property using @Value is a tedious process. So, Spring Boot introduced a mechanism to automatically bind a set of properties to a bean's properties in a type-safe manner.

Suppose you have the previous JDBC parameters and a DataSourceConfig class as follows:

```
public class DataSourceConfig
{
    private String driver;
    private String url;
    private String username;
    private String password;
    //setters and getters
}
```

Now you can simply annotate DataSourceConfig with @ConfigurationProperties(prefix="jdbc") to automatically bind the properties that start with jdbc.*.

```
@Component
@ConfigurationProperties(prefix="jdbc")
public class DataSourceConfig
{
...
...
}
```

Now you can inject the DataSourceConfig bean into other Spring beans and access the properties using getters.

Relaxed Binding

The bean property names need not be identical to the property key names. Spring Boot supports relaxed binding, where the bean property driverClassName will be mapped from any of these: driverClassName, driver-class-name, or DRIVER_CLASS_NAME.

Validating Properties with the Bean Validation API

To validate the property's values, you can use Bean Validation API annotations such as @NotNull,@Min, @Max, and so on.

```
@Component
@ConfigurationProperties(prefix="support")
public class Support
{
    @NotNull
    private String applicationName;
    @NotNull
    @Email
    private String email;
    @Min(1) @Max(5)
    private Integer severity;
    //setters and getters
}
```

If you configure invalid property values as per the configured validation annotations, an exception will be thrown at the application startup time. For more details on externalizing properties, see "Externalized Configuration" at https://docs.spring.io/spring-boot/docs/current/reference/htmlsingle/#boot-features-external-config.

To enable the above bean validation functionality in your project, you must add the starter dependency, spring-boot-starter-validation, to your pom.xml file.

```
<dependency>
    <groupId>org.springframework.boot</groupId>
    <artifactId>spring-boot-starter-validation</artifactId>
</dependency>
```

Developer Tools

During development, you may need to change the code often and restart the server to apply the code changes. Spring Boot provides developer tools (the spring-boot-devtools module) that support quick application restarts whenever the application classpath content changes.

When you include the `spring-boot-devtools` module during development, the caching of the view templates (Thymeleaf, Velocity, Freemarker, etc.) will be disabled automatically so that you can see the changes immediately. You can see the list of configured properties at `org.springframework.boot.devtools.env.DevToolsPropertyDefaultsPostProcessor`.

```
<dependency>
<groupId>org.springframework.boot</groupId>
<artifactId>spring-boot-devtools</artifactId>
<optional>true</optional>
</dependency>
```

Note that this specifies `spring-boot-devtools` as **optional** by using `<optional>true</optional>` so that it won't be packaged in a fat JAR.

The Spring Boot developer tools trigger application restarts automatically whenever there is a change to the classpath content.

Note   In Eclipse or STS, as soon as you change the classpath resources and save them, devtools will restart the server. In Intellij IDEA, you need to run Make Project to trigger a restart.

Whenever you change the class or properties files in the classpath, Spring Boot will automatically restart the server. You won't typically need to restart the server when static content, such as CSS, JS, and HTML, changes. So, by default, Spring Boot excludes these static resource locations from the file change watch list.

```
@ConfigurationProperties(prefix = "spring.devtools")
public class DevToolsProperties {
    ....
    ....
    public static class Restart {
        private static final String DEFAULT_RESTART_EXCLUDES =
        "META-INF/maven/**,"
        + "META-INF/resources/**,resources/**,"
        + "static/**,public/**,templates/**,"
```

```
    + "**/*Test.class,**/*Tests.class,git.properties, META-INF/build-
      info.properties ";
    /**
    * Patterns that should be excluded from triggering a full restart.
    */
    private String exclude = DEFAULT_RESTART_EXCLUDES;
    ....

    ....

  }
}
```

You can override this default exclusion list by configuring the `spring.devtools.restart.exclude` property.

```
spring.devtools.restart.exclude=assets/**,resources/**
```

If you want to add locations to the restart exclude/include paths, use the following properties:

```
spring.devtools.restart.additional-exclude=assets/**,setup-instructions/**
spring.devtools.restart.additional-paths=D:/global-overrides/
```

Spring Boot's restart mechanism helps increase developer productivity by automatically restarting the server after code changes. But at times, you may need to change multiple classes to implement some feature, and it would be annoying if the server kept restarting after every file change. In this case, you can use the `spring.devtools.restart.trigger-file` property to configure a file path to watch for changes. The server will restart only when the `trigger file` has changed.

```
spring.devtools.restart.trigger-file=restart.txt
```

Note   Once you configure the `spring.devtools.restart.trigger-file` and update the trigger file, the server will restart only if there are modifications to the watched files. Otherwise, Spring Boot won't restart the server.

The restart mechanism works by using two classloaders: one (the base classloader) to load classes that don't change (such as classes in third-party jars) and the other (the restart classloader) to load classes that frequently change (such as classes from your application code). Only the classes in the restart classloader will be recreated when the application restarts. This process will yield faster restarts.

You can disable restarting by setting the `spring.devtools.restart.enabled = false` property. This will still use two classloaders, but the restart classloader won't watch for file changes. If you want to completely turn off the restart mechanism, set the `spring.devtools.restart.enabled=false` property as the system property, as follows:

```
java -jar -Dspring.devtools.restart.enabled=false app.jar
```

Suppose you are developing many Spring Boot applications and want to apply the same devtools settings to all of them. In that case, you can configure global settings by creating a `.spring-bootdevtools.properties` file in the HOME directory. On Windows OS, it is `C:\Users\<username>\.spring-boot-devtools.properties` and on Linux/MacOS, it is `/home/<username>/.spring-boot-devtools.properties`. If you are more aligned with YML files, you can use the name `spring-boot-devtools.yaml` (or) `spring-boot-devtools.yml` to store the global settings.

You can read more about the Spring Boot developer tools at `https://docs.spring.io/spring-boot/docs/current/reference/htmlsingle/#using-boot-devtools`.

Summary

This chapter looked at some of the cool features of Spring Boot that help developers increase productivity. The next chapter covers how to work with relational databases using Spring Boot.

CHAPTER 4

Web Applications with Spring Boot

Spring MVC is the most popular Java web framework based on the Model-View-Controller (MVC) design pattern. In this chapter, you will look at developing web applications with Spring Boot using the power of Spring MVC. In the previous chapter, you built a basic Hello World application. In this chapter, you will build a simple blog application where users can post blog articles.

You will build upon this application for the rest of the book, slowly turning it into a non-trivial Spring Boot application with more complex functionality.

You will also build UI components using view templating technologies like Thymeleaf. Traditionally JSPs are used for view rendering, but many other view templating technologies have emerged over time, such as Thymeleaf, Mustache, Groovy Templates, and FreeMarker. Spring Boot provides nice out-of-the-box support for these view technologies.

Spring Boot also provides embedded servlet container support to build your applications as self-contained deployment units, so you can run your Spring Boot applications without deploying a standalone server. Spring Boot supports Tomcat, Jetty, and Undertow servlet containers and provides customization hooks to implement all server-level customizations.

In this chapter, you will learn how to use Thymeleaf View templates, implement form validations, upload files, and use resource bundles for internationalization (i18n).

Finally, you will also learn how to implement exception handling with the help of various annotations provided by Spring Boot.

© K. Siva Prasad Reddy, Sai Upadhyayula 2023
K. S. P. Reddy and S. Upadhyayula, *Beginning Spring Boot 3*, https://doi.org/10.1007/978-1-4842-8792-7_4

Introducing Spring MVC

Spring MVC is a robust web framework built on MVC and front controller design patterns. In Figure 4-1, you can view the Spring MVC request processing flow.

- When a client sends a request, `DispatcherServlet` acts as a front controller by receiving incoming requests to your application and delegates the processing to request handlers.

- We call these request handlers as controllers. The controller processes the request, fetches any data from the database if needed, and sends it back to the `DispatcherServlet`, which forwards it to the `ViewResolver`.

- The `ViewResolver` renders a view based on the view name and sends it back to `DispatcherServlet`, which finally sends it as a response back to the client.

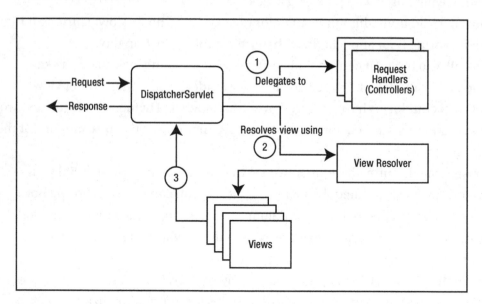

Figure 4-1. *SpringMVC request processing flow*

In the case of your Spring Blog application, whenever the web browser makes a request to your application, the `DispatcherServlet` will identify the respective controller based on the URL mapping (e.g., `http://springblog.com/posts`). The controller will fetch the post information from the database and will dispatch the request to the `ViewResolver`, which will return the HTML that is displayed by the web browser.

To keep things simple, in this chapter you will only store the blog posts in memory instead of storing them in a database. In the following chapters, you will enhance the application with various persistence technologies like JDBC, JPA, and JooQ, and you will also see how to interact with NoSQL databases like MongoDB.

Developing Web Application Using Spring Boot

Let's start developing your Spring Blog application. The first thing to do is to go to the Spring Initializer website, as you saw in Chapter 2. Generate a Spring Boot project with the following configuration:

- Project: Maven Project

- Language: Java

- Spring Boot: Latest possible release of Spring Boot (without SNAPSHOT, and M*)

- Project Metadata: Add the group, artifact, name, description, and package name details.

- Packaging: Jar

- Java: 17 (the latest LTS release as of writing this book)

- Dependencies: Add the following dependencies:

  - Spring Web: Adds the spring-boot-starter-web dependency, which is responsible for enabling Spring MVC in your application

  - Thymeleaf: Adds Thymeleaf capabilities using spring-boot-starter-thymeleaf dependency

  - Validation: Adds bean validation with Hibernate Validator

  - Lombok: A Java annotation library that helps to reduce boilerplate code

After adding all the dependencies, click the Generate button to download the starter project to your machine. After that, unzip the project and open it in your favorite IDE. You can view the dependency information in Figure 4-2.

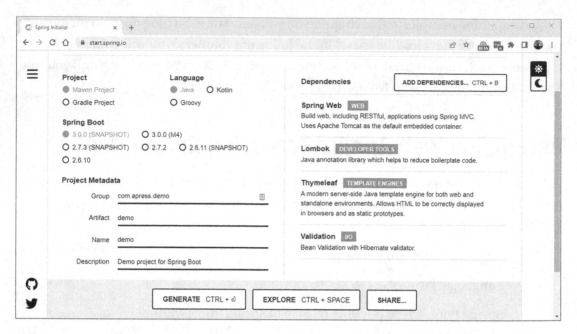

Figure 4-2. *Spring Initializer with dependencies*

Creating the Domain Model of a Spring Blog Application

Let's start building your Spring Blog application by creating domain classes, which are part of your domain model. A domain model is a core part of your application and it represents various objects in your application. For example, a blog typically contains blog posts, comments, and users.

To get started, you will create a package called domain and a class called Post.java, shown in Listing 4-1.

Listing 4-1. Post Class

```
package com.apress.demo.springblog.domain;

import lombok.AllArgsConstructor;
import lombok.Getter;
import lombok.NoArgsConstructor;
import lombok.Setter;
import java.time.LocalDateTime;
import java.util.List;
```

```
@Getter
@Setter
@AllArgsConstructor
@NoArgsConstructor
@Builder
public class Post {
    private Integer id;
    private String title;
    private String description;
    private String body;
    private String slug;
    private PostStatus postStatus;
    private LocalDateTime createdOn;
    private LocalDateTime updatedOn;
    private List<Comment> comments;
}
```

The Post class contains various fields like id, title, description, and body, which contain essential information for a blog post. Other than that, there are metadata-related fields like slug, which is a short, readable identifier for each blog post. The createdOn and updatedOn fields hold the timestamp information whenever you create or update a blog post.

You also have a PostStatus enum, which, as the name suggests, defines the status of each blog post, either as DRAFT or PUBLISHED. A blog post in DRAFT status is not visible to other users. It's only visible if the status is PUBLISHED. Refer to Listing 4-2 for the PostStatus enum.

Listing 4-2. PostStatus Enum

```
package com.apress.demo.springblog.domain;
public enum PostStatus {
    DRAFT, PUBLISHED
}
```

And lastly, each post can have one or more comments from other users. This Comment class contains fields like id, title, authorName, body, createdOn, and updatedOn, as shown in Listing 4-3.

Listing 4-3. Comment Class

```
package com.apress.demo.springblog.domain;
import lombok.AllArgsConstructor;
import lombok.Getter;
import lombok.NoArgsConstructor;
import lombok.Setter;
import java.time.LocalDateTime;

@Getter
@Setter
@AllArgsConstructor
@NoArgsConstructor
public class Comment {
    private Integer id;
    private String title;
    private String authorName;
    private String body;
    private LocalDateTime createdOn;
    private LocalDateTime updatedOn;
}
```

You may have observed that all of the above classes do not contain any of the usual boilerplate code you see in regular POJO classes like getters, setters, constructors, or equals(), hashCode(), and toString() methods.

All of these classes are auto-generated for you at compile time using a library called Lombok. It provides various annotations like @Getter, @Setter, @AllArgsConstructor, @NoArgsConstructor, and @EqualsAndHashCode. You can learn more about Lombok at https://projectlombok.org/. The installation instructions for this library in your favorite IDE are also available on the Lombok website. If you don't install this library, you may find many compilation errors when you run the code on your machine.

Lombok also helps you to implement the famous Builder pattern in your POJO classes, using the @Builder annotation. If you are not aware of the Builder pattern, you can read more about it at https://en.wikipedia.org/wiki/Builder_pattern.

You will make use of different annotations provided by Lombok throughout this book. Now let's go ahead and create a controller class to handle the incoming web requests in the Spring Blog application.

Creating a Controller Class

As discussed, controllers are responsible for handling the incoming HTTP requests, processing those requests, and dispatching the requests to the `ViewResolver`, which sends the HTML page as the response. If you are developing RESTful applications instead of standard web applications, the controller will directly send the data as the HTTP response body.

The controllers can handle HTTP requests like GET, POST, PUT, DELETE, and PATCH. Each HTTP request type can be handled by separate annotations like `@GetMapping`, `@PostMapping`, `@PutMappping`, and `@DeleteMapping`, as shown in Listing 4-4.

Listing 4-4. PostController Class

```
package com.apress.demo.springblog.controller;
import com.apress.demo.springblog.domain.Post;
import org.springframework.stereotype.Controller;
import org.springframework.ui.Model;
import org.springframework.web.bind.annotation.GetMapping;
import org.springframework.web.bind.annotation.RequestMapping;

@Controller
@RequestMapping("/posts")
public class PostController {
    @GetMapping
    public String postPage(Model model) {
        Post post = new Post();
        post.setTitle("Hello Spring Boot");
        post.setDescription("Spring Boot");
        post.setBody("Spring Boot is Awesome");
        model.addAttribute("post", post);
        return "post";
    }
}
```

You can observe that the PostController class is first annotated with the @Controller annotation to denote it as a Spring MVC controller. By adding this annotation, Spring Boot will automatically register this bean as a controller during the application startup. You also have a @RequestMapping annotation, which allows you to define the URL pattern your controller should handle. For example, if you receive a request with path http://localhost:8080/posts, Spring Boot's DispatcherServlet will identify that PostController, which is annotated with @RequestMapping("/posts") and will dispatch the request to the PostController class.

The postPage() method is annotated with the @GetMapping annotation. Whenever you receive an HTTP GET request for the URL with the base path of /posts, the postForm() method will return a String called "post". The ViewResolver will then look for an HTML page called post.html based on this string and will return the HTML as a response to the browser.

Before returning the string "post", the postPage() method creates an object called Post, with information like title, description, and body, and adds it as an attribute to the Model object. A Model acts as a placeholder for the data, which should be displayed by the view (in your case, the post.html page).

Creating Views

The next logical step after creating the controller is to create the view post.html page. You will use Thymeleaf as your view templating engine. The spring-boot-starter-thymeleaf dependency will automatically set up the required beans to work with Thymeleaf.

You can read more about Thymeleaf at www.thymeleaf.org/.

Now let's go ahead and create the post.html file inside the src/main/resources/templates folder, as shown in Listing 4-5.

Listing 4-5. Code for post.html

```
<!DOCTYPE html>
<html xmlns="http://www.w3.org/1999/xhtml"
    lang="en">
<head>
   <title>Spring Blog</title>
</head>
```

```
<body>
<h1>Welcome to Spring Blog</h1>

<h3 th:text="${post.title}"></h3>
<h6 th:text="${post.description}"></h6>
<div th:text="${post.body}"></div>
</body>
</html>
```

This listing contains the code for the post.html page, which is a Thymeleaf template. On this page, you display the title, description, and body of the blog post, using the th:text attribute from Thymeleaf, which looks for a model attribute with the key post and displays the corresponding values for the title, description, and body fields. Notice that you are using the ${} operator inside the th:text attribute to replace the expression with the value of the required field.

If you want to display multiple posts, you can use the th:each attribute, which loops through the list of objects provided to the Model object.

```
Post post = new Post();
post.setTitle("Hello Spring Boot");
post.setDescription("Spring Boot");
post.setBody("Spring Boot is Awesome");
Post post1 = new Post();
post1.setTitle("Hello Spring Boot 3");
post1.setDescription("Spring Boot 3");
post1.setBody("Spring Boot 3 is Awesome");
model.addAttribute("posts", Arrays.asList(post, post1));
```

If you send a list of posts instead of one single post, you can display them on the HTML page using the th:each and th:text attributes. The th:each attribute works similar to the forEach() method in Java, where it loops through each object in the list, and you display the required attribute of that object using the th:text attribute.

```
<div th:each="post : ${posts}">
    <h3 th:text="${post.title}"></h3>
    <h6 th:text="${post.description}"></h6>
    <div th:text="${post.body}"></div>
</div>
```

Now, if you start the application and open the URL `http://localhost:8080/posts`, you should see the web page in your browser, as shown in Figure 4-3.

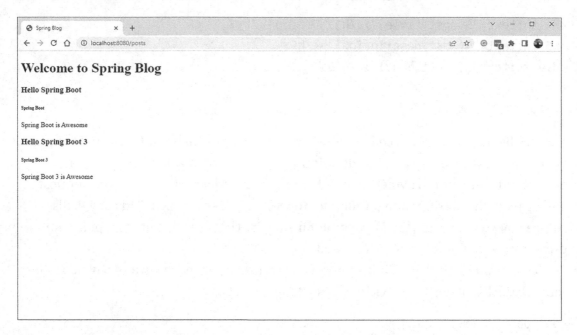

Figure 4-3. *Spring Blog home page*

Spring Boot, by default, serves the static resources (HTML, CSS, JS, images, etc.) from the following `CLASSPATH` locations found under the `src/main/resources` folder:

- `/static`
- `/public`
- `/META-INF/resources`

So, you can place the static files under any of the folders mentioned above.

Working with Thymeleaf Forms

Now let's go ahead and create another view called `addPost.html`. In this HTML page, you will mainly work with forms and look at how to use Thymeleaf features to work with those forms. Refer to Listing 4-6.

Listing 4-6. Code for addPost.html

```html
<!DOCTYPE html>
<html xmlns="http://www.w3.org/1999/xhtml"
    lang="en">
<head>
   <title>Spring Blog</title>
</head>

<body>
<h1>Welcome to Spring Blog</h1>
<form th:object="${post}" th:action="@{/posts}" method="post">
   <div>
      <label for="title">Title:</label>
      <input id="title" th:field="${post.title}" type="text"/>
   </div>
   <div>
      <label for="description">Description:</label>
      <input id="description" th:field="${post.description}" type="text"/>
   </div>
   <div>
      <label for="body">Body:</label>
      <textarea id="body" th:field="${post.body}"></textarea>
   </div>
   <div>
      <input type="submit">
   </div>
</form>
</body>
</html>
```

After the <h1> tag, you define a simple HTML form that contains fields for the input values of title and description and a text area for the field body. Apart from that, you can also observe the attributes th:object, th:field, and th:action.

- The th:object attribute binds the object post to the form. Each field defined inside the form can be mapped to this post object.

- The th:action attribute defines the URL you must invoke when the form is submitted. Notice that you are using the @{} expression from Thymeleaf to define the context-relative path of the URL. For example, instead of defining the whole URL, like http://localhost:8080/posts, you just define the relevant URL path like /posts by using the @{} expression.

- The th:field attribute binds the field inside your post object to the fields inside the form.

You can bind the object's fields to the form using the ${} expression by defining the object name followed by the corresponding field, such as ${post.title}, if you want to display the title of the post.

Instead of repeating the post object multiple times for each field, you can use the select variable expression *{} from Thymeleaf, which helps you define just the attribute name.

For example, instead of defining ${post.title}, ${post.description}, and ${post.body}, you can just write *{title}, *{description}, and *{body} in the above form like so:

```
<div>
    <label for="title">Title:</label>
    <input id="title" th:field="*{title}" type="text"/>
</div>
<div>
    <label for="description">Description:</label>
    <input id="description" th:field="*{description}" type="text"/>
</div>
<div>
    <label for="body">Body:</label>
    <textarea id="body" th:field="*{body}"></textarea>
</div>
<div>
    <input type="submit">
</div>
```

Now let's update the PostController.java class to add the endpoint to handle the addPost functionality, as shown in Listing 4-7.

Listing 4-7. PostController.java Class

```java
package com.apress.demo.springblog.controller;

import com.apress.demo.springblog.domain.Post;
import com.apress.demo.springblog.service.PostService;
import lombok.RequiredArgsConstructor;
import org.springframework.stereotype.Controller;
import org.springframework.ui.Model;
import org.springframework.web.bind.annotation.GetMapping;
import org.springframework.web.bind.annotation.ModelAttribute;
import org.springframework.web.bind.annotation.PostMapping;
import org.springframework.web.bind.annotation.RequestMapping;

import java.util.Arrays;

@Controller
@RequestMapping("/posts")
@RequiredArgsConstructor
public class PostController {

    private final PostService postService;

    @GetMapping
    public String postPage(Model model) {
        Post post = new Post();
        post.setTitle("Hello Spring Boot");
        post.setDescription("Spring Boot");
        post.setBody("Spring Boot is Awesome");

        Post post1 = new Post();
        post1.setTitle("Hello Spring Boot 3");
        post1.setDescription("Spring Boot 3");
        post1.setBody("Spring Boot 3 is Awesome");
        model.addAttribute("posts", Arrays.asList(post, post1));
        return "post";
    }
```

```
@GetMapping("/add")
public String addPostPage(Model model) {
    model.addAttribute("post", new Post());
    return "addPost";
}

@PostMapping
public String addPost(@ModelAttribute("post") Post post) {
    postService.addPost(post);
    return "redirect:/posts";
}
}
```

- You add two new methods in the `PostController` class. The first one is `addPostPage()` with a `@GetMapping("/add)` annotation on top of the method. You are adding an empty Post object as an attribute to the Model object and returning a string called `"addPost"` from the method.

- Whenever you type `http://localhost:8080/posts/add`, Spring Boot invokes the `addPostPage()` method and returns the `addPost.html` page as a response.

- You also have the `addPost()` method with a `@PostMapping` annotation. This method takes the Post object as the method parameter, which is annotated with the `@ModelAttribute` annotation with the name post. By adding this annotation, Spring Boot will look for the post object in the form the user submitted and automatically map the values from the form to the Post object.

- You define a class called `PostService`, which handles the business logic in your application. And you are using the `@RequiredArgsConstructor` annotation from Lombok to replace the argument constructor.

Let's go ahead and implement the business logic in the `PostService.java` class, as shown in Listing 4-8 and Listing 4-9.

Listing 4-8. PostService.java Class

```java
package com.apress.demo.springblog.service;

import com.apress.demo.springblog.domain.Post;
import com.apress.demo.springblog.repository.PostRepository;
import lombok.RequiredArgsConstructor;
import org.springframework.stereotype.Service;
import java.util.Set;

@Service
@RequiredArgsConstructor
public class PostService {

    private final PostRepository postRepository;

    public void addPost(Post post) {
        postRepository.addPost(post);
    }

    public Set<Post> findAllPosts() {
        return postRepository.findAllPosts();
    }
}
```

Listing 4-9. PostRepository.java Class

```java
package com.apress.demo.springblog.repository;

import com.apress.demo.springblog.domain.Post;
import org.springframework.stereotype.Repository;
import java.util.Set;
import java.util.concurrent.CopyOnWriteArraySet;

@Repository
public class PostRepository {
    private final Set<Post> posts = new CopyOnWriteArraySet<>();
    public void addPost(Post post) {
        posts.add(post);
    }
```

```
public Set<Post> findAllPosts() {
  return posts;
}
}
```

- The PostService.java class is annotated with @Service, a Stereotype annotation that defines your class as a Service class and a Spring Bean.

- The RequiredArgsConstructor annotation will generate the argument constructor at compile time, as you are using the PostRepository class as the dependency.

- You also have two methods: addPost() to add the post and findAllPosts() to retrieve all of the blog posts you stored in your application.

- The actual logic to perform the add and retrieve operations is defined inside the PostRepository.java class.

- Note that you are not using a database to store the post objects (at least for now). Instead, you are using an in-memory, thread-safe implementation of the Set interface data structure called CopyOnWriteArraySet.

You can also refactor the postPage() method inside the PostController.java class to retrieve the posts from memory using postService.findAllPosts() instead of hard-coding the Post objects.

```
@GetMapping
public String postPage(Model model) {
    model.addAttribute("posts", postService.findAllPosts());
    return "post";
}
```

Finally, let's update the post.html page with the code below so you can navigate to the addPost page.

```
<div>
<a href="/posts/add">Write new Blog Post</a>
</div>
```

Now you have a fully functional, minimalistic blog. Fire up the browser, go to `http://localhost:8080/posts`, click the link "Write new Blog Post," fill in the necessary details, and submit. The browser will redirect to the `/posts` page, and you should see the submitted blog post. Refer to Figure 4-4 and Figure 4-5.

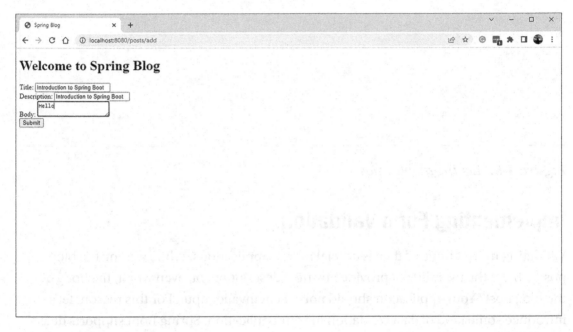

Figure 4-4. *Add Post page*

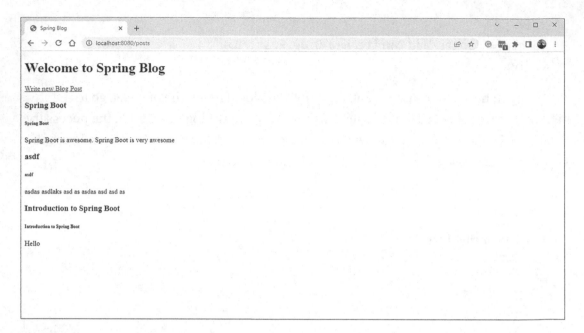

Figure 4-5. *Listing all blog posts*

Implementing Form Validation

Validating user-submitted data is crucial in web applications. While writing the blog post, what if the user did not provide any title, description, or, even worst, the body of the blog post? Your application should not accept invalid input. For this reason, let's introduce some kind of data validation in your application. Spring Boot supports data validation using its validation framework and supports the Java Bean Validation API (`https://beanvalidation.org/2.0-jsr380/`).

At the beginning, you added the following dependency to your `pom.xml` file:

```
<dependency>
        <groupId>org.springframework.boot</groupId>
        <artifactId>spring-boot-starter-validation</artifactId>
    </dependency>
```

This dependency will enable the bean validation capabilities in your application and allow you to access a bunch of annotations that enforce the data validation.

Now let's update the `Post.java` class with the validation rules.

```
public class Post {
        private Integer id;
        @NotNull
    @Size(min = 3, max = 50, message = "Title must be minimum 3
    characters, and maximum 50 characters long")
        private String title;
  @NotNull
        @Size(min = 3, max = 500, message = "Description must be minimum 3
        characters, and maximum 500 characters long")
        private String description;
  @NotNull
    @Size(min = 3, max = 5000 , message = "Body must be minimum 3
    characters, and maximum 5000 characters long")
        private String body;
        private String slug;
        private PostStatus postStatus;
        private LocalDateTime createdOn;
        private LocalDateTime updatedOn;
        private List<Comment> comments;
}
```

The @NotNull annotation, as the name suggests, verifies if the given field is not null. The @Size annotation verifies whether the input fits into the given min and max criteria or not. For example, the @Size annotation on top of the title field validates whether the title is a minimum of three characters and a maximum of 50 characters long. Notice that you can provide a custom error message using the message attribute of the annotation.

You can find the complete list of supported annotations at the Jakarta EE Bean Validation API documentation at https://jakarta.ee/specifications/bean-validation/3.0/jakarta-bean-validation-spec-3.0.html.

Let's also add the bean validation annotations to the Comment.java class, as shown in Listing 4-10.

Listing 4-10. Comment.java Class

```
package com.apress.demo.springblog.domain;

import jakarta.validation.constraints.NotNull;
import jakarta.validation.constraints.Size;
```

```
import lombok.AllArgsConstructor;
import lombok.Getter;
import lombok.NoArgsConstructor;
import lombok.Setter;

import java.time.LocalDateTime;

@Getter
@Setter
@AllArgsConstructor
@NoArgsConstructor
public class Comment {
    private Integer id;
    @NotNull
    @Size(min = 3, max = 50, message = "Title must be minimum 3 characters,
    and maximum 50 characters long")
    private String title;
    @NotNull
    private String authorName;
    @NotNull
    @Size(min = 3, max = 100 , message = "Body must be minimum 3 characters,
    and maximum 100 characters long")
    private String body;
    private LocalDateTime createdOn;
    private LocalDateTime updatedOn;
}
```

Triggering Validation During Form Binding

You have defined the rules to ensure the consistency of data. Now you must trigger the bean validation at the time of form binding. Spring Boot allows you to trigger bean validation when binding the form to the object with the @Valid annotation.

By adding this validation, Spring Boot will scan through all the rules defined for the Post bean and validate the form data against those rules. If any rules fail, it will automatically throw an error.

```
@PostMapping
public String addPost(@ModelAttribute("post") @Valid Post post, Errors
errors) {
    if (errors.hasErrors()) {
        return "addPost";
    }
    postService.addPost(post);
    return "redirect:/posts";
}
```

All validation errors can be captured and saved into the Errors object, and while executing the addPost() method, you can call the hasErrors() method of the Error object to check and act on the validation errors.

In the above code example, if you detect any errors, you return the addPost HTML page as the response to the browser.

Displaying Validation Errors to the User

In the previous section, you implemented the logic to implement the validation rules and detect whenever there are validation errors. In this section, let's understand how to display these validation errors to the user.

Thymeleaf provides the #fields.hasErrors() method in the templates so that you can access the Errors object and retrieve all the errors, as shown in Listing 4-11.

Listing 4-11. addPost.html Page with Validation Errors

```
<!DOCTYPE html>
<html xmlns:th="http://www.thymeleaf.org"
    lang="en">
<head>
    <title>Spring Blog</title>
</head>

<body>
<h1>Welcome to Spring Blog</h1>

<form th:object="${post}" th:action="@{/posts}" method="post">
    <div>
```

```html
        <label for="title">Title:</label>
        <input id="title" th:field="*{title}" type="text"/>
        <div style="color: red" th:if="${#fields.hasErrors('title')}"
        th:errors="*{title}">Invalid Title</div>
    </div>
    <div>
        <label for="description">Description:</label>
        <input id="description" th:field="*{description}" type="text"/>
        <div style="color: red" th:if="${#fields.hasErrors('description')}"
        th:errors="*{description}">Invalid
            Description
        </div>
    </div>
    <div>
        <label for="body">Body:</label>
        <textarea id="body" th:field="*{body}"></textarea>

        <div style="color:red" th:if="${#fields.hasErrors('body')}"
        th:errors="*{body}">Invalid Body</div>
    </div>
    <div>
        <input type="submit">
    </div>
</form>
</body>
</html>
```

In this code, you are displaying the validation errors for each field using the `#fields.hasErrors()` method.

```html
<div style="color: red" th:if="${#fields.hasErrors('title')}"
th:errors="*{title}">Invalid Title</div>
```

By adding the `th:if` attribute, it will only display the above `<div>` tag when there are validation errors for the given field. The `th:errors` attribute will replace the default message of the `<div>` with the error message coming from your backend. You can view the final output in Figure 4-6 after adding the above `<div>` tag for all the fields.

Figure 4-6. *Add Post page with validation errors*

Implementing Custom Validator

Until now, you have been using the in-built constraints from the Jakarta EE Bean Validation constraints to implement the validation rules. When those are not enough, you can implement your own custom validation constraints. You can apply this validation either on a field level or on a whole class level.

Let's go ahead and create a validator and a custom annotation that checks whether a blog post exists with a given exact title or not. This may not be a very appropriate use case for your application, but this can be applied to many different kinds of use cases, like checking if a username is available (or) not.

Listing 4-12 shows how you can create a custom annotation.

Listing 4-12. CustomValidator to Check If a Title Already Exists

```
package com.apress.demo.springblog.validation;

import jakarta.validation.Constraint;
import jakarta.validation.Payload;

import java.lang.annotation.ElementType;
import java.lang.annotation.Retention;
```

```
import java.lang.annotation.RetentionPolicy;
import java.lang.annotation.Target;

@Target(ElementType.TYPE)
@Retention(RetentionPolicy.RUNTIME)
@Constraint(validatedBy = BlogPostTitleValidator.class)
public @interface BlogPostTitleAlreadyExists {
    String message() default "Title Already Exists";

    Class<?>[] groups() default {};

    Class<? extends Payload>[] payload() default {};
}
```

The @Target(ElementType.TYPE) annotation denotes that
@BlogPostTitleAlreadyExists can be applied on a class level, and the @Constraint
annotation makes sure to use the BlogPostTitleValidator record to perform the actual
validation.

You can use the @BlogPostTitleAlreadyExists annotation on top of the Post.java
class, like so:

```
....
@BlogPostTitleAlreadyExists
public class Post {
  private Integer id;
  ...
  ...
}
```

Listing 4-13 shows the code for the BlogPostTitleValidator record.

Listing 4-13. BlogPostTitleValidator Record

```
package com.apress.demo.springblog.validation;

import com.apress.demo.springblog.domain.Post;
import com.apress.demo.springblog.service.PostService;
import jakarta.validation.ConstraintValidator;
import jakarta.validation.ConstraintValidatorContext;
import org.thymeleaf.util.StringUtils;
```

```java
public record BlogPostTitleValidator(
    PostService postService) implements ConstraintValidator<BlogPostTitle
    AlreadyExists, Post> {

  @Override
  public void initialize(BlogPostTitleAlreadyExists constraintAnnotation) {
    ConstraintValidator.super.initialize(constraintAnnotation);
  }

  @Override
  public boolean isValid(Post post, ConstraintValidatorContext
  constraintValidatorContext) {
    if (!StringUtils.isEmpty(post.getTitle()) && postService.
    postExistsWithTitle(post.getTitle())) {
      constraintValidatorContext.disableDefaultConstraintViolation();
      constraintValidatorContext.buildConstraintViolationWithTemplate
      ("Title Already Exists")
          .addPropertyNode("title")
          .addConstraintViolation();
      return false;
    }
    return true;
  }
}
```

This record implements the ConstraintValidator interface and overrides the initialize() and isValid() methods. You are mainly interested in the isValid() method, as this is where your custom validation logic goes. Here you are first calling the postExistsWithTitle() method from the PostService, which basically checks whether the Post object already exists for a given title and responds with either true or false.

If the title does exist, you disable the default constraint violation process, build your own custom error message for the property title, and return false from the method, indicating that the object is not valid.

Here is how the postExistsWithTitle() method can be implemented inside the PostService.java class:

```
public boolean postExistsWithTitle(String title) {
    return postRepository.findAllPosts().stream()
        .anyMatch(post -> post.getTitle().equals(title));
}
```

You can refer to Figure 4-7 to view the error message when you add a blog post with an existing title.

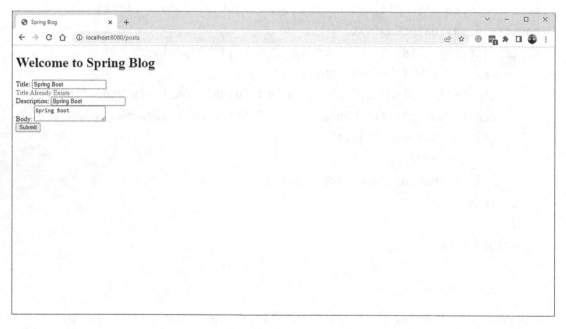

Figure 4-7. *Title already exists for a blog post*

Using the Tomcat, Jetty, and Undertow Embedded Servlet Containers

The Spring Boot Web starter includes Tomcat as the embedded servlet container by default. Instead of Tomcat, you can use other servlet containers like Jetty or Undertow.

To use Jetty as the embedded container, you simply need to exclude spring-boot-starter-tomcat and add spring-boot-starter-jetty.

```xml
<dependency>
    <groupId>org.springframework.boot</groupId>
    <artifactId>spring-boot-starter-web</artifactId>
    <exclusions>
        <exclusion>
            <groupId>org.springframework.boot</groupId>
            <artifactId>spring-boot-starter-tomcat</artifactId>
        </exclusion>
    </exclusions>
</dependency>
<dependency>
    <groupId>org.springframework.boot</groupId>
    <artifactId>spring-boot-starter-jetty</artifactId>
</dependency>
```

After adding the dependency, simply run the application, and you should see the following line in the logs:

```
o.s.b.web.embedded.jetty.JettyWebServer  : Jetty started on port(s) 8080
(http/1.1) with context path '/'
```

Undertow (http://undertow.io/) is a web server written in Java. It provides blocking and non-blocking APIs based on NIO. Spring Boot provides autoconfiguration support for the Undertow server as well. Similar to what you saw with Jetty, you can configure Spring Boot to use the Undertow embedded server instead of Tomcat as follows:

```xml
<dependency>
    <groupId>org.springframework.boot</groupId>
    <artifactId>spring-boot-starter-web</artifactId>
    <exclusions>
        <exclusion>
            <artifactId>spring-boot-starter-tomcat</artifactId>
            <groupId>org.springframework.boot</groupId>
        </exclusion>
    </exclusions>
</dependency>
```

```
<dependency>
    <groupId>org.springframework.boot</groupId>
    <artifactId>spring-boot-starter-undertow</artifactId>
</dependency>
```

After adding the above Undertow dependency, the Undertow server should be started at port 8080. You can observe this in the logs:

```
o.s.b.w.e.undertow.UndertowWebServer     : Undertow started on port(s)
                                           8080 (http)
```

You can customize various properties of the Tomcat, Jetty, and Undertow servlet containers using the `server.tomcat.*`, `server.jetty.*`, and `server.undertow.*` or `server.*` properties, respectively. Here are some of the properties and their default values:

```
server.tomcat.accesslog.directory=logs # Directory in which log files are
created.
server.tomcat.accesslog.enabled=false # Enable access log.
server.tomcat.accesslog.file-date-format=.yyyy-MM-dd # Date format to place
in log file name.
server.tomcat.basedir= # Tomcat base directory. If not specified a
temporary directory will be used.
server.tomcat.max-connections= 8192 # Maximum number of connections that
the server will accept and process at any given time.
server.max-http-header-size=8KB # Maximum size in bytes of the HTTP
message header.
server.tomcat.threads.max=200 # Maximum amount of worker threads.
server.tomcat.threads.min-spare=10 # Minimum amount of worker threads.
server.tomcat.remoteip.port-header=X-Forwarded-Port # Name of the HTTP
header used to override the original port value.
server.jetty.threads.acceptors= -1# Number of acceptor threads to use.
server.jetty.accesslog.append=false # Append to log.
server.jetty.accesslog.file-date-format=dd/MMM/yyyy:HH:mm:ss Z
server.jetty.accesslog.enabled=false # Enable access log.
server.jetty.accesslog.filename= # Log filename. If not specified, logs
will be redirected to "System.err".
```

```
server.jetty.max-http-form-post-size=200000B # Maximum size in bytes of the
HTTP post or put content.
server.undertow.accesslog.dir= # Undertow access log directory.
server.undertow.accesslog.enabled=false # Enable access log.
server.undertow.accesslog.rotate=true # Enable access log rotation.
server.undertow.accesslog.suffix=log # Log file name suffix.
server.undertow.buffer-size= # Size of each buffer in bytes.
server.undertow.threads.io= # Number of I/O threads to create for
the worker.
server.undertow.max-http-post-size=-1B # Maximum size in bytes of the HTTP
post content.
```

Use the `org.springframework.boot.autoconfigure.web.ServerProperties` class to see a complete list of server customization properties.

Customizing Embedded Servlet Containers

Spring Boot provides many customization options for configuring servlet containers using the `server.*` properties. You can customize the `port`, `connectionTimeout`, `contextPath`, and SSL configuration parameters and session configuration parameters by configuring these properties in the `application.properties` file.

But if you need more control, you can register embedded servlet containers programmatically by registering a bean of type `TomcatServletWebServerFactory`, `JettyServletWebServerFactory`, or `UndertowServletWebServerFactory` based on the embedded server you want to use.

One common scenario where you would want to register embedded servlet containers programmatically is to redirect the default HTTP request to the HTTPS protocol.

Suppose your application runs on `http://localhost:8080` and you want to use the HTTPS protocol. If anyone accesses `http://localhost:8080`, you want to redirect the request to `https://localhost:8443`.

First, you generate a self-signed SSL certificate using the following command:

```
keytool -genkey -alias mydomain -keyalg RSA -keysize 2048 -keystore
KeyStore.jks -validity 3650
```

After providing the answers to the questions that keytool asked, it will generate a KeyStore.jks file and copy it to the src/main/resources folder.

Now configure the SSL properties in the application.properties file as follows:

```
server.port=8443
server.ssl.key-store=classpath:KeyStore.jks
server.ssl.key-store-password=mysecret
server.ssl.keyStoreType=JKS
server.ssl.keyAlias=mydomain
```

The server.port property will change the default port of your application from 8080 to 8443, and the next few properties will define the local of the keystore, followed by the details of the keystore like password, keystore type, and alias. Using the Tomcat embedded container, you can register TomcatServletWebServerFactory programmatically, as shown in Listing 4-14.

Listing 4-14. Registering the Tomcat Embedded Container Programmatically

```
@Configuration
public class TomcatConfiguration
{
    @Value("${server.port}")
     int serverPort;
    @Bean
    public ServletWebServerFactory servletContainer() {
        TomcatServletWebServerFactory tomcat = new
        TomcatServletWebServerFactory() {
            @Override
            protected void postProcessContext(Context context) {
                SecurityConstraint securityConstraint = new
                SecurityConstraint();
                securityConstraint.setUserConstraint("CONFIDENTIAL");
                SecurityCollection collection = new SecurityCollection();
                collection.addPattern("/*");
                securityConstraint.addCollection(collection);
                context.addConstraint(securityConstraint);
            }
```

```
    };
    tomcat.addAdditionalTomcatConnectors(initiateHttpConnector());
    return tomcat;
  }
  private Connector initiateHttpConnector() {
    Connector connector = new Connector("org.apache.coyote.http11.
    Http11NioProtocol");
    connector.setScheme("http");
    connector.setPort(8080);
    connector.setSecure(false);
    connector.setRedirectPort(serverPort);
    return connector;
  }
}
```

With this customization, the request to http://localhost:8080/ will be automatically redirected to https://localhost:8443/. In this class, you basically created a bean called servletContainer, which will create an object for the class TomcatServletWebServerFactory, and you add a SecurityConstraint, that all the incoming traffic to our application must be confidential, by providing the pattern as /*, and after that you create a Connector object, which will redirect all the traffic coming to port 8080 to 8443.

Keep in mind that the certificate you created is a local self-signed certificate. For this reason, your web browser will rightly show you a warning message that the Certificate Authority is invalid. Just click to proceed, and you should see that the application is accessible at http://localhost:8443, as shown in Figure 4-8.

Figure 4-8. *SpringBlog with HTTPS*

Customizing SpringMVC Configuration

Most of the time, Spring Boot's default autoconfiguration, along with the customization properties, will be sufficient to tune your web application. But at times, you may need more control to configure the application components in a specific way to meet your application needs.

Suppose you want to take advantage of Spring Boot's autoconfiguration and add some MVC configuration (interceptors, formatters, view controllers, etc.). If so, you can create a configuration class without the @EnableWebMvc annotation, which implements WebMvcConfigurer and supplies additional configuration. See Listing 4-15.

Note   If you want complete control over the Spring MVC configuration, you can add your configuration class annotated with @EnableWebMvc. Spring Boot's WebMVC autoconfiguration will be completely turned off if you create a configuration class with the @Configuration and @EnableWebMvc annotations.

Listing 4-15. Customizing the SpringMVC Configuration

```
@Configuration
public class WebConfig implements WebMvcConfigurer
{
    @Override
    public void addViewControllers(ViewControllerRegistry registry){
        registry.addRedirectViewController("/", "/posts");
    }
    @Override
    public void addInterceptors(InterceptorRegistry registry) {
        //Add additional interceptors here
    }
    @Override
    public void addResourceHandlers(ResourceHandlerRegistry registry) {
        registry.addResourceHandler("/assets/").addResourceLocations
        ("/resources/assets/");
    }
```

```
@Override
public void configureDefaultServletHandling(DefaultServletHandlerConfig
urer configurer) {
    // Do Nothing
}
@Override
public void addFormatters(FormatterRegistry registry) {
    //Add additional formatters here
}
}
```

By adding the code `registry.addRedirectViewController("/", "/posts");` inside the `addViewControllers` method, you are basically asking Spring Boot to redirect all the requests for path / to `/posts`.

So, if you open the browser and go to URL `http://localhost:8080/`, you will be automatically redirected to `http://localhost:8080/posts`.

Similarly, you can also add different components like Interceptors, which are similar to Filters in Java EE. Interceptors are executed before your request is served by the `DispatcherServlet` (refer to the section "Using ResourceBundles for Internationalization" to understand how to use Interceptors). You can also add Resource Handlers and Formatters inside the WebConfig file.

Spring Boot Web Application as a Deployable WAR

The Spring Boot web application can be developed using WAR-type packaging also. If you want to build a deployable WAR file, the first thing you do is change the packaging type.

If you are using Maven, then in `pom.xml`, change the `packaging` type to `war`.

```
<packaging>war</packaging>
```

If you are using Gradle, you need to apply the WAR plugin.

```
apply plugin: 'war'
```

When you add the `spring-boot-starter-web` dependency, it will transitively add the `spring-boot-starter-tomcat` dependency as well. So, you need to add `spring-boot-starter-tomcat` as the `provided` scope so that it won't get packaged inside the WAR file.

```
<dependency>
    <groupId>org.springframework.boot</groupId>
    <artifactId>spring-boot-starter-tomcat</artifactId>
    <scope>provided</scope>
</dependency>
```

If you are using Gradle, add `spring-boot-starter-tomcat` with the `providedRuntime` scope as follows:

```
dependencies {
    ...
    providedRuntime 'org.springframework.boot:spring-boot-starter-tomcat'
    ...
}
```

Finally, you need to provide a `SpringBootServletInitializer` subclass and override its `configure()` method. You can simply make your application's entry point class extend `SpringBootServletInitializer`, as shown in Listing 4-16.

Listing 4-16. Implementing SpringBootServletInitializer

```
@SpringBootApplication
public class SpringbootWebDemoApplication extends
SpringBootServletInitializer {
    @Override
    protected SpringApplicationBuilder configure(SpringApplicationBuilder
    application) {
        return application.sources(SpringbootWebDemoApplication.class);
    }
    public static void main(String[] args) throws Exception {
        SpringApplication.run(SpringbootWebDemoApplication.class, args);
    }
}
```

Now if you try to build your application by running the `mvn package` command if you are running Maven or `gradlew build` if you are using Gradle, you will see the WAR file inside the target folder of your source code, as shown in Figure 4-9.

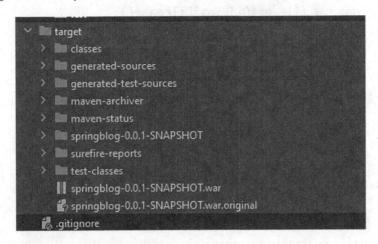

Figure 4-9. *WAR file generated from the build*

File Uploading

Spring Boot's `org.springframework.boot.autoconfigure.web.servlet. MultipartAutoConfiguration` enables multi-part uploads by default. You can create a form with `enctype="multipart/form-data"` to upload a file, as shown in Listing 4-17.

Listing 4-17. File Uploading Form

```
<form action="uploadMyFile" th:action="@{/uploadMyFile}"
        method="post" enctype="multipart/form-data">
  <input type="file" name="myFile" />
  <input type="submit" />
</form>
```

You can then implement the `FileUploadController` to handle the request, as shown in Listing 4-18.

Listing 4-18. FileUploadController.java

```
@PostMapping("/uploadMyFile")
public String handleFileUpload(@RequestParam("myFile") MultipartFile file)
```

```
{
    if (!file.isEmpty())
    {
        String name = file.getOriginalFilename();
        try
        {
            byte[] bytes = file.getBytes();
            Files.write(new File(name).toPath(), bytes);
        }
        catch (Exception e)
        {
            e.printStackTrace();
        }
    }
    return "redirect:/fileUpload";
}
```

Note that this example binds the file type input parameter myFile to the
MultipartFile argument with @RequestParam("myFile"), from which you can extract
byte[] or InputStream.

You can customize multipart configuration using the following properties:

```
spring.servlet.multipart.enabled=true
spring.servlet.multipart.max-file-size=1MB
spring.servlet.multipart.max-request-size=10MB
spring.servlet.multipart.file-size-threshold=0B
```

Using ResourceBundles for Internationalization

You can easily implement multilanguage support in your applications (also called
internationalization or i18n) with the help of Spring Boot. All you have to do is add a
file called messages.properties in the src/main/resources folder. For each language
you want to support, you can add the messages_<language-code>.properties file.
For example, if you want to add support for Spanish, you can add the messages_
es.properties file and define your translations in that file.

This file must contain a key and a value for each piece of text that needs to be translated. Then you can refer to those translations by using the #{} expression from Thymeleaf templates inside the th:text attribute.

To get started, you can add the name of the properties file under the property spring.messages.basename. In addition, Spring Boot provides the following customization properties:

```
spring.messages.basename=messages
spring.messages.cache-duration= # Cached for ever by default.
spring.messages.encoding=UTF-8
spring.messages.fallback-to-system-locale=true #Looks for the default
messages.properties file, when no translation file is available for a
language.
```

Let's update the default ResourceBundle messages.properties in src/main/resources/ folder as follows:

```
blog.title=Welcome to Spring Blog
blog.newpost=Write new Blog Post
```

Now create another file called messages_de.properties under the src/main/resources folder, which stores the translations in German.

```
post.title=Willkommen im Spring Blog
post.newpost=Schreiben Sie einen neuen Blog-Beitrag
```

The next step is to use the above properties inside your HTML files. For this, you can replace the <h1> and <a> tags inside the addPost.html and post.html files.

```
<h1 th:text="#{blog.title}">Welcome to Spring Blog</h1>
<a href="/posts/add" th:text="#{blog.newpost}">Write new Blog Post</a>
```

Leave the default value as it is, so that if something goes wrong, you will still see the text in English.

This is all well and good, but how do you toggle/select which translation your application must display? To address this, you can send a query parameter called lang to your application, and you can configure an Interceptor to intercept all the incoming requests and plug in the LocaleChangeInterceptor based on the query parameter. You can also store this value in the browser's cookie by defining a bean of type CookieLocaleResolver.

```
@Override
public void addInterceptors(InterceptorRegistry registry) {
    registry.addInterceptor(localeInterceptor());
}
@Bean
public LocaleResolver localeResolver() {
    return new CookieLocaleResolver();
}
@Bean
public LocaleChangeInterceptor localeInterceptor() {
    LocaleChangeInterceptor localeInterceptor = new
    LocaleChangeInterceptor();
    localeInterceptor.setParamName("lang");
    return localeInterceptor;
}
```

After adding the above configuration, if you open the URL http://localhost:8443/ posts?lang=de, you can see the output in Figure 4-10.

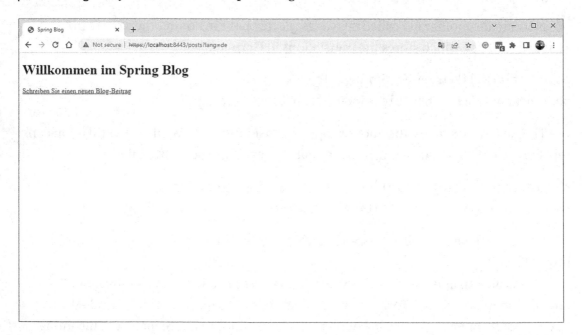

Figure 4-10. *German translation of the Spring Blog application*

Now, if you retry the request by excluding the language query parameter, you will see that the application still renders the text in German, as the LOCALE value is stored in the browser's cookie. Refer to Figure 4-11.

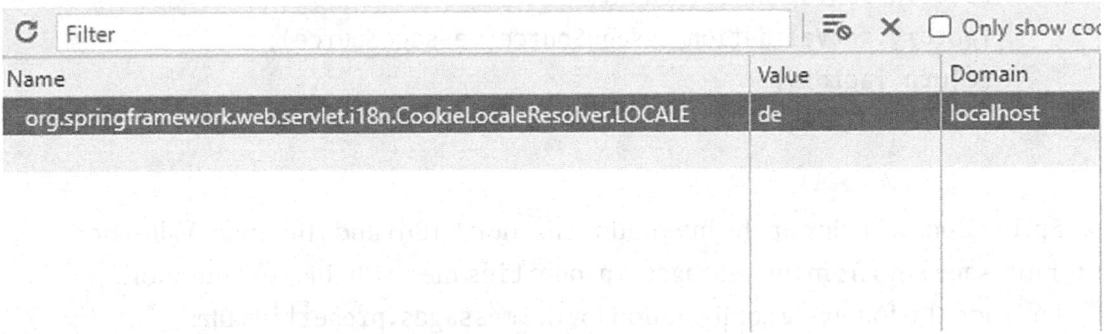

C Filter		☰ₒ ✕ ☐ Only show co
Name	Value	Domain
org.springframework.web.servlet.i18n.CookieLocaleResolver.LOCALE	de	localhost

Figure 4-11. *Browser cookie storing the value of LOCALE*

If you delete this cookie and reload the page, you can observe that the transitions will be rendered in the default language of English.

ResourceBundles for Hibernate Validation Errors

In the previous section, you saw how to use the translations for the website text. You also defined validation error messages in your application code, which is hard-coded in English. Let's see how to handle those messages.

Spring Boot uses Hibernate Validator as the bean validation API implementation. Hibernate validation looks for the ValidationMessages.properties file in the root classpath for failure message keys. You can register the Validator bean for i18n and Hibernate Validation error messages. Refer to Listing 4-19.

Listing 4-19. Using MessageSource for Hibernate Validation Messages

```
@Configuration
public class WebConfig implements WebMvcConfigurer
{
    ...
    ...
    @Autowired
    private MessageSource messageSource;
```

```
    @Override
    public Validator getValidator() {
        LocalValidatorFactoryBean factory = new
        LocalValidatorFactoryBean();
        factory.setValidationMessageSource(messageSource);
        return factory;
    }
}
```

Spring Boot will pick up the internationalization (i18n) and Hibernate Validation error message keys from the messages*.properties files with this configuration.

Let's add the following configuration for the messages.properties file:

```
blog.title=Welcome to Spring Blog
blog.newpost=Write new Blog Post
blog.label.title=Title
blog.label.description=Description
blog.label.body=Body

#Validation Error Messages
Size.post.title=Title must be minimum 3 characters, and maximum 50
characters long
Size.post.description=Description must be minimum 3 characters, and maximum
500 characters long
Size.post.body=Body must be minimum 3 characters, and maximum 5000
characters long
TitleAlreadyExists=Title Already Exists
```

Now let's add the properties for the messages_de.properties file:

```
blog.title=Willkommen im Spring Blog
blog.newpost=Schreiben Sie einen neuen Blog-Beitrag
blog.label.title=Titel
blog.label.description=Bezeichnung
blog.label.body=Text
```

```
#Validation Error Messages
Size.post.title=Der Titel muss mindestens 3 Zeichen und maximal 50 Zeichen
lang sein
Size.post.description=Die Beschreibung muss mindestens 3 Zeichen und
maximal 500 Zeichen lang sein
Size.post.body=Der Text muss mindestens 3 Zeichen lang und maximal 5000
Zeichen lang sein
TitleAlreadyExists=Titel existiert bereits
```

For the validation error messages, you first define the name of the annotation, followed by the object name and then the field name. Spring Boot uses these three items as the keys to identify and fetch the error message for each language.

You also add the field `TitleAlreadyExists`, which replaces the hard-coded error message you defined inside the `BlogPostTitleValidator` record. After adding all these properties and adjusting the HTML files, the final output should look like Figure 4-12 when you open the browser and point to `https://localhost:8443/posts`.

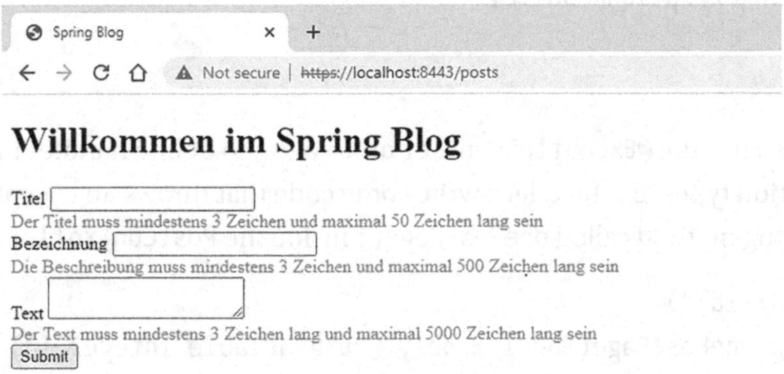

Figure 4-12. *Validation error messages in German*

Error Handling

You can handle exceptions in Spring MVC applications by registering the `SimpleMappingExceptionResolver` bean and configuring which view to render for what type of exception, as shown in Listing 4-20.

Listing 4-20. Handling Exceptions Using SimpleMappingExceptionResolver

```
@Configuration
@EnableWebMvc
public class WebMvcConfig implements WebMvcConfigurer
{
    @Bean(name="simpleMappingExceptionResolver")
    public SimpleMappingExceptionResolver simpleMappingExceptionResolver()
    {
        SimpleMappingExceptionResolver exceptionResolver = new
        SimpleMappingExceptionResolver();
        Properties mappings = new Properties();
        mappings.setProperty("SpringBlogException", "genericError");
        mappings.setProperty("RuntimeException", "error");
        exceptionResolver.setExceptionMappings(mappings);
        exceptionResolver.setDefaultErrorView("error");
        return exceptionResolver;
    }
}
```

You can also use the `@ExceptionHandler` annotation to define handler methods for specific exception types. But first, let's write some code that throws an exception. Let's add the following method called `onePostPage()` inside the `PostController.java` class:

```
@GetMapping("/{id}")
public String onePostPage(Model model, @PathVariable Integer id) {
    model.addAttribute("posts", postService.findOnePost(id));
    return "onePost";
}
```

This method takes an Integer value id as the `PathVariable`, coming in as a URL Path variable. For example, if the user types in the URL `http://localhost:8080/posts/1`, Spring Boot automatically detects the number 1 and maps it to the `id` variable.

The above method will throw a compilation error because you did not yet create the method `findOnePost()` inside the `PostService` class, so go ahead and create the method. Now, inside the `PostRepository.java` class, add a new method named `findOnePost()`:

```
public Post findOnePost(Integer postId) {
    return posts.stream().filter(post -> post.getId().equals(postId))
        .findFirst()
        .orElseThrow(() -> new SpringBlogException("Cannot find post by
        id: " + postId));
}
```

You are throwing an exception of type SpringBlogException, which is nothing but a custom exception class you created, like so:

```
public class SpringBlogException extends RuntimeException {
    public SpringBlogException(String message) {
        super(message);
    }
}
```

Lastly, let's update the findOnePost() method inside the PostService.java class with a call to the postRepository.findOnePost(id) method.

```
public Post findOnePost(Integer postId) {
    return postRepository.findOnePost(postId);
}
```

As you now have some logic in your code, which throws some exceptions, let's see how to handle those exceptions using the @ExceptionHandler annotation, as shown in Listing 4-21.

Listing 4-21. Handling Exceptions Using Controller Level @ExceptionHandler

```
@Controller
public class PostController
{

    ...

    @ExceptionHandler(SpringBlogException.class)
    public ModelAndView handleSpringBlogException(SpringBlogException ex) {
        ModelAndView model = new ModelAndView("error");
        model.addObject("exception", ex);
        return model;
    }

}
```

The handleSpringBlogException() method in PostController will only handle the exception SpringBlogException raised from PostController @RequestMapping methods.

You can handle exceptions globally by creating an exception handler class annotated with @ControllerAdvice. The @ExceptionHandler methods in the @ControllerAdvice class handle errors in any controller request handling method. See Listing 4-22.

Listing 4-22. Global Exception Handler Using @ControllerAdvice

```
package com.apress.demo.springblog.exception;

import lombok.extern.slf4j.Slf4j;
import org.springframework.web.bind.ServletRequestBindingException;
import org.springframework.web.bind.annotation.ControllerAdvice;
import org.springframework.web.bind.annotation.ExceptionHandler;

@ControllerAdvice
@Slf4j
public class GlobalExceptionHandler {

    @ExceptionHandler(SpringBlogException.class)
    public String servletRequestBindingException(ServletRequestBindingExce
    ption e) {
        log.error("SpringBlogException occurred: " + e.getMessage());
        return "error";
    }
}
```

You use the @Slf4j annotation from Lombok to generate an SLF4J-backed logger in your class at compile time.

Summary

This chapter discussed developing web applications using Spring Boot with Thymeleaf view templates. It also looked at performing form validations using the Bean Validation API and Spring's validation framework. You learned how to handle exception scenarios at the controller level and globally. In the next chapter, you will learn about persisting the data of your Spring Blog application in the database using JDBC.

## CHAPTER 5

Working with JDBC

Data persistence is a crucial part of software systems. Most software applications use relational databases as datastores, but recently NoSQL data stores like MongoDB, Redis, and Cassandra are getting popular. Java provides the JDBC API to talk to the database, but it is a low-level API that requires lots of boilerplate coding. The JavaEE platform provides the Java Persistence API (JPA) specification, an object-relational mapping (ORM) framework. Hibernate and EclipseLink are the most popular JPA implementations. Other popular persistence frameworks, such as MyBatis and JOOQ, are more SQL-focused.

Spring provides a nice abstraction on top of the JDBC API, using `JdbcTemplate`, and offers excellent transaction management capabilities using an annotation-based approach. Spring Data is an umbrella project that supports integration with the most widespread data access technologies, such as JPA, MongoDB, Redis, Cassandra, Solr, and ElasticSearch. Spring Boot makes working with these persistence technologies easier by automatically configuring the required beans based on various criteria.

This chapter looks at how you can add database support for your Spring blog application, first by using JDBC support of Spring without Spring Boot, and then you will learn how Spring Boot makes it easy to use JDBC without much coding or configuration. You will also learn about performing database migration using Flyway. If you are unaware of JDBC, you can go through this documentation to get a quick overview of it: `https://docs.oracle.com/javase/tutorial/jdbc/basics/index.html`.

Introduction to JdbcTemplate

Before the Spring Framework, application developers used to write a lot of boilerplate code for trivial database logic in applications using JDBC. Let's take the following code as an example:

```
public Optional<Post> findById(String id) {
```

© K. Siva Prasad Reddy, Sai Upadhyayula 2023
K. S. P. Reddy and S. Upadhyayula, *Beginning Spring Boot 3*, https://doi.org/10.1007/978-1-4842-8792-7_5

```
Connection connection = null;
PreparedStatement statement = null;
ResultSet resultSet = null;
try {
    connection = dataSource.getConnection();
    statement = connection.prepareStatement(
            "select id, title, description, body, slug, post_status,
            created_on, updated_on from posts where id=?");
    statement.setString(1,id);
    resultSet = statement.executeQuery();
    Post post = null;
    if(resultSet.next()) {
        post = new Post(
                resultSet.getInt("id"),
                resultSet.getString("title"),
                resultSet.getString("description"),
                resultSet.getString("body"),
                resultSet.getString("slug"),
                PostStatus.valueOf(resultSet.getString("post_status")),
                convertToLocalDate(resultSet.getDate("created_on")),
                convertToLocalDate(resultSet.getDate("updated_on"))
                    );
    }
    return Optional.of(post);
} catch (SQLException e) {
} finally {
    if (resultSet != null) {
        try {
            resultSet.close();
        } catch (SQLException e) {}
    }
    if (statement != null) {
        try {
            statement.close();
        } catch (SQLException e) {}
```

```
    }
    if (connection != null) {
        try {
            connection.close();
        } catch (SQLException e) {}
    }
}
return Optional.empty();
}
```

As the method name suggests, this code is used to find a post by its id. Even though the logic is straightforward, it has a lot of boilerplate code to handle exceptions, opening, and closing database connections, and such.

Spring Framework introduced a class called as `JdbcTemplate`, which implements the famous Template Design Pattern to abstract away all the boilerplate code for us and perform all the error handling and database connection management in the background. So let's go ahead and learn how to implement this using Spring Framework without using the Spring Boot starter for JDBC.

Using JdbcTemplate Without Spring Boot

First, let's take a quick look at how you can generally use Spring's `JdbcTemplate` (without Spring Boot) by registering the `DataSource`, `TransactionManager`, and `JdbcTemplate` beans. The `DataSource` is the interface that contains the blueprint to interact with the database of your choice. Each database driver has an implementation of this `DataSource` interface, and it is responsible for creating the database connection.

The `TransactionManager` bean is used to manage transactions. No prizes for guessing that this means creating, committing, and rolling back the database transactions.

To get started, add the following dependencies to the `pom.xml` file of the Spring blog application:

```
<dependency>
    <groupId>org.springframework</groupId>
    <artifactId>spring-jdbc</artifactId>
</dependency>
```

```
<dependency>
    <groupId>mysql</groupId>
    <artifactId>mysql-connector-java</artifactId>
    <scope>runtime</scope>
</dependency>
<dependency>
    <groupId>org.apache.commons</groupId>
    <artifactId>commons-dbcp2</artifactId>
    <version>2.9.0</version>
</dependency>
```

These dependencies add the JDBC support from Spring Framework to your project, along with the MySQL database driver, followed by the commons-dbcp2 database connection pooling library.

Now create a class called AppConfig.java inside the config folder with the following code:

```
@Configuration
@ComponentScan
@EnableTransactionManagement
@PropertySource(value = { "classpath:application.properties" })
public class AppConfig {
    @Autowired
    private Environment env;
    @Bean
    public static PropertySourcesPlaceholderConfigurer
    placeHolderConfigurer()
    {
        return new PropertySourcesPlaceholderConfigurer();
    }
    @Value("${init-db:false}")
    private String initDatabase;
    @Bean
    public JdbcTemplate jdbcTemplate(DataSource dataSource)
    {
        return new JdbcTemplate(dataSource);
```

```
    }
    @Bean
    public PlatformTransactionManager transactionManager(DataSource
    dataSource)
    {
        return new DataSourceTransactionManager(dataSource);
    }
    @Bean
    public DataSource dataSource()
    {
        BasicDataSource dataSource = new BasicDataSource();
        dataSource.setDriverClassName(env.getProperty("jdbc.
        driverClassName"));
        dataSource.setUrl(env.getProperty("jdbc.url"));
        dataSource.setUsername(env.getProperty("jdbc.username"));
        dataSource.setPassword(env.getProperty("jdbc.password"));
        return dataSource;
    }
    @Bean
    public DataSourceInitializer dataSourceInitializer(DataSource
    dataSource)
    {
        DataSourceInitializer dataSourceInitializer = new
        DataSourceInitializer();
        dataSourceInitializer.setDataSource(dataSource);
        ResourceDatabasePopulator databasePopulator = new
        ResourceDatabasePopulator();
        databasePopulator.addScript(new ClassPathResource("data.sql"));
        dataSourceInitializer.setDatabasePopulator(databasePopulator);
        dataSourceInitializer.setEnabled(Boolean.
        parseBoolean(initDatabase));
        return dataSourceInitializer;
    }
}
```

This code first enables transaction management using the
@EnableTransactionManagement annotation and then it defines a bean for
JdbcTemplate, a bean for DataSource with a connection pool, a bean for
TransactionManager, and a bean that initializes the database at the startup of the
application, based on the property init-db. If this property is true, you can initialize the
database at startup using a database script called data.sql.

You should configure the JDBC connection parameters in src/main/resources/
application.properties as follows:

```
jdbc.driverClassName=com.mysql.cj.jdbc.Driver
jdbc.url=jdbc:mysql://localhost:3306/springblog
jdbc.username=root
jdbc.password=admin
init-db=true
```

You can then create a database setup script called data.sql in src/main/resources
as follows:

```
DROP TABLE IF EXISTS COMMENTS;
DROP TABLE IF EXISTS POSTS;
CREATE TABLE POSTS
(
    ID int NOT NULL AUTO_INCREMENT,
    TITLE varchar(50) NOT NULL,
    DESCRIPTION varchar(500) NOT NULL,
    BODY LONGTEXT DEFAULT NULL,
    SLUG varchar(60) DEFAULT NULL,
    POST_STATUS ENUM ('DRAFT','PUBLISHED'),
    CREATED_ON datetime DEFAULT NULL,
    UPDATED_ON datetime DEFAULT NULL,
    PRIMARY KEY (ID)
);

CREATE TABLE COMMENTS
(
    ID int NOT NULL AUTO_INCREMENT,
    POST_ID int NOT NULL,
```

```
TITLE varchar(200) NOT NULL,
AUTHOR_NAME varchar(200) NOT NULL,
BODY LONGTEXT DEFAULT NULL,
CREATED_ON datetime DEFAULT NULL,
UPDATED_ON datetime DEFAULT NULL,
PRIMARY KEY (ID),
FOREIGN KEY (POST_ID) REFERENCES POSTS(ID)
);
```

If you prefer to keep the schema generation script and seed the data insertion script separately, you can put them in separate files and add them as follows:

```
databasePopulator.addScripts(new ClassPathResource("schema.sql"),
                        new ClassPathResource("seed-data.sql") );
```

With this configuration in place, let's make some small changes to your domain model. Let's change the type of createdOn and updatedOn from LocalDateTime to LocalDate because the default jakarta.sql.Date class does not store the time component, only the date.

```
        private LocalDate createdOn;
        private LocalDate updatedOn;
```

Now let's create another class called JdbcPostRepository.java, which contains the actual code to interact with the database using the JdbcTemplate class.

```
package com.apress.demo.springblog.repository;
import com.apress.demo.springblog.domain.Post;
import lombok.RequiredArgsConstructor;
import org.springframework.jdbc.core.JdbcTemplate;
import org.springframework.stereotype.Repository;
import java.sql.PreparedStatement;
import java.sql.Statement;
import java.util.Set;
import java.util.stream.Collectors;
@Repository
@RequiredArgsConstructor
```

```java
public class JdbcPostRepository {
    private final JdbcTemplate jdbcTemplate;

    public Set<Post> findAllPosts() {
        return jdbcTemplate.queryForStream("select id, title, description,
        body, slug, post_status, created_on, updated_on from posts", new
        PostMapper())
                .collect(Collectors.toSet());
    }
    public void addPost(Post post) {
        final String sql = "insert into posts(title, description, body,
        slug, post_status, created_on, updated_on) " +
                        "values (?,?,?,?,?,?,?)";
      jdbcTemplate.update(con -> {
            PreparedStatement preparedStatement = con.prepareStatement(sql,
            Statement.RETURN_GENERATED_KEYS);
            preparedStatement.setString(1, post.getTitle());
            preparedStatement.setString(2, post.getDescription());
            preparedStatement.setString(3, post.getBody());
            preparedStatement.setString(4, post.getSlug());
            preparedStatement.setObject(5, post.getPostStatus());
            preparedStatement.setDate(6, java.sql.Date.valueOf(post.
            getCreatedOn()));
            preparedStatement.setDate(7, java.sql.Date.valueOf(post.
            getUpdatedOn()));
            return preparedStatement;
        });
    }
}
```

- The @Repository annotation will mark your JdbcRepository as a
  Spring Repository bean.

- Using the constructor injection, you inject the JdbcTemplate class
  into the JdbcRepository class. The constructors will be generated at
  compile time by the @RequiredArgsConstructor.

- The findAllPosts() method uses the queryForStream() method of the JdbcTemplate object to execute the select statement and returns a stream of Post objects, which are collected into a Set.

- Lastly, the addPost() method uses the update() method of jdbcTemplate to execute the insert statement. You are using the PreparedStatement class to map the data to the query because PreparedStatement is, in general, faster than the Statement class and also it helps mitigate SQL injection attacks.

You must also create a class to map the data from the ResultSet, while querying for the posts, inside the findAllPosts() method into the Post object. For that, you must create the following PostMapper class, which implements an interface called RowMapper:

```java
public class PostMapper implements RowMapper<Post> {
    @Override
    public Post mapRow(ResultSet rs, int rowNum) throws SQLException {
        Post post = new Post();
        post.setId(rs.getInt("id"));
        post.setTitle(rs.getString("title"));
        post.setDescription(rs.getString("description"));
        post.setBody(rs.getString("body"));
        post.setPostStatus((PostStatus) rs.getObject("post_status"));
        post.setCreatedOn(convertToLocalDateTime(rs.getDate("created_on")));
        post.setUpdatedOn(convertToLocalDateTime(rs.getDate("updated_on")));
        return post;
    }
    private LocalDate convertToLocalDateTime(Date date) {
        if (date == null) {
            return null;
        } else {
            return date.toLocalDate();
        }
    }
}
```

The mapRow() method goes through all the fields inside the Post object and maps each field from ResultSet. Notice that for mapping the createdOn and updatedOn fields, you must create custom mapping logic because you defined these fields as type LocalDate instead of jakarta.sql.Date.

Before testing your changes, you need to make a few more changes inside the PostService class: replace the usage of PostRepository with the JdbcPostRepository class, and also adapt the logic inside the addPost() method to set the createdOn and updatedOn fields, before saving the Post object to the database.

```java
package com.apress.demo.springblog.service;
import com.apress.demo.springblog.domain.Post;
        import com.apress.demo.springblog.repository.JdbcPostRepository;
        import lombok.RequiredArgsConstructor;
        import org.springframework.stereotype.Service;

        import java.time.LocalDate;
        import java.util.Set;
        @Service
        @RequiredArgsConstructor
        public class PostService {
    private final JdbcPostRepository postRepository;
    public void addPost(Post post) {
        post.setCreatedOn(LocalDate.now());
        post.setUpdatedOn(LocalDate.now());
        postRepository.addPost(post);
    }
    public Set<Post> findAllPosts() {
        return postRepository.findAllPosts();
    }
    public boolean postExistsWithTitle(String title) {
        return postRepository.findAllPosts().stream()
                .anyMatch(post -> post.getTitle().equals(title));
    }
}
```

Now, let's see how to use JdbcTemplate without manually configuring all these beans inside the AppConfig.java class by using Spring Boot.

Using JdbcTemplate with Spring Boot

Using Spring Boot's autoconfiguration feature, you don't have to configure beans manually. To get started, replace the `spring-jdbc` dependency in the `pom.xml` file with the `spring-boot-starter-jdbc` module.

```
<dependency>
    <groupId>org.springframework.boot</groupId>
    <artifactId>spring-boot-starter-jdbc</artifactId>
</dependency>
```

By adding the `spring-boot-starter-jdbc` module, you get the following autoconfiguration features:

- The `spring-boot-starter-jdbc` module transitively pulls the `com.zaxxer.HikariCP` dependency, which is used to configure the `DataSource` bean.

- If you have not defined a `DataSource` bean explicitly and if you have any embedded database drivers in the classpath, such as H2, HSQL, or Derby, then Spring Boot will automatically register the `DataSource` bean using the in-memory database settings.

- If you haven't registered any of the following beans, Spring Boot registers them automatically:

  - `PlatformTransactionManager` (`DataSourceTransactionManager`)

  - `JdbcTemplate`

  - `NamedParameterJdbcTemplate`

- You can have the `schema.sql` and `data.sql` files in the root classpath, which Spring Boot will automatically use to initialize the database.

Initializing the Database

Spring Boot uses the `spring.sql.init.mode` property value to determine whether to initialize the database. If the `spring.sql.init.mode` property is set to `always`, Spring Boot will use the `schema.sql` and `data.sql` files in the root classpath to initialize the database.

In addition to `schema.sql` and `data.sql`, Spring Boot will load the `schema-${platform}.sql` and `data-${platform}.sql` files if they are available in the root classpath. Here, the platform value is the value of the `spring.sql.init.platform` property, which can be `hsqldb`, `h2`, `oracle`, `mysql`, `postgresql`, and so on.

You can customize the default names of the scripts using the following properties:

```
spring.datasource.schema=create-db.sql
spring.datasource.data=seed-data.sql
```

If you want to turn off the database initialization, you can set `spring.sql.init.initialize=never`. If there are script execution errors, the application will fail to start. If you want to continue, you can set `spring.sql.init.continue-on-error=true`.

Testing JDBC Code

Let's write tests to make sure that your JDBC code is working. For this, you can use h2 as in the in-memory test database. To add the h2 database driver to the `pom.xml` file, you use the following code:

```
<dependency>
    <groupId>com.h2database</groupId>
    <artifactId>h2</artifactId>
    <scope>test</scope>
</dependency>
```

Now you can create a JUnit test class to test the `JdbcPostRepository` methods, as shown in Listing 5-1.

Listing 5-1. JdbcPostRepositoryTest.java

```
package com.apress.demo.springblog;

import com.apress.demo.springblog.domain.Post;
import com.apress.demo.springblog.repository.JdbcPostRepository;
import org.assertj.core.api.Assertions;
import org.junit.jupiter.api.Test;
import org.springframework.beans.factory.annotation.Autowired;
import org.springframework.boot.test.autoconfigure.jdbc.JdbcTest;
import org.springframework.context.annotation.Import;
```

```
import java.time.LocalDate;

@JdbcTest
@Import(JdbcPostRepository.class)
class JdbcRepositoryTest {

    @Autowired
    private JdbcPostRepository postRepository;

    @Test
    void testFindAllPosts() {
        Post post = new Post();
        post.setTitle("sample blog post");
        post.setDescription("sample blog post");
        post.setBody("sample blog post");
        post.setSlug("sample-blog-post");
        post.setUpdatedOn(LocalDate.now());
        post.setCreatedOn(LocalDate.now());
        postRepository.addPost(post);

        Assertions.assertThat(postRepository.findAllPosts()).hasSize(1);
    }
}
```

In this test class, you use an annotation called @JdbcTest, which is a sliced annotation provided by Spring Boot to test the JDBC-related functionality in your application. This annotation will create all the required beans needed to create an application context, run the JDBC code, and auto-configure the test database, transaction management features, and all the necessary beans required to run the JDBC code. Normally, many developers use another annotation called @SpringBootTest, which does all of the above and beyond. This annotation will load the complete Spring Boot application context, including beans like Controllers, Services, and other Config classes defined in your code.

Since your main goal is to test the JDBC-related code in isolation, it doesn't make sense to load the whole application context for your JDBC-related unit tests. It makes perfect sense to use the @SpringBootTest annotation when you want to test multiple classes together or when you want to create an integration test. We will discuss testing-related concepts in much more detail in a dedicated chapter.

> **Note**   By default, the Spring Boot features, such as external properties, and logging, are available in the `ApplicationContext` only if you use `SpringApplication`. So, Spring Boot provides the `@SpringBootTest` annotation to configure the `ApplicationContext` for tests that use `SpringApplication` behind the scenes.

Using Other Connection Pooling Libraries

Spring Boot, by default, pulls in the `com.zaxxer.hikari.HikariCP` jar and uses `com.zaxxer.hikari.HikariDataSource` to configure the `DataSource` bean.

Spring Boot checks the availability of the following classes and uses the first one available in the classpath:

- `com.zaxxer.hikari.HikariDataSource`

- `org.apache.tomcat.jdbc.pool.DataSource`

- `org.apache.commons.dbcp2.BasicDataSource`

If you want to use `Tomcat's DataSource`, you can exclude `HikariCP` and add the `tomcat-jdbc` dependency as follows:

```
<dependency>
    <groupId>org.springframework.boot</groupId>
    <artifactId>spring-boot-starter-jdbc</artifactId>
    <exclusions>
        <exclusion>
            <groupId>com.zaxxer</groupId>
            <artifactId>HikariCP</artifactId>
        </exclusion>
    </exclusions>
</dependency>
<dependency>
    <groupId>org.apache.tomcat</groupId>
    <artifactId>tomcat-jdbc</artifactId>
</dependency>
```

You can configure specific settings for the connection pool library as follows:

```
spring.datasource.tomcat.*= # Tomcat Datasource specific settings
spring.datasource.hikari.*= # Hikari DataSource specific settings
spring.datasource.dbcp2.*= # Commons DBCP2 specific settings
```

For example, you can set the `HikariCP` connection pool settings as follows:

```
spring.datasource.hikari.allow-pool-suspension=true
spring.datasource.hikari.connection-test-query=SELECT 1
spring.datasource.hikari.transaction-isolation=TRANSACTION_READ_COMMITTED
spring.datasource.hikari.connection-timeout=45000
```

Using Spring Data JDBC

You can observe that using Spring Boot JDBC support is also not that easy to implement, as you must write the `JdbcTemplate` logic to query and update the database and then create an instance of `RowMapper` to map the query result set to your domain objects. This will become a laborious task if you have many entities to manage in your application. Luckily, Spring Team introduced a simpler way to work with JDBC using the Spring Data JDBC framework.

Spring Data JDBC comes under the umbrella of the Spring Data project, which abstracts the logic to interact with different databases without worrying about the implementation details.

For example, you can delete your `PostMapper.java` class and `JdbcPostRepository.java` classes and replace them with the following `PostJdbcRepository.java` interface:

```java
public interface PostJdbcDataRepository extends CrudRepository<Post,
Integer> {
    @Query("select * from posts where title= :title")
    Optional<Object> findByTitle(@Param("title") String title);
}
```

Shocking, isn't it ? All that boilerplate code is replaced by hardly four lines of code. Spring Data JDBC acts like an object relational mapping (ORM) framework under the hood and provides a mapping between your Java classes and the database tables.

You will learn about Spring Data in much detail in Chapter 8 when we discuss Spring Data JPA, another project under the Spring Data umbrella that helps us work with JPA.

The CrudRepository interface provides all the functionality to save, update, read, and delete (CRUD operations) on the database. The Spring Data project provides the implementations dynamically for these operations based on the underlying framework.

Similar to the CrudRepository interface, the PagingAndSortingRepository interface automatically provides pagination and sorting support.

You can also write custom SQL queries by using the @Query annotation. The `:title` placeholder will be replaced with the title String variable at the time of query execution.

Database Migration with Flyway

Having a proper database migration plan for enterprise applications is crucial. The new versions of the application may be released with new features or enhancements that involve changes to the database schema. It is strongly recommended to version the database scripts to track which changes were introduced in which release and restore the database to a particular version if required.

This section looks at one popular database migration tool, Flyway, which Spring Boot supports out of the box.

You can create database migration scripts as `.sql` files following a specific naming pattern so that Flyway can run these scripts in order based on the current schema version. Flyway creates a database table called `schema_version` that keeps track of the current schema version so that it will run any pending migration scripts while performing the migration operation (Figure 5-1).

installed_rank	version	description	type	script	checksum	installed_by	installed_on	executi...	success
1	1.1	init	SQL	V1_1__init.sql	72970307	root	2017-03-26 09:01	300	1
2	1.2	Add Col Dob	SQL	V1_2__Add_Col_Dob.sql	487040151	root	2017-03-26 09:01	583	1
(NULL)	(NULL)	(NULL)	(NULL)	(NULL)	(NULL)	(NULL)	CURRENT_TIMESTAM	(NULL)	(NULL)

Figure 5-1. *Flyway schema_version table*

You should follow this naming convention when naming the migration scripts to run in the correct order:

```
V{Version}__{Description}.sql
```

Here, {Version} is the.version number and it can contain dots (.) and underscores (_). The {Description} can contain text describing the migration changes. A separator should separate {Version} and {Description}; the default is two consecutive underscores (__), but this option is configurable.

Examples:

```
V1__Init.sql
V1.1_CreatePostTable.sql
V1_2__UpdatePostTable.sql
```

To add Flyway migration support to a Spring Boot application, you just need to add the flyway-core dependency and place the migration scripts in the db/migration directory in the classpath.

```
<dependency>
    <groupId>org.flywaydb</groupId>
    <artifactId>flyway-mysql</artifactId>
</dependency>
```

Create the two migration scripts shown in Listings 5-2 and 5-3 in the src/main/resources/db/migration directory.

Listing 5-2. V1.0__Init.sql

```
DROP TABLE IF EXISTS COMMENTS;
DROP TABLE IF EXISTS POSTS;
CREATE TABLE POSTS
(
    ID int NOT NULL AUTO_INCREMENT,
    TITLE varchar(50) NOT NULL,
    DESCRIPTION varchar(500) NOT NULL,
    BODY LONGTEXT DEFAULT NULL,
    SLUG varchar(60) DEFAULT NULL,
    POST_STATUS ENUM ('DRAFT','PUBLISHED'),
    CREATED_ON datetime DEFAULT NULL,
    UPDATED_ON datetime DEFAULT NULL,
    PRIMARY KEY (ID)
);
```

```
CREATE TABLE COMMENTS
(
    ID int NOT NULL AUTO_INCREMENT,
    POST_ID int NOT NULL,
    TITLE varchar(200) NOT NULL,
    AUTHOR_NAME varchar(200) NOT NULL,
    BODY LONGTEXT DEFAULT NULL,
    CREATED_ON datetime DEFAULT NULL,
    UPDATED_ON datetime DEFAULT NULL,
    PRIMARY KEY (ID),
    FOREIGN KEY (POST_ID) REFERENCES POSTS(ID)
);
```

Listing 5-3. V1.1__Add_Description_Column.sql

```
ALTER TABLE COMMENTS ADD COLUMN DESCRIPTION varchar(50) DEFAULT NULL;
```

Now, when you start the application, it will check the current schema version number (maximum of the `schema_version.version` column value) and run if there are any pending migration scripts with a higher version value.

If you have an existing database with tables, you can take the dump of the current database structure and make it the baseline script so that you can clean the database and start from scratch. If you don't want to dump and rerun the initial script (common in production environments), you can set `spring.flyway.baseline-on-migrate=true`, which will insert a baseline record in the `schema_version` table with the version set to 1. Now you can add migration scripts with version numbers higher than 1—say 1.1, 1_2, etc.

For more information about Flyway migrations, see `https://flywaydb.org/`.

Summary

In this chapter, you learned how to use `JdbcTemplate` easily in Spring Boot and connect to databases like h2 and MySQL. The chapter also used SQL scripts and various connection pooling libraries to initialize a database. The next chapter explains how to use MyBatis with Spring Boot.

## CHAPTER 6

Working with MyBatis

MyBatis is an open-source Java persistence framework that abstracts JDBC boilerplate code and provides a simple and easy-to-use API to interact with the database.

Unlike Hibernate, a full-blown ORM framework, MyBatis is a SQL mapping framework. It automates the process of populating the SQL resultset into Java objects, and it persists data into tables by extracting the data from the Java objects.

This chapter covers how to use the Spring Boot MyBatis starter, execute database queries using MyBatis XML, and use annotation-based mappers.

Using the Spring Boot MyBatis Starter

The MyBatis community built the Spring Boot starter for MyBatis, which you can use while creating the Spring Boot project from the Spring Initializer or the IDE. You can explore the source code on GitHub at `https://github.com/mybatis/spring-boot-starter`.

Let's see how to use the Spring Boot MyBatis starter to quickly use MyBatis in Spring Boot applications.

1. Create a Spring Boot Maven project and configure the MyBatis Starter dependency and H2/MySQL driver dependencies.

```
<dependency>
    <groupId>org.mybatis.spring.boot</groupId>
    <artifactId>mybatis-spring-boot-starter</artifactId>
    <version>2.2.2</version>
</dependency>
<dependency>
    <groupId>com.h2database</groupId>
    <artifactId>h2</artifactId>
</dependency>
```

119

© K. Siva Prasad Reddy, Sai Upadhyayula 2023
K. S. P. Reddy and S. Upadhyayula, *Beginning Spring Boot 3*, https://doi.org/10.1007/978-1-4842-8792-7_6

```
<dependency>
    <groupId>mysql</groupId>
    <artifactId>mysql-connector-java</artifactId>
</dependency>
```

This example reuses the User.java, schema.sql, and data.sql files created in the previous chapter.

2. Create the MyBatis SQL Mapper interface UserMapper.java with a few database operations, as shown in Listing 6-1.

Listing 6-1. com.apress.demo.mappers.UserMapper.java

```
package com.apress.demo.mappers;
public interface UserMapper
{
    void insertUser(User user);
    User findUserById(Integer id);
    List<User> findAllUsers();
}
```

3. You must create mapper XML files to define the queries for the SQL statements mapped to the corresponding mapper interface methods. Create the UserMapper.xml file in the src/main/resources/com/apress/demo/mappers/ directory, as shown in Listing 6-2.

Listing 6-2. src/main/resources/com/apress/demo/mappers/UserMapper.xml

```
<!DOCTYPE mapper
    PUBLIC "-//mybatis.org//DTD Mapper 3.0//EN"
    "http://mybatis.org/dtd/mybatis-3-mapper.dtd">
<mapper namespace="com.apress.demo.mappers.UserMapper">
<resultMap id="UserResultMap" type="User">
    <id column="id"  property="id"  />
    <result column="name"  property="name"  />
    <result column="email"  property="email"  />
</resultMap>
```

```
<select id="findAllUsers" resultMap="UserResultMap">
        select id, name, email from users
</select>
<select id="findUserById" resultMap="UserResultMap">
        select id, name, email from users WHERE id=#{id}
</select>
<insert id="insertUser" parameterType="User" useGeneratedKeys="true"
            keyProperty="id">
        insert into users(name,email) values(#{name},#{email})
</insert>
</mapper>
```

A few things to observe here are the following:

- The namespace in the mapper XML should be the same as the Fully Qualified Name (FQN) of the mapper interface.

- The statement id values should be the same as the mapper interface method names.

- Suppose the query result column names are different from the bean property names. If so, you can use the `<resultMap>` configuration to provide the mapping between column names and their corresponding bean property names.

4. MyBatis also provides annotation-based query configurations without requiring mapper XMLs. You can create the UserMapper. java interface and configure the mapped SQLs using annotations, as shown in Listing 6-3.

Listing 6-3. com.apress.demo.mappers.UserMapper.java

```
public interface UserMapper
{
    @Insert("insert into users(name,email) values(#{name},#{email})")
    @SelectKey(statement="call identity()", keyProperty="id",
                before=false, resultType=Integer.class)
    void insertUser(User user);
    @Select("select id, name, email from users WHERE id=#{id}")
```

```
    User findUserById(Integer id);
    @Select("select id, name, email from users")
    List<User> findAllUsers();
}
```

5. Next, you must configure the starter configuration parameters. Configure the type-aliases-package and mapper-locations parameters in application.properties as follows:

```
mybatis.type-aliases-package=com.apress.demo.domain
mybatis.mapper-locations=classpath*:/mappers/*.xml
```

6. Create the entry point class called SpringbootMyBatisDemoApplication.java, as shown in Listing 6-4.

Listing 6-4. com.apress.demo.SpringbootMyBatisDemoApplication.java

```
@SpringBootApplication
@MapperScan("com.apress.demo.mappers")
public class SpringbootMyBatisDemoApplication
{
    public static void main(String[] args)
    {
        SpringApplication.run(SpringbootMyBatisDemoApplication.
        class, args);
    }
}
```

Note   This example uses the @MapperScan("com.apress.demo.mappers") annotation to specify where to look for the mapper interfaces. Instead of using @MapperScan, you could also use annotated mapper interfaces with the new @Mapper annotation that shipped with MyBatis 3.4.0.

7. Create a JUnit test class and test the `UserMapper` methods, as shown in Listing 6-5.

Listing 6-5. com.apress.demo.SpringbootMyBatisDemoApplicationTests.java

```
@SpringBootTest
public class SpringbootMyBatisDemoApplicationTests
{
    @Autowired
    private UserMapper userMapper;
    @Test
    public void findAllUsers()  {
        List<User> users = userMapper.findAllUsers();
        assertNotNull(users);
        assertTrue(users.isEmpty());
    }
    @Test
    public void findUserById()  {
        User user = userMapper.findUserById(1);
        assertNotNull(user);
    }
    @Test
    public void createUser() {
        User user = new User(0, "george", "george@gmail.com");
        userMapper.insertUser(user);
        User newUser = userMapper.findUserById(user.getId());
        assertEquals("george", newUser.getName());
        assertEquals("george@gmail.com", newUser.getEmail());
    }
}
```

The Spring Boot MyBatis starter provides the following MyBatis configuration parameters, which you can use to customize your MyBatis settings:

```
mybatis.config-location =  #mybatis config filename
mybatis.check-config-location=  # Indicates whether to perform presence
                                 check of the MyBatis xml config file
```

```
mybatis.mapper-locations =  #mappers file locations
mybatis.type-aliases-package =  #domain object's package
mybatis.type-handlers-package =  #handler's package
mybatis.check-config-location =  #check the mybatis configuration exists
mybatis.executor-type =  #mode of execution. Default is SIMPLE
mybatis.configuration-properties=  #externalized properties for mybatis
                                 configuration
```

You can read more about MyBatis at http://blog.mybatis.org/p/products.
html and https://mybatis.org/spring-boot-starter/mybatis-spring-boot-
autoconfigure/.

Summary

In this chapter, you learned how to work with MyBatis in Spring Boot applications. The next chapter covers how to use another popular Java persistence framework with Spring Boot, called JOOQ.

CHAPTER 7

Working with JOOQ

JOOQ (Java Object Oriented Querying) is a persistence framework that embraces SQL. JOOQ provides the following features:

- Typesafe SQL using DSL API

- Typesafe database object referencing using code generation

- Easy-to-use API for querying and data fetching

- SQL logging and debugging

This chapter covers using the Spring Boot JOOQ Starter, using the JOOQ Maven Codegen plugin to generate code from the database schema, and performing various operations.

Introduction to JOOQ

JOOQ is a Java persistence framework that provides a Fluent API to write typesafe SQL queries. JOOQ provides code generation tools to generate code based on the database schema, and you can use that generated code to build typesafe queries.

Listing 7-1 shows code to query a database. In the coming sections, we will dig deeper and see how to implement this in your Spring blog application.

Listing 7-1. Using the JOOQ DSL API

```
String userName = "root";
String password = "admin";
String url = "jdbc:mysql://localhost:3306/test";
Class.forName('com.mysql.jdbc.Driver');
Connection conn = DriverManager.getConnection(url, userName, password);
DSLContext jooq = DSL.using(conn, SQLDialect.MYSQL);
```

© K. Siva Prasad Reddy, Sai Upadhyayula 2023
K. S. P. Reddy and S. Upadhyayula, *Beginning Spring Boot 3*, https://doi.org/10.1007/978-1-4842-8792-7_7

```
Result<Record> result = jooq.select().from(POST).fetch();
for (Record r : result)
{
    Integer id = r.getValue(POST.ID);
    String title = r.getValue(POST.TITLE);
    String content = r.getValue(POST.CONTENT);
    System.out.println("Id: " + id + " title: " + title + " content: " +
    content);
}
```

This code snippet created a database named Connection and instantiated the DSLContext object, which is the entry point for using JOOQ QueryDSL. Using the DSLContext object, it queried the POST table and iterated through the resultset.

You can integrate JOOQ with the Spring Framework so that you don't have to manually create a connection and instantiate DSLContext. See www.jooq.org/doc/3.17/ manual-single-page/#code-generation learn how to integrate Spring with JOOQ.

Spring Boot provides JOOQ Starter to get up and running with JOOQ quickly. You do this by leveraging its autoconfiguration mechanism.

Using Spring Boot's JOOQ Starter

Spring Boot provides a starter called spring-boot-starter-jooq, which allows you to integrate with JOOQ quickly. This section shows how to use spring-boot-starter-jooq via a step-by-step approach.

Configuring Spring Boot JOOQ Starter

Create a Spring Boot Maven-based project and add the spring-boot-starter-jooq dependency along with H2 and MySQL driver dependencies.

```
<dependency>
    <groupId>org.springframework.boot</groupId>
    <artifactId>spring-boot-starter-jooq</artifactId>
</dependency>
<dependency>
    <groupId>org.springframework.boot</groupId>
```

```
        <artifactId>spring-boot-starter-test</artifactId>
        <scope>test</scope>
</dependency>
<dependency>
        <groupId>com.h2database</groupId>
        <artifactId>h2</artifactId>
</dependency>
<dependency>
        <groupId>mysql</groupId>
        <artifactId>mysql-connector-java</artifactId>
</dependency>
```

This example uses the H2 in-memory database first. Later you will see how to use MySQL.

Database Schema

Create a simple database with two tables named POSTS and COMMENTS. Create the database creation script called src/main/resources/data.sql, as shown in Listing 7-2.

Listing 7-2. The src/main/resources/data.sql File

```
DROP TABLE IF EXISTS COMMENTS;
DROP TABLE IF EXISTS POSTS;
CREATE TABLE POSTS
(
    ID int NOT NULL AUTO_INCREMENT,
    TITLE varchar(50) NOT NULL,
    DESCRIPTION varchar(500) NOT NULL,
    BODY LONGTEXT DEFAULT NULL,
    SLUG varchar(60) DEFAULT NULL,
    POST_STATUS ENUM ('DRAFT','PUBLISHED'),
    CREATED_ON datetime DEFAULT NULL,
    UPDATED_ON datetime DEFAULT NULL,
    PRIMARY KEY (ID)
);
```

```
CREATE TABLE COMMENTS
(
    ID int NOT NULL AUTO_INCREMENT,
    POST_ID int NOT NULL,
    TITLE varchar(200) NOT NULL,
    AUTHOR_NAME varchar(200) NOT NULL,
    BODY LONGTEXT DEFAULT NULL,
    CREATED_ON datetime DEFAULT NULL,
    UPDATED_ON datetime DEFAULT NULL,
    PRIMARY KEY (ID),
    FOREIGN KEY (POST_ID) REFERENCES POSTS(ID)
);
```

Code Generation Using the JOOQ Maven Codegen Plugin

JOOQ provides the JOOQ Maven Codegen plugin to generate database artifacts using Maven goals. This section shows how to use Maven profiles to configure the jooq-codegen-maven configuration properties based on database type. See Listing 7-3.

Listing 7-3. The jooq-codegen-maven Plugin Configuration in the pom.xml File

```xml
<profiles>
    <profile>
        <id>h2</id>
        <activation>
            <activeByDefault>true</activeByDefault>
        </activation>
        <build>
            <plugins>
                <plugin>
                    <groupId>org.codehaus.mojo</groupId>
                    <artifactId>sql-maven-plugin</artifactId>
                    <version>1.5</version>
                    <executions>
                        <execution>
                            <phase>generate-sources</phase>
                            <goals>
```

```xml
                    <goal>execute</goal>
                </goals>
            </execution>
        </executions>
        <dependencies>
            <dependency>
                <groupId>com.h2database</groupId>
                <artifactId>h2</artifactId>
                <version>${h2.version}</version>
            </dependency>
        </dependencies>
        <configuration>
            <driver>org.h2.Driver</driver>
            <url>jdbc:h2:~/springbootjooq</url>
            <srcFiles>
                <srcFile>${basedir}/src/main/resources/reset.
                sql</srcFile>
                <srcFile>${basedir}/src/main/resources/schema.
                sql</srcFile>
            </srcFiles>
        </configuration>
    </plugin>
    <plugin>
        <groupId>org.jooq</groupId>
        <artifactId>jooq-codegen-maven</artifactId>
        <executions>
            <execution>
                <goals>
                    <goal>generate</goal>
                </goals>
            </execution>
        </executions>
        <dependencies>
            <dependency>
                <groupId>com.h2database</groupId>
                <artifactId>h2</artifactId>
```

```
                        <version>${h2.version}</version>
                    </dependency>
                </dependencies>
                <configuration>
                    <jdbc>
                        <driver>org.h2.Driver</driver>
                        <url>jdbc:h2:~/springbootjooq</url>
                    </jdbc>
                    <generator>
                        <name>org.jooq.codegen.JavaGenerator</name>
                        <database>
                            <name>org.jooq.meta.h2.H2Database</name>
                            <includes>.*</includes>
                            <excludes/>
                            <inputSchema>PUBLIC</inputSchema>
                        </database>
                        <target>
                            <packageName>com.apress.demo.jooq.domain
                            </packageName>
                            <directory>gensrc/main/java</directory>
                        </target>
                    </generator>
                </configuration>
            </plugin>
        </plugins>
    </build>
</profile>
<profile>
    <id>mysql</id>

    <build>
        <plugins>
            <plugin>
                <groupId>org.codehaus.mojo</groupId>
                <artifactId>sql-maven-plugin</artifactId>
                <version>1.5</version>
```

```xml
        <executions>
            <execution>
                <phase>generate-sources</phase>
                <goals>
                    <goal>execute</goal>
                </goals>
            </execution>
        </executions>
        <dependencies>
            <dependency>
                <groupId>mysql</groupId>
                <artifactId>mysql-connector-java</artifactId>
                <version>${mysql.version}</version>
            </dependency>
        </dependencies>
        <configuration>
            <driver>com.mysql.cj.jdbc.Driver</driver>
            <url>jdbc:mysql://localhost:3306/springblog</url>
            <username>root</username>
            <password>mysql</password>
            <srcFiles>
                <srcFile>${basedir}/src/main/resources/schema.
                sql</srcFile>
            </srcFiles>
        </configuration>
    </plugin>
    <plugin>
        <groupId>org.jooq</groupId>
        <artifactId>jooq-codegen-maven</artifactId>
        <executions>
            <execution>
                <goals>
                    <goal>generate</goal>
                </goals>
            </execution>
        </executions>
```

```
                    <dependencies>
                        <dependency>
                            <groupId>mysql</groupId>
                            <artifactId>mysql-connector-java</artifactId>
                            <version>${mysql.version}</version>
                        </dependency>
                    </dependencies>
                    <configuration>
                        <jdbc>
                            <driver>com.mysql.cj.jdbc.Driver</driver>
                            <url>jdbc:mysql://localhost:3306/
                            springblog</url>
                            <user>root</user>
                            <password>mysql</password>
                        </jdbc>
                        <generator>
                            <name>org.jooq.codegen.JavaGenerator</name>
                            <database>
                                <name>org.jooq.meta.mysql.
                                MySQLDatabase</name>
                                <includes>.*</includes>
                                <excludes/>
                                <inputSchema>springblog</inputSchema>
                            </database>
                            <target>
                                <packageName>com.apress.demo.jooq.domain
                                </packageName>
                                <directory>gensrc/main/java</directory>
                            </target>
                        </generator>
                    </configuration>
                </plugin>
            </plugins>
        </build>
    </profile>
</profiles>
```

This example configures two profiles (h2 and mysql) with the appropriate JDBC configuration parameters. It generates the code artifacts and places them in the com. apress.demo.jooq.domain package within the gensrc/main/java directory.

You can run the Maven build that activates the h2 or mysql profile as follows:

```
mvn clean verify -P h2 (or) mvn clean verify -P mysql
```

Using JOOQ DSL

DSLContext is the main entry point for the JOOQ DSL API. You will see how to implement the data persistence methods using the JOOQ DSL API.

First, you create the PostRepository class with the DSLContext object injected into the class, as shown in Listing 7-4.

Listing 7-4. com.apress.demo.repository.PostRepository.java

```
@Repository
@RequiredArgsConstructor
public class PostRepository {

    private final DSLContext dslContext;
    ...
    ...
}
```

When you query the database using JOOQ, you will get a Record that represents the database record and from which you can extract the required data. The following example queries the Post table, denoted as POSTS:

```
@Repository
public class PostRepository
{
        ...
        ...
public Optional<Post> findOnePost(Integer postId) {
    Record postRecord = dslContext.select().
            from(POSTS)
            .where(POSTS.ID.eq(postId))
```

```
            .fetchOne();
    if (postRecord != null) {
        return Optional.of(getPostEntity(postRecord));
    }
    return Optional.empty();
}

private Post getPostEntity(Record r) {
    Integer id = r.getValue(POSTS.ID, Integer.class);
    String title = r.getValue(POSTS.TITLE, String.class);
    String description = r.getValue(POSTS.DESCRIPTION, String.class);
    String body = r.getValue(POSTS.BODY, String.class);
    String slug = r.getValue(POSTS.SLUG, String.class);
    Post post = new Post();
    post.setId(id);
    post.setTitle(title);
    post.setDescription(description);
    post.setBody(body);
    post.setSlug(slug);
    return post;
}

}
```

In this code example, under the findOnePost() method, you run a SELECT
command on the POSTS table to retrieve the posts that match the given postId. The logic
inside this method can be translated into the following SQL query:

```
select `springblog`.`posts`.`ID`, `springblog`.`posts`.`TITLE`, `s
pringblog`.`posts`.`DESCRIPTION`, `springblog`.`posts`.`BODY`,
`springblog`.`posts`.`SLUG`, `springblog`.`posts`.`POST_STATUS`,
`springblog`.`posts`.`CREATED_ON`, `springblog`.`posts`.`UPDATED_ON` from
`springblog`.`posts` where `springblog`.`posts`.`ID` = 1
```

So now that you have viewed the SQL query, let's see how the JOOQ DSL API
correlates with the above query.

The SELECT command operation is taken care of by the `dslContext.select()` method from the JOOQ DSL API, followed by the `from()` and `where()` method calls to denote the rest of the SQL query. Finally, you use the `fetchOne()` method to fetch the result set from the database, and in the `getPostEntity()` method, you map the result set values from the database to your Post Entity.

Now let's implement the methods to insert a new `Post` in `PostRepository.java` as follows:

```
public void addPost(Post post) {
    dslContext.insertInto(POSTS)
            .set(POSTS.TITLE, post.getTitle())
            .set(POSTS.DESCRIPTION, post.getDescription())
            .set(POSTS.BODY, post.getBody())
            .set(POSTS.SLUG, post.getSlug())
            .returning(POSTS.ID)
            .fetchOne();
}
```

The example uses the `dsl.insertInto()` method to insert a new record and specifies the `returning()` method to return the auto-generated primary key column value. It also calls the `fetchOne()` method to return the newly inserted record.

Now implement fetching a list of `Posts` using JOOQ DSL as follows:

```
public List<Post> findAllPosts() {
    List<Post> posts = new ArrayList<>();

    Result<Record> recordResult = dslContext.select().from(POSTS).fetch();
    for (Record r : recordResult) {
        posts.add(getPostEntity(r));
    }
    return posts;
}
```

Similar to the `fineOnePost()` method, the `findAllPosts()` method fetches all rows from the POSTS table using `dsl.select().from()`, which returns `Result<Record>`. The example loops through `Result<Record>` and converts the record into a `Post` domain object using the `getPostEntity()` utility method you created earlier.

Finally, let's implement the method to delete a comment in the CommentRepository.java file:

```
public void deletePost(Integer postId) {
    dslContext.deleteFrom(POSTS).where(POSTS.ID.equal(postId)).execute();
}
```

You don't need to make any changes to the PostService.java class, as all the changes are done inside the PostRepository.java class methods.

You have learned how to perform various operations, like inserting new records and querying and deleting records using JOOQ DSL.

Assuming you have generated code using the H2 profile, you can run the application without any further configuration. But if you have generated code using the Mysql profile, you will have to configure the following properties in application.properties:

```
spring.datasource.driver-class-name=com.mysql.jdbc.Driver
spring.datasource.url=jdbc:mysql://localhost:3306/test
spring.datasource.username=root
spring.datasource.password=admin
spring.jooq.sql-dialect=MYSQL
```

After adding the above properties, start the application and go to http://localhost:8080/ and add some new posts. You should see that the data is persisted successfully using JOOQ.

Next, let's write some tests for the Repository classes, as shown in Listing 7-5.

Listing 7-5. PostRepositoryJooqTest.java

```
@JooqTest
@Import(PostRepository.class)
class PostRepositoryJooqTest {

    @Autowired
    private PostRepository postRepository;

    @Test
    void findAllPosts() {
        List<Post> posts = postRepository.findAllPosts();
```

```
    assertNotNull(posts);
    assertFalse(posts.isEmpty());
}

@Test
void findPostById() {
    Post post = postRepository.findOnePost(1)
            .orElseThrow(() -> new IllegalArgumentException("Cannot find
            any post withd id 1"));
    assertNotNull(post);
}

@Test
void createPost() {
    Post post = new Post();
    post.setTitle("Test");
    post.setDescription("Test");
    postRepository.addPost(post);
    assertTrue(postRepository.findAllPosts()
            .stream()
            .anyMatch(savedPost -> savedPost.getTitle().equals(post.
            getTitle())));
}
}
```

The PostRepositoryJooqTest.java test class spins up the Spring application context with beans required to test the JOOQ-related logic, with the help of the @JooqTest. This way, you don't need to load the whole application context to test your Repository layer. These are called test slices. You will learn more about them in Chapter 14.

Note   Use the correct SQL dialect for the database; otherwise, you may get SQL syntax errors at runtime.

For more info on JOOQ, visit www.jooq.org/learn/.

Summary

This chapter explained how to use the JOOQ framework by using the Spring Boot JOOQ Starter. The next chapter explains how to work with JPA (with the Hibernate implementation) in your Spring Boot applications.

CHAPTER 8

Working with JPA

The Java Persistence API (JPA) is an object-relational mapping (ORM) framework that's part of the Java EE platform. JPA simplifies the implementation of the data access layer by letting developers work with an object-oriented API instead of writing SQL queries by hand. The most popular JPA implementations are Hibernate, EclipseLink, and OpenJPA.

The Spring Framework provides a Spring ORM module to integrate easily with ORM frameworks. You can also use Spring's declarative transaction management capabilities with JPA. In addition to the Spring ORM module, the Spring Data portfolio project provides a consistent, Spring-based programming model for data access to relational and NoSQL datastores.

Spring Data integrates with most of the popular data access technologies, including JPA, MongoDB, Redis, Cassandra, Solr, and ElasticSearch.

This chapter explores the Spring Data JPA, explains how to use it with Spring Boot, and looks into how you can work with multiple databases in the same Spring Boot application.

Introducing the Spring Data JPA

Chapter 1 discussed developing a web application using SpringMVC and JPA without Spring Boot. Without using Spring Boot, you must configure beans like `DataSource`, `TransactionManager`, and `LocalContainerEntityManagerFactoryBean`. You can use the Spring Boot JPA Starter `spring-boot-starter-data-jpa` to get up and running with JPA quickly. Let's look at Spring Data JPA.

As noted in Chapter 5, Spring Data is an umbrella project that supports most of the popular data access technologies, including JPA, MongoDB, Redis, Cassandra, Solr, and ElasticSearch, in a consistent programming model. The Spring Data JPA is one of the modules for working with relational databases using JPA.

139

At times, you may need to implement data management applications to store, edit, and delete data. For those applications, you just need to implement CRUD (Create, Read, Update, Delete) operations for entities. Instead of implementing the same CRUD operations again and again or rolling out your own generic CRUD DAO implementation, Spring Data provides various repository abstractions, such as CrudRepository, PagingAndSortingRepository, and JpaRepository. They provide out-of-the-box support for CRUD operations, pagination, and sorting.

```java
public interface JpaRepository<T, ID> extends CrudRepository<T, ID>,
PagingAndSortingRepository<T, ID>, QueryByExampleExecutor<T> {

    @Override
    List<T> findAll();

    @Override
    List<T> findAll(Sort sort);

    @Override
    List<T> findAllById(Iterable<ID> ids);

    @Override
    <S extends T> List<S> saveAll(Iterable<S> entities);

    void flush();

    <S extends T> S saveAndFlush(S entity);

    <S extends T> List<S> saveAllAndFlush(Iterable<S> entities);

    void deleteAllInBatch(Iterable<T> entities);

    void deleteAllByIdInBatch(Iterable<ID> ids);

    void deleteAllInBatch();

    T getReferenceById(ID id);

    @Override
    <S extends T> List<S> findAll(Example<S> example);

    @Override
    <S extends T> List<S> findAll(Example<S> example, Sort sort);
}
```

The `JpaRepository` provides several methods for CRUD operations, along with the following interesting methods:

- `long count()`; returns the total number of entities available.

- `boolean existsById(ID id)`; returns whether an entity with the given ID exists.

- `List<T> findAll(Sort sort)`; returns all entities sorted by the given options.

- `Page<T> findAll(Pageable pageable)`; returns a page of entities meeting the paging restriction provided in the `Pageable` object. This method can be found in the `PagingAndSortingRepository.java`, like so:

```
@NoRepositoryBean
public interface PagingAndSortingRepository<T, ID> extends
Repository<T, ID> {
    Iterable<T> findAll(Sort sort);
    Page<T> findAll(Pageable pageable);
}
```

The Spring Data JPA not only provides CRUD operations out of the box, it also supports dynamic query generation based on the method names.

For example,

- By defining a `User findByEmail(String email)` method, Spring Data will automatically generate the query with a `where` clause, as in `"where email = ?1"`.

- By defining a `User findByEmailAndPassword(String email, String password)` method, Spring Data will automatically generate the query with a `where` clause, as in `"where email = ?1 and password=?2"`.

Note   You can also use other operators such as OR, LIKE, Between, LessThan, LessThanEqual, and so on. Refer to `http://docs.spring.io/spring-data/jpa/docs/current/reference/html/#jpa.query-methods.query-creation` for a complete list of supporting operations.

But sometimes you may not be able to express your criteria using method names or the method names look ugly. Spring Data provides the flexibility to configure the query explicitly using the @Query annotation.

```
@Query("select u from User u where u.email=?1 and u.password=?2 and
u.enabled=true")
User findByEmailAndPassword(String email, String password);
```

You can also perform data update operations using @Modifying and @Query, as follows:

```
@Modifying
@Query("update User u set u.enabled=:status")
int updateUserStatus(@Param("status") boolean status)
```

This example uses the named parameter status instead of the positional parameter ?1.

Using Spring Data JPA with Spring Boot

Now let's add the Spring Data JPA support to your Spring blog project by adding the following dependencies to the pom.xml file:

```
<dependencies>
    <dependency>
        <groupId>org.springframework.boot</groupId>
        <artifactId>spring-boot-starter-data-jpa</artifactId>
    </dependency>
<dependency>
    <groupId>mysql</groupId>
    <artifactId>mysql-connector-java</artifactId>
    <scope>runtime</scope>
  </dependency>

</dependencies>
```

The spring-boot-starter-data-jpa dependency will auto-configure all the required beans to work with JPA in your application. You also added the dependency to download the MySQL Java Driver, which enables you to communicate with the MySQL database from your application.

The next step is making small changes in your domain classes so that Spring Boot understands how to persist them to the database. Listing 8-1 shows the `Post.java` class.

Listing 8-1. JPA Entity Post.java

```
package com.apress.demo.springblog.domain;

import com.apress.demo.springblog.validation.BlogPostTitleAlreadyExists;
import jakarta.persistence.*;
import jakarta.validation.constraints.NotNull;
import jakarta.validation.constraints.Size;
import lombok.*;

import java.time.LocalDateTime;
import java.util.List;

@Entity
@Table
@Getter
@Setter
@AllArgsConstructor
@NoArgsConstructor
@Builder
@BlogPostTitleAlreadyExists
public class Post {
    @Id
    @GeneratedValue(strategy = GenerationType.AUTO)
    private Long id;
    @NotNull
    @Size(min = 3, max = 50, message = "Title must be minimum 3 characters,
    and maximum 50 characters long")
    private String title;
    @NotNull
    @Size(min = 3, max = 500, message = "Description must be minimum 3
    characters, and maximum 500 characters long")
    private String description;
    @NotNull
```

```
@Size(min = 3, max = 5000, message = "Body must be minimum 3 characters,
and maximum 5000 characters long")
private String body;
private String slug;
@Column(name = "post_status")
private PostStatus postStatus;
@Column(name = "created_on")
private LocalDateTime createdOn;
@Column(name = "updated_on")
private LocalDateTime updatedOn;
@OneToMany(mappedBy = "post",
        cascade = CascadeType.ALL,
        orphanRemoval = true)
private List<Comment> comments;

}
```

- First, you add the @Entity and @Table annotations from JPA to denote that your Post class is a JPA Entity and Spring Data JPA should map it to the post table in the database.

- You add @Id annotation on top of the id field to denote that it's a primary key. You also add the @GeneratedValue annotation with strategy as AUTO, which will auto-increment the primary key whenever a new record is added to the table.

- The @Column annotation can be added if you want to add a custom name for the column. If you don't specify the annotation, the default name applies.

- Lastly, you add the @OneToMany annotation on top of the comments fields to determine the one-to-many relationship between the Post and Comment objects. Similarly, you add the @ManyToOne annotation on the post field inside the Comment class to establish a bidirectional mapping between the Post and Comment objects.

- You define the cascade attribute of the @OneToMany association as CascadeType.ALL with orphanRemoval=true. This means whenever a post is deleted, you also delete the related Comment records from the database.

```
package com.apress.demo.springblog.domain;

import jakarta.persistence.*;
import lombok.AllArgsConstructor;
import lombok.Getter;
import lombok.NoArgsConstructor;
import lombok.Setter;

import java.time.LocalDateTime;

@Entity
@Table
@Getter
@Setter
@AllArgsConstructor
@NoArgsConstructor
public class Comment {
    @Id
    @GeneratedValue(strategy = GenerationType.AUTO)
    private Long id;
    private String title;
    private String authorName;
    private String body;
    @Column(name = "created_on")
    private LocalDateTime createdOn;
    @Column(name = "updated_on")
    private LocalDateTime updatedOn;
    @ManyToOne(fetch = FetchType.LAZY)
    private Post post;
}
```

The @ManyToOne association uses the FetchType of LAZY, which offers better performance than EAGER fetching.

The next step is to refactor the PostRepository.java and CommentRepository.java classes to interfaces and extend them with the JpaRepository, as shown in Listings 8-2 and 8-3.

Listing 8-2. JPA Repository Interface PostRepository.java

```
package com.apress.demo.springblog.repository;

import com.apress.demo.springblog.domain.Post;
import org.springframework.data.jpa.repository.JpaRepository;

public interface PostRepository extends JpaRepository<Post, Long> {
    boolean existsByTitle(String title);
}
```

Listing 8-3. JPA Repository Interface CommentRepository.java

```
package com.apress.demo.springblog.repository;

import com.apress.demo.springblog.domain.Comment;
import org.springframework.data.jpa.repository.JpaRepository;
import org.springframework.stereotype.Repository;

@Repository
public interface CommentRepository extends JpaRepository<Comment, Integer> {
}
```

The JpaRepository interface provides many general-purpose database operation methods out of the box. But you can also define your methods and customize the repository according to your needs.

In Listing 8-2, you define a new method called existsByTitle. Spring Data JPA will parse the method name and understand that you want to check if the post exists or not with a given title.

Using the Sort and Pagination Features

Suppose you want to get all posts by title in ascending order. You can use the findAll(Sort sort) method as follows:

```
postRepository.findAll(Sort.by(Sort.Direction.ASC, "title"));
```

You can also apply sorting on multiple properties as follows:

```
postRepository.findAll(Sort.by(new Sort.Order(Sort.Direction.ASC, "title"),
new Sort.Order(Sort.Direction.DESC, "id")));
```

The posts will be ordered first by title in ascending order and then by ID in descending order.

In many web applications, you want to show data page by page. Spring Data makes it very easy to load data in the pagination style. Suppose you want to load the first 25 users on one page. You can use `Pageable` and `PageRequest` to get results by page as follows:

```
int size = 25;
int page = 0; //zero-based page index.
Pageable pageable = PageRequest.of(page, size);
Page<Post> postsPage = postRepository.findAll(pageable);
```

The `postsPage` will only contain the first 25 user records. You can get additional details, like the total number of pages, the current page number, whether there is a next page, whether there is a previous page, and more.

- `postsPage.getTotalElements();` returns the total amount of elements.

- `postsPage.getTotalPages();` returns the total number of pages.

- `postsPage.hasNext();`

- `postsPage.hasPrevious();`

- `List<Post> posts = postsPage.getContent();`

You can also apply pagination along with sorting as follows:

```
Sort sort = new Sort(Direction.ASC, "title");
Pageable pageable = PageRequest.of(page, size, sort);
Page<Post> postsPage = postRepository.findAll(pageable);
```

Note   To learn more about Spring Data JPA, visit the official Spring Data JPA documentation at `http://docs.spring.io/spring-data/jpa/docs/current/reference/html`.

Summary

This chapter covered Spring Data JPA and its use with Spring Boot. The next chapter explains how to work with MongoDB in your Spring Boot applications.

CHAPTER 9

Working with MongoDB

MongoDB is one of the most popular document-oriented NoSQL databases. Spring Data MongoDB provides support for working with MongoDB with a consistent Spring-based programming model similar to Spring Data JPA. Spring Boot provides a starter for Spring Data Mongo, which makes it even easier to use by implementing its autoconfiguring mechanism.

This chapter discusses MongoDB, including installing a MongoDB server on various platforms like Windows, macOS, and Linux. It also explains how to perform various database operations from Mongo Shell. Then you will explore how to use Spring Data Mongo features by using Spring Boot's `spring-boot-starter-data-mongodb` starter.

Introducing MongoDB

MongoDB is an open-source document-oriented NoSQL database. MongoDB uses document storage and a data interchange format called BSON, which provides a binary representation of JSON-like documents. MongoDB stores documents in collections. *Collections* are analogous to tables in relational databases. Unlike a table, a collection does not require documents with the same schema. See Listing 9-1.

Listing 9-1. A Sample Blog Post Document in a MongoDB Collection

```
{
    "_id" : ObjectId("13f345492b7c8eb21818bd09"),
    "title" : "Working with MongoDB in SpringBoot app",
    "url": "http://localhost:8080/blog/working-with-mongodb",
    "created_on" : ISODate("2016-10-01T00:00:00Z"),
    "tags" : ["NoSQL","MongoDB","SpringBoot"],
    "content" : "Long Blog post content goes here",
    "comments": [
```

© K. Siva Prasad Reddy, Sai Upadhyayula 2023
K. S. P. Reddy and S. Upadhyayula, *Beginning Spring Boot 3*, https://doi.org/10.1007/978-1-4842-8792-7_9

```
    {
        "name" : "John",
        "email": "john@gmail.com",
        "message": "Nice tutorial",
        "created_on" : ISODate("2016-10-01T00:00:00Z"),
    },
    {

        "name" : "Remo",
        "email": "remo@gmail.com",
        "message": "Thanks for the tutorial",
        "created_on" : ISODate("2016-10-04T00:00:00Z"),
    }
    ]
}
```

Installing MongoDB

MongoDB supports various platforms, including Windows, Linux, and macOS operating systems. To get a complete list of supported platforms, see `www.mongodb.com/docs/manual/installation/#supported-platforms`.

Note   We use the MongoDB Community Server in this book.

Installing MongoDB on Windows

Download the latest version of MongoDB from `www.mongodb.com/try/download/community`. Run the MSI installer and choose an installation directory, say `C:\Apps`. In that case, MongoDB server will be installed at `C:\Apps\MongoDB\Server\<version-number>`. Note that the text <version-number> should be replaced with the version of MongoDB installed on your machine. At the time of writing this chapter, the latest version is 6.0.1.

MongoDB requires a data directory to store its files. The default location for the MongoDB data folder in Windows is `C:\data\db`. You can either create the data directory structure `C:\data\db` or pass a custom location of the data directory as an argument, as follows:

```
C:\Apps\MongoDB\Server\<version-number>\bin>mongod.exe --dbpath " C:\Apps\
MongoDB\Server\<version-number>\data"
```

After you run this command, MongoDB should start on default port 27017. Instead of running this command and passing all the configuration options every time, you can create a config file and batch script to start MongoDB.

For example, you can create mongod.cfg in the C:\Apps\MongoDB\Server\5.0.8 directory with the content shown in Listing 9-2.

Listing 9-2. MongoDB Server Configuration File Called mongod.cfg

```
systemLog:
    destination: file
    path: C:/Apps/MongoDB/Server/<version-number>/logs/mongo.log
storage:
    dbPath: C:/Apps/MongoDB/Server/<version-number>/data/db
net:
    bindIp: 127.0.0.1
    port: 27017
```

You create start-mongo.bat in the C:\Apps\MongoDB\Server\<version-number> directory as follows:

```
bin\mongod.exe --config C:\Apps\MongoDB\Server\<version-number>\mongod.cfg
```

Now you can simply start the MongoDB server as follows:

```
C:\Apps\MongoDB\Server\4.4>start-mongo.bat
```

Note   Make sure that the data and logs directories are already created before starting MongoDB.

You can learn more about the MongoDB server configuration options at www.mongodb.com/docs/manual/reference/configuration-options/.

Installing MongoDB on macOS

The easiest way to install the MongoDB server on macOS is by using Homebrew. See `https://brew.sh/` on how to install Homebrew. Once Homebrew is installed, you need to update Homebrew's package database and install the MongoDB package as follows:

```
> brew update
> brew install mongodb
```

On macOS, the default data directory is `/data/db`. Make sure that the data directory has read-write permission. You can start the Mongo server without specifying the `dbpath`, which means it will use the default data directory, or you can pass a custom data directory location as follows:

```
> mongod --dbpath /Users/username/mongodb/data
```

For alternative options for installing MongoDB on MacOS, see `www.mongodb.com/docs/manual/tutorial/install-mongodb-on-os-x/`.

Installing MongoDB on Linux

MongoDB provides packages for most of the popular Linux distributions. For installation instructions of your specific Linux distribution, refer to `www.mongodb.com/docs/manual/administration/install-on-linux/`.

Getting Started with MongoDB Using the Mongo Shell

Once the MongoDB server starts, you can connect to the MongoDB server by starting the Mongo Shell. Download the Mongo Shell software from the link `www.mongodb.com/try/download/shell`. Open the terminal, navigate to the downloaded folder, and run the `mongosh.exe` command.

```
>mongosh
```

Current Mongosh Log ID: 62f5f90fff3157371a9b40e3
Connecting to: mongodb://127.0.0.1:27017/?directConnection=true&serverSelectionTimeoutMS=2000&appName=mongosh+1.5.4

Using MongoDB: 6.0.0

Using Mongosh: 1.5.4

You can use the `show dbs` command to check the list of available databases:

```
> show dbs
```

By default, you are connected to the default database called `test`. You can use the `use db_name` command to switch to another database.

```
> use users
switched to db users
```

You can insert a user document into the `users` collection as follows:

```
> db.users.insertOne({"username": "siva","password": "secret" })
```

If the collection does not exist, it will be created automatically.

You can query the database to return all the documents as follows:

```
> db.users.find()
```

You can apply filters to a query as follows:

```
> db.users.find({"username": "siva" })
```

You can get the count of number of documents as follows:

```
> db.users.countDocuments()
```

Note   Covering MongoDB in depth is out of the scope of this book. Visit the official documentation at `www.mongodb.com/docs/manual/` to learn more about MongoDB.

Introducing Spring Data MongoDB

The Spring Data umbrella project provides the Spring Data Mongo module, which supports performing CRUD (Create, Read, Update, Delete) operations and dynamic queries based on method names similar to Spring Data JPA.

The Spring Data MongoDB module provides the `MongoTemplate`, which provides a higher level abstraction over the MongoDB Java driver API `com.mongodb.Mongo`.

If you are not using Spring Boot, you need to configure the MongoDB components using JavaConfig, as shown in Listing 9-3.

Listing 9-3. MongoDB Components Configuration Using JavaConfig

```
@Configuration
public class MongoConfiguration
{
@Bean
public MongoClient mongoClient() {
    return MongoClients.create("mongodb://localhost:27017");
}
@Bean
public MongoTemplate mongoTemplate() {
    return new MongoTemplate(mongoClient(), "springblog");
}
}
```

Spring Boot provides the `spring-boot-starter-data-mongodb` starter to easily work with MongoDB by autoconfiguring the MongoDB components without requiring manual configuration.

```
<dependency>
    <groupId>org.springframework.boot</groupId>
    <artifactId>spring-boot-starter-data-mongodb</artifactId>
</dependency>
```

By adding the `spring-boot-starter-data-mongodb` dependency, Spring Boot will autoconfigure `MongoClient` and `MongoTemplate` and connect to the local MongoDB server at `mongodb://localhost/test`.

You can customize the `mongodb` server URL by configuring the `spring.data.mongodb.uri` property in the `application.properties` file.

```
spring.data.mongodb.uri=mongodb://localhost:27017/springblog
```

You can map a domain object to a particular MongoDB collection using the `@Document` annotation, similar to how you used the `@Table` annotation in Spring Data JPA. By default, the collection will be created with the default name of the class, but you can override that using the collection attribute of `@Document`.

```
package com.apress.demo.springblog.domain;

import com.apress.demo.springblog.validation.BlogPostTitleAlreadyExists;
import jakarta.validation.constraints.NotNull;
import jakarta.validation.constraints.Size;
import lombok.*;
import org.springframework.data.annotation.Id;
import org.springframework.data.mongodb.core.mapping.Document;
import org.springframework.data.mongodb.core.mapping.Field;

import java.time.LocalDateTime;
import java.util.List;

@Getter
@Setter
@AllArgsConstructor
@NoArgsConstructor
@Builder
@BlogPostTitleAlreadyExists
@Document
public class Post {
    @Id
    private String id;
    @NotNull
    @Size(min = 3, max = 50, message = "Title must be minimum 3 characters,
    and maximum 50 characters long")
    private String title;
    @NotNull
    @Size(min = 3, max = 500, message = "Description must be minimum 3
    characters, and maximum 500 characters long")
    private String description;
    @NotNull
    @Size(min = 3, max = 5000, message = "Body must be minimum 3 characters,
    and maximum 5000 characters long")
    private String body;
    private String slug;
    @Field(name = "post_status")
```

155

```
    private PostStatus postStatus;
    @Field(name = "created_on")
    private LocalDateTime createdOn;
    @Field(name = "updated_on")
    private LocalDateTime updatedOn;
    private List<Comment> comments;
}
```

By default, MongoDB generates an `ObjectId` primary key called `_id`. But you can map any existing property to be used as the primary key, simply by using the `@Id` annotation. The unique ID in MongoDB is of type String, so you migrated the data type from Long to String while using MongoDB. The ID looks like this: 630d50e9f8f7575dec88d62e

You can define a custom field name for the document using the `@Field` annotation similar to `@Column` annotation in Spring Data JPA.

Finally, you didn't add any OneToMany or ManyToOne annotations here because in MongoDB there is no need to create complex relationships and joins like in relational databases. All the data is stored under one document.

However, there are some best practices you need to be aware of when designing MongoDB schemas. Refer to this article for further reference: `www.mongodb.com/ developer/products/mongodb/mongodb-schema-design-best-practices/`.

Let's create the `PostRepository` interface under the repository package. This interface should extend the `MongoRepository` interface, as shown in Listing 9-4.

Listing 9-4. PostRepository.java

```
package com.apress.demo.springblog.repository;

import com.apress.demo.springblog.domain.Post;
import org.springframework.data.mongodb.repository.MongoRepository;

public interface PostRepository extends MongoRepository<Post, String> {

    boolean existsByTitle(String title);
}
```

Now you can perform various CRUD operations as follows:

```
List<Post> posts= postRepository.findAll();
Optional<Post> post = postRepository.findById("1");

Post post = new Post();
post.setTitle("sample blog");
Post savedPost= postRepository.save(post);

// delete post by primary key
postRepository.deleteById("1");

// delete post by object
postRepository.delete(post);

// get total count of user documents in users collection
postRepository.count();
```

You can perform sorting and pagination similar to Spring Data JPA repositories.

```
List<Post> users = postRepository.findAll(Sort.of(Direction.ASC, "title"));
```

You can express the query criteria using @Query as follows:

```
@Query("{ 'title' : ?0 }")
Post findByTitle(String title);
```

Since you introduced a new interface for PostRepository and changed the data type of the id field, you also need to make some changes inside the PostService.java and PostController.java classes, respectively.

```
@Service
@RequiredArgsConstructor
public class PostService {

    private final PostRepository postRepository;

    public void addPost(Post post) {
        postRepository.save(post);
    }
```

```
public List<Post> findAllPosts() {
    return postRepository.findAll();
}

public Post findOnePost(String postId) {
    return postRepository.findById(postId).orElseThrow(() -> new Illegal
    ArgumentException("Cannot find Post by id - " + postId));
}

public boolean postExistsWithTitle(String title) {
    return postRepository.existsByTitle(title);
}
}
```

In the PostService.java class, you simply change the input method parameter of the findOnePost to String. For the postExistsWithTitle method, you are now calling the postRepository.existsByTitle method from the PostRepository.java interface, which is used in the BlogPostTitleValidator class.

Finally, let's also adapt the onePostPage() method to receive the id as a String inside the PostController.java class:

```
@GetMapping("/{id}")
public String onePostPage(Model model, @PathVariable String id) {
    model.addAttribute("posts", postService.findOnePost(id));
    return "onePost";
}
```

Using Embedded Mongo for Testing

Using an embedded MongoDB for testing purposes would be more convenient, especially in continuous integration environments.

You can use the following embedded Mongo (https://github.com/flapdoodle-oss/de.flapdoodle.embed.mongo) dependency, which Spring Boot can autoconfigure so that you can run tests without setting up an actual MongoDB server:

```
<dependency>
    <groupId>de.flapdoodle.embed</groupId>
    <artifactId>de.flapdoodle.embed.mongo</artifactId>
</dependency>
```

You can also initialize sample data by implementing the `CommandLineRunner` interface, which executes the `public void run(String... args)` method upon application startup, as shown in Listing 9-5.

Listing 9-5. SpringBlogApplication.java

```java
package com.apress.demo.springblog;

import com.apress.demo.springblog.domain.Post;
import com.apress.demo.springblog.domain.PostStatus;
import com.apress.demo.springblog.repository.PostRepository;
import lombok.RequiredArgsConstructor;
import org.springframework.boot.CommandLineRunner;
import org.springframework.boot.SpringApplication;
import org.springframework.boot.autoconfigure.SpringBootApplication;

import java.time.LocalDateTime;

@SpringBootApplication
@RequiredArgsConstructor
public class SpringblogApplication implements CommandLineRunner {

    private final PostRepository postRepository;

    public static void main(String[] args) {
        SpringApplication.run(SpringblogApplication.class, args);
    }

    @Override
    public void run(String... args) throws Exception {
        Post post = Post.builder()
                .title("Sample Blog Post")
                .description("Sample Blog Post")
                .body("Sample Blog Post")
                .slug("sample_blog_post")
```

```
            .postStatus(PostStatus.DRAFT)
            .createdOn(LocalDateTime.now())
            .updatedOn(LocalDateTime.now())
            .build();
        postRepository.save(post);
    }
}
```

To learn more about the Spring Data Mongo features, see the Spring Data MongoDB reference documentation at `http://docs.spring.io/spring-data/data-mongo/docs/current/reference/html`.

Now, if you run the application and open the link `http://localhost:8080/`, you should see the home page of your Spring blog application. You should see a blog post with the title "Sample Blog Post."

Summary

This chapter explained how to install and use the MongoDB server. It explored how to work with Spring Data MongoDB in Spring Boot applications. In the next chapter, you will develop REST APIs using Spring Boot and SpringMVC.

## CHAPTER 10

Building REST APIs Using Spring Boot

REST is an architectural style for building distributed systems that provide interoperability between heterogeneous systems. The need for REST APIs has increased significantly with the drastic increase in mobile devices. It became logical to build REST APIs and let web and mobile clients consume the API instead of developing separate applications.

SpringMVC provides first-class support for building RESTful web services. As Spring's REST support is built on top of SpringMVC, you can leverage the knowledge of SpringMVC for building REST APIs.

Spring Data REST is a spring portfolio project that can expose Spring Data repositories as REST endpoints. You can expose Spring Data JPA, Spring Data Mongo, and Spring Data Cassandra repositories as REST endpoints without much effort.

This chapter covers RESTful web services, including how you can build REST APIs using SpringMVC. You will build a REST API for your Spring blog application, and you will also learn about building REST APIs using the Spring Data REST project.

Introduction to RESTful Web Services

REST stands for *representational state transfer* and is an architectural style for designing distributed hypermedia systems. Roy Fielding coined the term REST in 2000 in his doctoral dissertation, which you can find at `www.ics.uci.edu/~fielding/pubs/dissertation/rest_arch_style.htm`.

The fundamental concept of a REST-based system is the *resource,* which can be identified by a Uniform Resource Identifier (URI). HTTP is the most commonly used protocol for communicating with external systems for web-based systems. You can identify a unique resource using a URI.

161

For example, a blog post can be identified by the URI `http://www.myblog.com/posts/restful-architecture`. A resource can be a *collection resource*, representing a grouped set of resources. For example, the URI `http://www.myblog.com/posts/` represents the `posts` resource, which may contain zero or more `Post` resources, each of which can be identified by its own URI. The various operations performed on a resource can be expressed using its URI and the appropriate HTTP method (`GET`, `POST`, `PUT`, `DELETE`, etc.).

As you build a REST API for a blog application, you can identify resources in a blog domain as posts, comments, and users.

Following the REST principles, you can use the following HTTP verbs:

- `GET` to get a collection or a single resource

- `POST` to create a new resource

- `PUT` to update an existing resource

- `DELETE` to delete a collection or a single resource

Now consider how you can define URIs for a blog system's resources:

- `GET-http://localhost:8080/myblog/posts/` returns a list of all posts.

- `GET-http://localhost:8080/myblog/posts/2` returns a post whose ID is 2.

- `POST—http://localhost:8080/myblog/posts/` creates a new Post resource.

- `PUT—http://localhost:8080/myblog/posts/2` updates a POST resource whose ID is 2.

- `DELETE—http://localhost:8080/myblog/posts/2` deletes a POST resource whose ID is 2.

- `GET—http://localhost:8080/myblog/posts/2/comments` returns all the comments of the post whose ID is 2.

- `POST—http://localhost:8080/myblog/posts/2/comments` creates a new comment for the POST whose ID is 2.

- `DELETE—http://localhost:8080/myblog/posts/2/comments` deletes all the comments of the POST whose ID is 2.

JSON and XML are the most commonly used data exchange formats (`ContentTypes`). The typical practice of determining the input request content and output response types in web-based systems is based on the `ContentType` and `Accept` header values.

REST API Using SpringMVC

SpringMVC supports building RESTful web services, and Spring Boot makes it much easier with its autoconfiguration mechanism.

Listing 10-1 shows a SpringMVC-based REST endpoint.

Listing 10-1. SpringMVC REST Controller

```
@Controller
@RequiredArgsConstructor
public class PostController
{
    private final PostService postService;

    @ResponseBody
    @GetMapping("/posts")
    public List<Post> listPosts()
    {
        return postService.findAll();
    }
}
```

It just looks like a regular SpringMVC controller, with two noticeable differences:

- Unlike standard controller methods, which return a view name or a `ModelAndView` object, the `listPosts()` method returns a list of `Post` objects.

- The `listPosts()` request handler method is annotated with `@ResponseBody`.

The `@ResponseBody` annotation on the request handler method indicates that the return value should be bound to the response body. If you make a `GET` request to the `/posts` URL, you might get a JSON or XML representation of the list of `Post` objects based on the `Accept` header value.

Listing 10-2 shows another method used to create a new post.

Listing 10-2. REST Controller Method Using the @RequestBody Annotation

```
@Controller
@RequiredArgsConstructor
public class PostController
{
    private final PostService postService;
    ...
    ...
    @ResponseBody
    @PostMapping("/posts")
    public Post createPost(@RequestBody Post post)
    {
        return postService.save(post);
    }
}
```

The interesting part of the `createPost()` handler method is the `@RequestBody` annotation. The `@RequestBody` annotation will bind the web request body to the method parameter with the help of the registered `HttpMessageConverters`. So, when you make a `POST` request to the `/post` URL with a `Post` JSON body, a bean registered automatically by Spring Boot with the name of `HttpMessageConverters` converts the JSON request body into a `Post` object and passes it to the `savePost()` method.

If all of your handler methods are REST endpoint handler methods, you can have a `@ResponseBody` at the class level instead of adding it to each method. Even better, you can use `@RestController`, a composed annotation of `@Controller` and `@ResponseBody`.

If you open the source of the `@RestController` in your IDE, you can find the following definition. As you can see, it has both `@Controller` and `@RestController` annotations.

```
@Target({ElementType.TYPE})
@Retention(RetentionPolicy.RUNTIME)
@Documented
@Controller
@ResponseBody
```

```
public @interface RestController {
    @AliasFor(
        annotation = Controller.class
    )
    String value() default "";
}
```

Using Data Transfer Objects

In your PostController class, you are directly exposing the Post.java class as the
ResponseBody, which is part of the domain model. Usually, it's advisable not to expose
the domain classes directly to the outside world in real-world applications, as an API
response should be according to the consumer's needs. When you expose the whole
domain class like Post.java, you may also reveal some unnecessary fields to the users.
For this reason, you can use a temporary class, a Data Transfer Object, to send and
receive the data between the client and the server.

Go ahead and create a class called PostDto.java in a new package called dto, as
shown in Listing 10-3.

Listing 10-3. PostDto.java Class

```
package com.apress.demo.springblog.dto;

import com.apress.demo.springblog.domain.PostStatus;
import com.apress.demo.springblog.validation.BlogPostTitleAlreadyExists;
import jakarta.validation.constraints.NotNull;
import jakarta.validation.constraints.Size;
import lombok.Builder;
import lombok.Data;
import lombok.NoArgsConstructor;
import lombok.AllArgsConstructor;

import java.time.LocalDateTime;

@Data
@NoArgsConstructor
@AllArgsConstructor
@Builder
```

```
@BlogPostTitleAlreadyExists
public class PostDto {
    private Long id;
    @NotNull
    @Size(min = 3, max = 50, message = "Title must be minimum 3 characters,
    and maximum 50 characters long")
    private String title;
    @NotNull
    @Size(min = 3, max = 500, message = "Description must be minimum 3
    characters, and maximum 500 characters long")
    private String description;
    @NotNull
    @Size(min = 3, max = 5000, message = "Body must be minimum 3 characters,
    and maximum 5000 characters long")
    private String body;
    private String slug;
    private PostStatus postStatus;
    private LocalDateTime createdOn;
    private LocalDateTime updatedOn;
}
```

You have a regular POJO class, `PostDto.java`, annotated with `@Data` that generates all the necessary methods like getters, setters, equals, and hashCode. The required constructors for the class can be generated using the `@NoArgsConstructor` and `@AllArgsConstructor` annotations.

You also add the `@BlogPostTitleAlreadyExists` annotation that performs the bean validation on top of the `PostDto.java` class. It makes sense to perform the validation on the class exposed to the outside world instead of the `Post.java` class, mainly used to persist your data in the database.

So now, let's refactor the `PostController.java` and `PostService.java` classes to use `PostDto.java` to expose the post information to the clients. Also, don't forget to replace the usage of `Post` with `PostDto` inside the `BlogPostTitleValidator` record, as shown in Listings 10-4 and 10-5.

Listing 10-4. Refactoring PostController.java Class to Use PostDto.java

```java
package com.apress.demo.springblog.controller;

import com.apress.demo.springblog.dto.PostDto;
import com.apress.demo.springblog.service.PostService;
import lombok.RequiredArgsConstructor;
import org.springframework.web.bind.annotation.*;

import java.util.List;

@RestController
@RequestMapping("/api/posts")
@RequiredArgsConstructor
public class PostController {

    private final PostService postService;

    @GetMapping
    public List<PostDto> listPosts() {
        return postService.findAllPosts();
    }

    @PostMapping
    public PostDto createPost(@RequestBody PostDto postDto) {
        return postService.save(postDto);
    }
}
```

Listing 10-5. Refactoring PostService.java Class to Use PostDto.java

```java
package com.apress.demo.springblog.service;

import com.apress.demo.springblog.domain.Post;
import com.apress.demo.springblog.dto.PostDto;
import com.apress.demo.springblog.mapper.PostMapper;
import com.apress.demo.springblog.repository.PostRepository;
import lombok.RequiredArgsConstructor;
import org.springframework.stereotype.Service;

import java.util.List;
```

```java
@Service
@RequiredArgsConstructor
public class PostService {

    private final PostRepository postRepository;
    private final PostMapper postMapper;

    public PostDto save(PostDto postDto) {
        Post post = postMapper.mapToPost(postDto);
        Post savedPost = postRepository.save(post);
        postDto.setId(savedPost.getId());
        return postDto;
    }

    public List<PostDto> findAllPosts() {
        return postRepository.findAll().stream().
        map(postMapper::mapToPostDto).toList();
    }

    public boolean postExistsWithTitle(String title) {
        return postRepository.existsByTitle(title);
    }
}
```

In the `PostService.java` class, inside the `findAllPosts()` and the `save()` method, you use the `PostRepository.java` interface to save the posts and retrieve the posts from the database. But since you are receiving the objects from the `PostController.java` class as the `PostDto` objects, you need to map these objects from the `PostDto` to the `Post` object manually. For this reason, you create a class called `PostMapper`, whose responsibility is only to map the `Post` object from `PostDto` and vice versa. You can find the code of the `PostMapper.java` class in Listing 10-6.

Listing 10-6. PostMapper.java Class

```java
package com.apress.demo.springblog.mapper;

import com.apress.demo.springblog.domain.Post;
import com.apress.demo.springblog.dto.PostDto;
import org.springframework.stereotype.Component;
```

```
@Component
public class PostMapper {

    public Post mapToPost(PostDto postInput) {
        return Post.builder()
                .title(postInput.getTitle())
                .description(postInput.getDescription())
                .body(postInput.getBody())
                .slug(postInput.getSlug())
                .postStatus(postInput.getPostStatus())
                .build();
    }

    public PostDto mapToPostDto(Post post) {
        return PostDto.builder()
                .id(post.getId())
                .title(post.getTitle())
                .description(post.getDescription())
                .body(post.getBody())
                .slug(post.getSlug())
                .postStatus(post.getPostStatus())
                .build();
    }
}
```

The `mapToPost` and `mapToPostDto` methods are just regular methods, just mapping from and to `Post` and `PostDto` objects. It's always nice to separate the responsibilities of each layer into its own class when you are dealing with large, real-world applications.

As you generate the getters, setters, and other boilerplate code of Java using Lombok, you can also generate the mapping methods between two objects using libraries like Mapstruct, ModelMapper, and Dozer.

You can read more about these libraries here:

- Mapstruct, `https://mapstruct.org/`

- ModelMapper, `http://modelmapper.org/`

- Dozer, `https://dozermapper.github.io/`

Continue Building the REST API

Let's continue building the REST API. You have already created two methods, findAllPosts and save, to read and create post information. Let's create some methods to handle the update and delete operations. First, let's create the update method in the PostController.java class.

```
@PutMapping
public PostDto updatePost(@RequestBody PostDto postDto) {
    return postService.update(postDto);
}
```

As you saw at the beginning of this chapter, you can use the PUT HTTP verb when you want to update a particular resource using a REST API. For this reason, use the specialized @PutMapping annotation to denote this operation, and inside the method, call the update method inside the PostService.java class.

```
public PostDto update(PostDto postDto) {
    Post post = postRepository.findById(postDto.getId())
            .orElseThrow(() -> new SpringBlogException("Cannot find Post with
            Id " + postDto.getId()));
    Post savedPost = postMapper.mapToPost(postDto);
    savedPost.setId(post.getId());
    postRepository.save(savedPost);
    return postDto;
}
```

This method updates a given post in the database with the new post details coming in from the client. You first query if a post exists with a given id. If not, you throw a SpringBlogException with a customized error message of "Cannot find Post with id" followed by the id provided by the client.

Then you simply save the updated post to the database and return the postDto object to the PostController.java class.

Now let's implement the delete operation to delete a given post in the database. Update PostController.java first.

```
@DeleteMapping("/{id}")
public void deletePost(@PathVariable Long id) {
    postService.delete(id);
}
```

Like @PutMapping, you also have the @DeleteMapping annotation to denote that this endpoint is responsible for handling the DELETE operation. Here you read the post's id as a PathVariable and pass on the id to the PostService to delete the post by its id.

```
public void delete(Long id) {
    postRepository.deleteById(id);
}
```

Let's also create another endpoint to read a post by its slug attribute. You can create a method called findPostBySlug inside the PostController.java.

```
@GetMapping("/{slug}")
public PostDto findPostBySlug(@PathVariable String slug) {
    return postService.findBySlug(slug);
}
```

And inside the PostService.java class:

```
public PostDto findBySlug(String slug) {
    Post post = postRepository.findBySlug(slug)
            .orElseThrow(() -> new SpringBlogException("Cannot find Post with
            Slug - " + slug));
    return postMapper.mapToPostDto(post);
}
```

The findBySlug() method queries the database for a post by the slug attribute through the Spring Data JPA PostRepository interface. If there are no posts, it throws a SpringBlogException with a message "Cannot find Post with Slug" followed by the slug provided by the client.

You can define the findBySlug method inside the PostRepository.java interface as follows:

```
public interface PostRepository extends JpaRepository<Post, Long> {

    boolean existsByTitle(String title);

    Optional<Post> findBySlug(String slug);
}
```

Defining an HTTP Response for the API

All API methods implemented using Spring Boot will, by default, return the HTTP Response as 200 OK. According to the HTTP specification, each HTTP verb should return an appropriate response code.

- Reading data from the server using GET: 200 OK

- Creating a resource using POST: 201 CREATED

- Update a resource using PUT: 200 OK or 204

- Delete a resource using DELETE: 200 OK or 204

Let's see how to add these custom response codes to the PostController.java class methods. Spring Boot provides the @ResponseStatus annotation that lets you define the response code you need to return for each API endpoint.

```
@GetMapping
@ResponseStatus(HttpStatus.OK)
public List<PostDto> listPosts() {
    return postService.findAllPosts();
}

@PostMapping
@ResponseStatus(HttpStatus.CREATED)
public PostDto createPost(@RequestBody PostDto postDto) {
    return postService.save(postDto);
}

@PutMapping
@ResponseStatus(HttpStatus.OK)
```

```java
public PostDto updatePost(@RequestBody PostDto postDto) {
    return postService.update(postDto);
}

@DeleteMapping("/{id}")
@ResponseStatus(HttpStatus.NO_CONTENT)
public void deletePost(@PathVariable Long id) {
    postService.delete(id);
}

@GetMapping("/{slug}")
@ResponseStatus(HttpStatus.OK)
public PostDto findPostBySlug(@PathVariable String slug) {
    return postService.findBySlug(slug);
}
```

The ResponseStatus annotation has an attribute of type HttpStatus, an enum that defines all the possible HTTP status codes. For the deletePost() method, you return the HTTP status as 204 (No Content) because the resource is already deleted on the server and there is no need to send any response of the resource back to the client.

CORS (Cross-Origin Resource Sharing) Support

For security reasons, browsers don't allow you to make AJAX requests to resources residing outside of the current origin. An origin can be defined as a combination of the HTTP scheme (http/https), the hostname where the application is running, and the port where the application is running. If your REST API runs at http://localhost:8080, and if you have a single page application (SPA) developed using frameworks like React/Angular/Vue running at http://localhost:3000 or http://localhost:4200, the web browser will not allow you to make a call from the SPA to your REST API because the origin is different. In this case, the only difference is the port. By definition, the application's port is also considered part of its origin. The web browser will block the requests to the REST API from the SPA. The CORS specification (www.w3.org/TR/2020/SPSD-cors-20200602/) provides a way to specify which cross-origin requests are permitted. SpringMVC provides support for enabling CORS for REST API endpoints so that the API consumers, such as web clients and mobile devices, can make calls to REST APIs.

Class- and Method-Level CORS Configuration

You can enable CORS at the controller or method level using the @CrossOrigin annotation. You'll see how to enable CORS support on a specific request handling method.

```
@RestController
@RequestMapping("/api/posts")
public class PostController
{
    @CrossOrigin
    @GetMapping("/{slug}")
    public PostDto findPostBySlug(@PathVariable String slug) {
        // ...
    }
    @DeleteMapping("/{id}")
    public void deletePost(@PathVariable Long id) {
        // ...
    }
}
```

The CORS support is enabled only for the findPostBySlug() method using the default configuration.

- All headers and origins are permitted.

- Credentials are allowed.

- The maximum age is set to 30 minutes.

- The list of HTTP methods is set to the methods on the @RequestMethod annotation.

You can customize these properties by providing options on the @CrossOrigin annotation.

```
@CrossOrigin(origins={"http://domain1.com", "http://domain2.com"},
             allowedHeaders="X-AUTH-TOKEN",
             allowCredentials="false",
             maxAge=15*60,
```

```
            methods={RequestMethod.GET, RequestMethod.POST }
        )
@GetMapping("/{slug}")
public PostDto findPostBySlug(@PathVariable String slug) {
    // ...
}
```

Similarly, you can apply the @CrossOrigin annotation at the controller class level.

```
@CrossOrigin
@RestController
@RequestMapping("/api/posts")
public class PostController
{
    ....
    ....
}
```

When applied at the class level, the same @CrossOrigin configuration is applied to all @RequestMapping methods. If the @CrossOrigin annotation is specified at both the class and method levels, Spring will derive the CORS configuration by combining attributes from both annotations.

Global CORS Configuration

In addition to specifying CORS configuration at the class and method levels, you can configure it globally by implementing the WebMvcConfigurer.addCorsMappings() method. See Listing 10-7.

Listing 10-7. SpringMVC Global CORS Configuration

```
@Configuration
public class WebConfig implements WebMvcConfigurer
{
    @Override
    public void addCorsMappings(CorsRegistry registry) {
        registry.addMapping("/api/**")
        .allowedOrigins("http://localhost:3000")
```

```
        .allowedMethods("*")
        .allowedHeaders("*")
        .allowCredentials(false)
        .maxAge(3600);
    }
}
```

This configuration enables the CORS for URL pattern /api/** from the origin http://localhost:3000 only. You can specify allowedOrigins("*") to allow requests from any origin.

REST API Using Spring Data REST

In the previous section, you implemented the REST API with CRUD operations for JPA entities. You created a PostController class to handle the presentation layer logic, a PostService class to handle the business logic, and the PostRepository Spring Data interface to handle the database operations.

If your application needs to be a simple REST API with CRUD operations on top of database tables, you can use Spring Data REST. By using Spring Data REST, all you need to create is a Spring Data Repository interface and define the corresponding Spring Data entities, and you have a fully working REST API ready to use.

Spring Data REST builds on top of the Spring Data repositories and automatically exports them as REST resources. The Spring Data REST configuration is defined in the configuration class RepositoryRestMvcConfiguration, and you can import it simply by using @Import(RepositoryRestMvcConfiguration.class) to activate it in your application.

Spring Boot will automatically enable Spring Data REST if you add spring-boot-starter-data-rest to your application.

```
<dependency>
<groupId>org.springframework.boot</groupId>
<artifactId>spring-boot-starter-data-rest</artifactId>
</dependency>
```

You don't need any extra configuration to expose the Spring Data repositories as REST resources with the defaults.

Let's go ahead and delete the `PostController.java` and `PostService.java` classes and see what happens if you start your application and access the URL `http://localhost:8080/posts`. It should return the response shown in Listing 10-8.

Listing 10-8. Spring Data REST Collection Resource Response

```
{
    "_embedded": {
        "posts": [
            {
                "title": "Spring Boot",
                "description": "Spring Boot",
                "body": "Spring Boot",
                "slug": "spring_boot",
                "postStatus": "PUBLISHED",
                "createdOn": "2022-08-07T19:47:36.072253",
                "updatedOn": "2022-08-07T19:47:36.071253",
                "_links": {
                    "self": {
                        "href": "http://localhost:8080/posts/302"
                    },
                    "post": {
                        "href": "http://localhost:8080/posts/302"
                    },
                    "comments": {
                        "href": "http://localhost:8080/posts/302/comments"
                    }
                }
            }
        ]
    },
    "_links": {
        "self": {
            "href": "http://localhost:8080/posts"
        },
        "profile": {
```

```
            "href": "http://localhost:8080/profile/posts"
        },
        "search": {
            "href": "http://localhost:8080/posts/search"
        }
    },
    "page": {
        "size": 20,
        "totalElements": 1,
        "totalPages": 1,
        "number": 0
    }
}
```

You can create a new Post by invoking the POST request on http://localhost:8080/
posts with the Accept and Content-Type headers set to application/json. Pass the
Post details to be created as JSON in request body.

```
{
    "title": "Spring Boot Created",
    "description": "Spring Boot Created",
    "body": "Spring Boot Created",
    "slug": "spring_boot_created",
    "postStatus": "PUBLISHED",
    "createdOn": "2022-08-07T19:47:36.072253",
    "updatedOn": "2022-08-07T19:47:36.071253"
}
```

Similarly, you can update POST with id=4 by using the PUT request on http://
localhost:8080/posts/4.

```
{
    "title": "Spring Boot Created",
    "description": "Spring Boot Created",
    "body": "Spring Boot Created",
    "slug": "spring_boot_created",
    "postStatus": "PUBLISHED",
```

```
    "createdOn": "2022-08-07T19:47:36.072253",
    "updatedOn": "2022-08-07T19:47:36.071253"
}
```

You can delete POST with id=4 by using the DELETE request on `http://localhost:8080/posts/4`.

The Spring Data REST serves up the REST resources at the root URI, /. You can customize the path using the `spring.data.rest.basePath` property in `application.properties`.

```
spring.data.rest.basePath=/api
```

Sorting and Pagination

If the `Repository` extends `PagingAndSortingRepository`, then Spring Data REST endpoints support pagination and sorting out of the box.

You can use the `size` query parameter to limit the number of entries returning.

```
http://localhost:8080/posts/?size=10
```

Use the page and size query parameters to retrieve the second-page entries with five entries per page.

```
http://localhost:8080/posts?page=1&size=5
```

To retrieve entries sorted by some property, use the `sort` query parameter.

```
http://localhost:8080/posts?sort=createdOn,desc
```

Spring Data REST, by default, exposes all the public repository interfaces without requiring any extra configuration. But if you want to customize the defaults, you can use the @RepositoryRestResource and @RestResource annotations. You can disable a repository from being exposed as a REST resource by adding @RepositoryRestResource(exported = false).

```
@RepositoryRestResource(exported = false)
public interface CommentRepository extends JpaRepository<Comment, Integer>
{
}
```

CORS Support in Spring Data REST

Like SpringMVC REST endpoints, you can enable CORS support for Spring Data REST endpoints using the @CrossOrigin annotation at the repository level or globally.

```
@CrossOrigin
public interface PostRepository extends JpaRepository<Post, Integer>
{
}
```

To enable CORS support globally, you can extend RepositoryRestConfigurerAdapter and provide CORS configuration, as shown in Listing 10-9.

Listing 10-9. Spring Data REST Global CORS Configuration

```
@Configuration
public class RepositoryConfig extends RepositoryRestConfigurer
{
    @Override
    public void configureRepositoryRestConfiguration(RepositoryRestConfigur
    ation config)
    {
        config.getCorsRegistry()
                    .addMapping("/api/**")
                        .allowedOrigins("http://localhost:3000")
                        .allowedMethods("*")
                        .allowedHeaders("*")
                        .allowCredentials(false)
                        .maxAge(3600);
    }
}
```

Note   SpringMVC's CORS configuration is NOT applied to Spring Data REST endpoints.

To learn more about Spring Data REST, visit the Spring Data REST documentation at `http://docs.spring.io/spring-data/rest/docs/current/reference/html/`.

Exception Handling

You can handle exceptions in REST API in the same way you handle them in the SpringMVC-based web application: by using the `@ExceptionHandler` and `@ControllerAdvice` annotations. Instead of rendering a view, you can return `ResponseEntity` with the appropriate HTTP status code and exception details.

Instead of simply throwing an exception with the HTTP status code, it is better to provide more details about the issue, such as the error code, message, developer message, and such.

Create a class called `ErrorDetails`, as shown in Listing 10-10.

Listing 10-10. ErrorDetails.java

```java
public class ErrorDetails
{
    private String errorCode;
    private String errorMessage;
    private String devErrorMessage;
    private Map<String, Object> additionalData = new HashMap<>();
    //setters & getters
}
```

In the controller handler method, you can throw an exception based on error conditions and handle those exceptions using the `@ExceptionHandler` methods, as shown in Listing 10-11.

Listing 10-11. Handling REST API Exception at Controller Level @ExceptionHandler Methods

```java
@RestController
@RequestMapping(value="/posts")
public class PostController
{
```

```
    ...
    ...
    @DeleteMapping("/{id}")
    public void deletePost(@PathVariable("id") Integer id)
    {
        Post post = postRepository.findById(id)
                .orElseThrow(() -> new ResourceNotFoundException("No post
                found with id="+id));
        try {
            postRepository.deleteById(post.getId());
        } catch (Exception e) {
            throw new PostDeletionException("Post with id="+id+" can't be
            deleted");
        }
    }
    ...
    ...
    @ExceptionHandler(PostDeletionException.class)
    public ResponseEntity<?> servletRequestBindingException(PostDeletionEx
    ception e)
    {
        ErrorDetails errorDetails = new ErrorDetails();
        errorDetails.setErrorMessage(e.getMessage());
        StringWriter sw = new StringWriter();
        PrintWriter pw = new PrintWriter(sw);
        e.printStackTrace(pw);
        errorDetails.setDevErrorMessage(sw.toString());
        return new ResponseEntity<>(errorDetails, HttpStatus.INTERNAL_
        SERVER_ERROR);
    }
}
```

You can handle exceptions globally using the @ControllerAdvice class with the @ExceptionHandler methods, as shown in Listing 10-12.

Listing 10-12. Handling REST API Exceptions Globally Using
@ExceptionHandler Methods

```
@ControllerAdvice
public class GlobalExceptionHandler
{
    @ExceptionHandler(ServletRequestBindingException.class)
    public ResponseEntity<?> servletRequestBindingException(ServletRequest
    BindingException e) {
        ErrorDetails errorDetails = new ErrorDetails();
        errorDetails.setErrorMessage(e.getMessage());
        errorDetails.setDevErrorMessage(getStackTraceAsString(e));
        return new ResponseEntity<>(errorDetails, HttpStatus.BAD_REQUEST);
    }

    @ExceptionHandler(Exception.class)
    public ResponseEntity<?> exception(Exception e) {
        ErrorDetails errorDetails = new ErrorDetails();
        errorDetails.setErrorMessage(e.getMessage());
        errorDetails.setDevErrorMessage(getStackTraceAsString(e));
        return new ResponseEntity<>(errorDetails, HttpStatus.INTERNAL_
        SERVER_ERROR);
    }
    private String getStackTraceAsString(Exception e)
    {
        StringWriter sw = new StringWriter();
        PrintWriter pw = new PrintWriter(sw);
        e.printStackTrace(pw);
        return sw.toString();
    }
}
```

The global exception handling mechanism helps you handle exceptions (like database communication errors and third-party service invocation failures) in a central place instead of handling them in each controller class.

Exercise

In this chapter, you implemented the CRUD API on how to create, read, update, and delete posts in your Spring blog application. As an exercise, you can implement a similar CRUD API for the Comments object. If you are stuck, feel free to check out the GitHub repository that contains the implementation of the Comments API.

Summary

This chapter discussed creating REST APIs using SpringMVC and Spring Data REST. It also looked at handling exceptions at the controller level and globally. In the next chapter, you will learn how to build reactive web applications using Spring WebFlux.

CHAPTER 11

Reactive Programming Using Spring WebFlux

Modern IT business needs have changed significantly compared to a few years ago. The amount of data that is being generated from various sources like social media sites, IoT devices, sensors, and the like is humongous. The traditional data processing models may not be suitable for processing such a huge volume of data. Even though we have better hardware support these days, many of the existing APIs are synchronous and blocking APIs, which become bottlenecks to better throughput.

Reactive programming is a programming paradigm that promotes an asynchronous, non-blocking, event-driven approach to data processing. Reactive programming is gaining momentum, and many programming languages provide reactive frameworks and libraries.

In Java, there are reactive libraries like RxJava and Reactor that support reactive programming. As interest in reactive programming grows in the Java community, a new reactive streams initiative is starting to provide a standard for asynchronous stream processing with non-blocking back pressure. Reactive stream support is available from JDK 9.

Spring Framework 5 introduces support for reactive programming with the new WebFlux module. Spring Boot also provides a starter to create reactive applications using WebFlux quickly. This chapter teaches you how to build reactive web applications using Spring WebFlux.

© K. Siva Prasad Reddy, Sai Upadhyayula 2023
K. S. P. Reddy and S. Upadhyayula, *Beginning Spring Boot 3*, https://doi.org/10.1007/978-1-4842-8792-7_11

Introduction to Reactive Programming

Reactive programming involves modeling data and events as observable data streams and implementing data processing routines to react to the changes in those streams. A group of people put together a *Reactive Manifesto* at www.reactivemanifesto.org/ to describe the characteristics of a reactive system.

Reactive programming is becoming popular, and there are already reactive frameworks or libraries for many of the popular programming languages.

- Project Reactor, https://projectreactor.io/

- RxJava, https://github.com/ReactiveX/RxJava

- Akka Streams, https://doc.akka.io/docs/akka/2.5.32/stream/index.html

- RxJS, https://github.com/ReactiveX/rxjs

- Rx.NET, https://github.com/dotnet/reactive

- RxScala, http://reactivex.io/rxscala

- RxClojure, https://github.com/ReactiveX/RxClojure

- RxSwift, https://github.com/ReactiveX/RxSwift

Reactive Streams

Reactive streams (www.reactive-streams.org/) is an initiative to provide a standard for asynchronous stream processing with non-blocking back pressure. The key components of reactive streams are the Publisher and Subscriber.

A Publisher is a provider of an unbounded number of sequenced elements published according to the demand received from the subscriber(s).

```
public interface Publisher<T> {
    public void subscribe(Subscriber<? super T> s);
}
```

A Subscriber subscribes to the Publisher for callbacks. Publishers don't automatically push data to Subscribers unless they request the data.

```
public interface Subscriber<T> {
    public void onSubscribe(Subscription s);
    public void onNext(T t);
    public void onError(Throwable t);
    public void onComplete();
}
```

Two popular implementations of reactive streams are RxJava (https://github.com/ReactiveX/RxJava) and Project Reactor (https://projectreactor.io/).

Project Reactor

Project Reactor is an implementation of the reactive streams specification with non-blocking and back pressure support. Reactor provides two composable reactive types, Flux and Mono, that implement the publisher but also provide a rich set of operators. A Flux represents a reactive sequence of 0..N items, whereas a Mono represents a single value or an empty result.

A Flux<T> is a standard Publisher<T> representing an asynchronous sequence of 0 to N emitted items, optionally terminated by either a success signal or an error.

A Mono<T> is a specialized Publisher<T> that emits at most one item and then optionally terminates with an onComplete signal or an onError. A Mono can be used to represent no-value asynchronous processes returning Mono<Void>.

Now you'll see how to create Mono and Flux types and how to consume data from them.

```
Mono<String> mono = Mono.just("Spring");
Mono<String> mono = Mono.empty();

Flux<String> flux = Flux.just("Spring", "SpringBoot", "Reactor");
Flux<String> flux = Flux.fromArray(new String[]{"Spring", "SpringBoot",
"Reactor"});
Flux<String> flux = Flux.fromIterable(Arrays.asList("Spring", "SpringBoot",
"Reactor"));
```

Until you subscribe to Publisher, no data flow will happen. You must enable logging and subscribe to the flux.

```
Flux<String> flux = Flux.just("Spring", "SpringBoot", "Reactor");
flux.log().subscribe();
```

When you run this code it will log the underlying callback method invocations as follows:

```
[main] INFO reactor.Flux.Array.1 - | onSubscribe([Synchronous Fuseable]
FluxArray.ArraySubscription)
[main] INFO reactor.Flux.Array.1 - | request(unbounded)
[main] INFO reactor.Flux.Array.1 - | onNext(Spring)
[main] INFO reactor.Flux.Array.1 - | onNext(SpringBoot)
[main] INFO reactor.Flux.Array.1 - | onNext(Reactor)
[main] INFO reactor.Flux.Array.1 - | onComplete()
```

Looking at the log statements, you can see that when you subscribe to Publisher, the following happens:

- The onSubscribe() method is called when you subscribe to Publisher(Flux).

- When you call subscribe() on Publisher, a subscription is created. This subscription requests data from the publisher. In this example, it defaults to *unbounded* and hence it requests every element available.

- The onNext() callback method is called for every element.

- The onComplete() callback method is called last after receiving the last element.

- If an error occurs while consuming the next element, then onError() callback is called.

Note   Covering Project Reactor in depth is out of the scope of this book. Refer to the Project Reactor documentation at `http://projectreactor.io/docs/core/release/reference/` for more details.

The Spring WebFlux Reactive framework is built on top of Project Reactor, which implements the reactive streams specification.

Reactive Web Applications Using Spring WebFlux

Spring Framework 5 comes with a new module called `spring-webflux` to support building reactive web applications. Spring WebFlux, by default, uses Project Reactor, which implements reactive streams for reactive support. But you can use other reactive stream implementations like RxJava. The `spring-webflux` module supports creating the reactive server and client applications using REST, HTML browsers, and WebSocket-style communications.

Spring WebFlux can run on servlet containers with support for Servlet 3.1 non-blocking I/O APIs and other async runtimes like Netty and Undertow. See Figure 11-1.

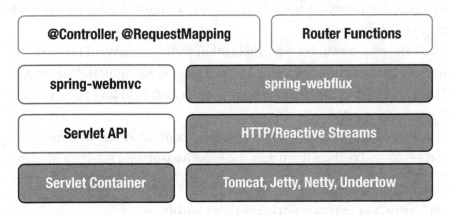

Figure 11-1. *Spring WebFlux runtime support*

Each runtime is adapted to a reactive `ServerHttpRequest` and `ServerHttpResponse`, thus exposing the body of a request and response as `Flux<DataBuffer>` instead of `InputStream` and `OutputStream` with reactive back pressure. REST-style JSON and XML serialization and deserialization and HTML view rendering is supported on top as a `Flux<Object>`.

You can develop Reactive web applications using the `spring-webflux` module in two ways:

- Using the SpringMVC style annotation based approach with `@Controller` & `@RestController`

- Using the functional style with routers and handlers

WebFlux Using the Annotation-Based Programming Model

You can build reactive web applications using the familiar Spring MVC annotations `@Controller` or `@RestController`, which also work with WebFlux. When used with WebFlux, the underlying framework components like `HandlerMapping` and `HandlerAdapter` are non-blocking and operate on the reactive `ServerHttpRequest` and `ServerHttpResponse` rather than on `HttpServletRequest` and `HttpServletResponse`.

Even though you use WebFlux reactive support at the controller layer, if you use a blocking API for data access like JDBC or JPA, your application will not be fully reactive. As of now, relational database vendors haven't provided non-blocking driver implementations. Some NoSQL datastores, such as MongoDB, Cassandra, and Redis, provide reactive drivers.

Now you'll develop a reactive web application with Spring WebFlux using the annotation-based programming model. You will use the MongoDB Reactive Stream Driver (http://mongodb.github.io/mongo-java-driver/) to take full advantage of MongoDB's reactive support.

In your Spring blog application, remove `spring-boot-starter-web` and `spring-boot-starter-data-jpa` and replace them with the Reactive web and Reactive Mongo starters.

```
<dependency>
    <groupId>org.springframework.boot</groupId>
    <artifactId>spring-boot-starter-webflux</artifactId>
</dependency>
<dependency>
    <groupId>org.springframework.boot</groupId>
    <artifactId>spring-boot-starter-data-mongodb-reactive</artifactId>
</dependency>
```

You will use the same POJO for the `Post.java` class, as defined in Chapter 9 when working with MongoDB, as shown in Listing 11-1.

Listing 11-1. Post.java

```
package com.apress.demo.springblog.domain;

import com.apress.demo.springblog.validation.BlogPostTitleAlreadyExists;
import jakarta.validation.constraints.NotNull;
import jakarta.validation.constraints.Size;
```

```java
import lombok.*;
import org.springframework.data.annotation.Id;
import org.springframework.data.mongodb.core.mapping.Document;
import org.springframework.data.mongodb.core.mapping.Field;

import java.time.LocalDateTime;
import java.util.List;

@Getter
@Setter
@AllArgsConstructor
@NoArgsConstructor
@Builder
@BlogPostTitleAlreadyExists
@Document
public class Post {
    @Id
    private String id;
    @NotNull
    @Size(min = 3, max = 50, message = "Title must be minimum 3 characters,
    and maximum 50 characters long")
    private String title;
    @NotNull
    @Size(min = 3, max = 500, message = "Description must be minimum 3
    characters, and maximum 500 characters long")
    private String description;
    @NotNull
    @Size(min = 3, max = 5000, message = "Body must be minimum 3 characters,
    and maximum 5000 characters long")
    private String body;
    private String slug;
    @Field(name = "post_status")
    private PostStatus postStatus;
    @Field(name = "created_on")
    private LocalDateTime createdOn;
    @Field(name = "updated_on")
```

```
    private LocalDateTime updatedOn;
    private List<Comment> comments;
}
```

The Spring Data Mongo library provides ReactiveCrudRepository, which is similar to CrudRepository but with reactive support, which will interact with the MongoDB Reactive driver under the hood.

Now create a Spring Data Repository for Post, as shown in Listing 11-2.

Listing 11-2. PostReactiveRepository.java

```
import org.springframework.data.repository.reactive.ReactiveCrudRepository;

public interface PostReactiveRepository extends
ReactiveCrudRepository<Post, String>
{
}
```

The Spring WebFlux annotation-based controllers look very similar to SpringMVC controllers, except that the input and return types will use the Reactor types Mono or Flux.

Now you can implement the CRUD operations for Post, as shown in Listing 11-3.

Listing 11-3. PostController.java Following the Annotation-Based Reactive Programming Model

```
import com.apress.demo.springblog.dto.PostDto;
import com.apress.demo.springblog.service.PostService;
import jakarta.validation.Valid;
import lombok.RequiredArgsConstructor;
import org.springframework.http.HttpStatus;
import org.springframework.web.bind.annotation.*;
import reactor.core.publisher.Flux;
import reactor.core.publisher.Mono;

@RestController
@RequestMapping("/api/posts")
@RequiredArgsConstructor
```

```java
public class PostController {

    private final PostService postService;

    @GetMapping
    @ResponseStatus(HttpStatus.OK)
    public Flux<PostDto> listPosts() {
        return postService.findAllPosts();
    }

    @PostMapping
    @ResponseStatus(HttpStatus.CREATED)
    public Mono<PostDto> createPost(@RequestBody @Valid PostDto postDto) {
        return postService.save(postDto);
    }
    @PutMapping
    @ResponseStatus(HttpStatus.OK)
    public Mono<PostDto> updatePost(@RequestBody @Valid PostDto postDto) {
        return postService.update(postDto);
    }
    @DeleteMapping("/{id}")
    @ResponseStatus(HttpStatus.NO_CONTENT)
    public Mono<Void> deletePost(@PathVariable String id) {
        return postService.delete(id);
    }

    @GetMapping("/{slug}")
    @ResponseStatus(HttpStatus.OK)
    public Mono<PostDto> findPostBySlug(@PathVariable String slug) {
        return postService.findBySlug(slug);
    }
}
```

You have the usual @RestController and @RequestMapping annotations on top of
the PostController class to define it as a standard Spring MVC Rest Controller. You have
the @RequiredArgsConstructor annotation to generate the argument-constructor for
the PostController class.

Inside the class are four endpoints:

- The listPosts() method, defined with @GetMapping, returns a
  Flux<PostDto> object since you can receive one (or) more posts as a
  response from this API.

- The createPost() method will receive a Mono<PostDto> as you will
  receive only one PostDto object as a response from this method.

- findPostBySlug also returns a Mono<PostDto> as you will receive a
  PostDto object based on the slugname.

- Finally, you have the deletePost() method, which returns a
  Mono<Void> because it has no return type.

Let's see the PostService.java class that contains the actual business logic:

```
@Service
@RequiredArgsConstructor
public class PostService {

    private final PostReactiveRepository postReactiveRepository;
    private final PostMapper postMapper;

    public Mono<PostDto> save(PostDto postDto) {
        Post post = postMapper.mapToPost(postDto);
        post.setCreatedOn(LocalDateTime.now());
        post.setUpdatedOn(LocalDateTime.now());
        return postReactiveRepository.save(post).map(p -> {
                    postDto.setId(p.getId());
                    return postDto;
                }
        );
    }
    public Flux<PostDto> findAllPosts() {
        return postReactiveRepository.findAll()
                .map(postMapper::mapToPostDto)
                .switchIfEmpty(Flux.empty());
    }
```

```java
    public Boolean postExistsWithTitle(String title) {
        return postReactiveRepository.existsByTitle(title).block();
    }
    public Mono<PostDto> update(PostDto postDto) {
        return postReactiveRepository.findById(postDto.getId())
                .flatMap(savedPost -> {
                    Post post = postMapper.mapToPost(postDto);
                    post.setId(savedPost.getId());
                    return postReactiveRepository.save(post);
                })
                .map(postMapper::mapToPostDto);
    }

    public Mono<Void> delete(String id) {
        return postReactiveRepository.deleteById(id);
    }
    public Mono<PostDto> findBySlug(String slug) {
        Mono<Post> postMono = postReactiveRepository.findBySlug(slug);
        return postMono.map(postMapper::mapToPostDto);
    }
}
}
```

In the PostService.java class, you perform the same operations as you saw in Chapter 10 while building the REST APIs; the only difference is the repository now returns a value of type Mono<PostDto> or Flux<PostDto>.

For this reason, you must handle the mapping between Post and PostDto objects a bit differently.

In the save() method, you first map PostDto to the Post object using the PostMapper.java class, and once the post object is saved in the database, to be able to access the id of the newly saved post and set it to the PostDto object, you use the map() function, and inside this function, you map the id field of the newly saved post object to the postDto object.

For the findAllPosts() method, you return Flux<Post> objects as response from the repository. The mapping from the Post object to postDto is repeated using the map() function. If there are no entries coming in from the database, the switchIfEmpty() function will be executed, which just returns an empty Flux object.

As the `postExistsWithTitle()` is called internally when the form validation is triggered, you evaluate this method synchronously instead of using reactive way by using the `.block()` method.

Next is the `update()` method, which uses the `flatMap()` method to loop through the existing post object, update the post, and save it back to the database. Finally, you use the `map()` method to map the `updatedPost` object to `PostDto` object and send it back as the response.

WebFlux Using a Functional Programming Model

Spring Framework 5 introduces a new functional-style programming model built on top of the reactive foundation and the annotation-based programming model.

Instead of using annotations to define request handling methods, you can implement `HandlerFunctions` as Java 8 lambdas and map the request URL patterns to `HandlerFunctions` using `RouterFunctions`. This programming model enables you to write Spring Code without using annotations.

```
HandlerFunction<ServerResponse> echoHandlerFn =
            ( request ) -> ServerResponse.ok().body(fromValue(request.
            queryParam("name")));
RequestPredicate predicate = RequestPredicates.GET("/echo");
RouterFunction<ServerResponse> routerFunction = RouterFunctions.
route(predicate, echoHandlerFn);
```

This example mapped the URL pattern GET /echo to echoHandlerFn, which returns the request parameter "name" value as the response body. You can write the same code block using Java 8 lambdas and static imports in a much more concise way, as follows:

```
route(GET("/echo"), request -> ok().body(fromValue(request.
queryParam("name")))));
```

Now let's explore the key components of the functional web framework.

HandlerFunction

The `HandlerFunction` is a functional interface that takes `ServletRequest` and returns `ServletResponse`.

```
@FunctionalInterface
public interface HandlerFunction<T extends ServerResponse>
{
    Mono<T> handle(ServerRequest request);
}
```

Here, ServerRequest and ServerResponse are immutable interfaces built on top of Reactor types. You can convert a request body into Reactor's Mono or Flux types and you can send any instance of a reactive stream's Publisher as a response body.

ServerRequest

The org.springframework.web.reactive.function.server.ServerRequest interface represents a server-side HTTP request. You can retrieve information from an input HTTP request from ServerRequest using various methods as follows:

```
HttpMethod method = request.method();
String path = request.path();
String id = request.pathVariable("id");
Map<String, String> pathVariables = request.pathVariables();
Optional<String> email = request.queryParam("email");
URI uri = request.uri();
```

You can convert a request body into a Mono or Flux using the bodyToMono() and bodyToFlux() methods.

```
Mono<User> userMono = request.bodyToMono(User.class);
Flux<User> usersFlux = request.bodyToFlux(User.class);
```

The bodyToMono() and bodyToFlux() methods are actually instances of BodyExtractor, which is used to extract the request body and deserialize it into an object.

You can use the BodyExtractors utility class to extract a request body into a Mono or Flux as follows:

```
Mono<User> userMono = request.body(BodyExtractors.toMono(User.class));
Flux<User> userFlux = request.body(BodyExtractors.toFlux(User.class));
```

You can use `ParameterizedTypeReference` if you want to convert a request body into a generic type.

```
ParameterizedTypeReference<Map<String, List<User>>> typeReference = new
ParameterizedTypeReference<Map<String, List<User>>>() {};
Mono<Map<String, List<User>>> mapMono = request.body(BodyExtractors.
toMono(typeReference));
```

ServerResponse

The `org.springframework.web.reactive.function.server.ServerResponse` interface represents a server-side HTTP response. The `ServerResponse` is an immutable interface and provides many static builder methods to construct the response with `status`, `contentType`, `cookies`, `headers`, `body`, and so on.

The following are a few examples of how you can construct `ServerResponse` using builder methods:

```
ServerResponse.ok().contentType(APPLICATION_JSON).body(userMono,
User.class);
ServerResponse.ok().contentType(APPLICATION_JSON).body(BodyInserters.
fromObject(user));
ServerResponse.created(uri).build();
ServerResponse.notFound().build();
```

You can also render the view templates using the `render()` method as follows:

```
Map<String,?> modelAttributes = new HashMap<>();
modelAttributes.put("user",user);
ServerResponse.ok().render("home", modelAttributes);
```

So, essentially using these `ServerResponse` builder methods, you can construct the return value of the `HandlerFunction.handle(ServerRequest)` method.

RouterFunction

`RouterFunction` maps the incoming request to a `HandlerFunction` using `RequestPredicate`. You can use the `RouterFunctions` utility class static methods to build the `RouterFunction` as follows:

```
RouterFunctions.route(GET("/echo"), request -> ServerResponse.ok().
body(fromValue(request.queryParam("name"))));
```

You can compose multiple route definitions into a new route definition that routes to the first handler function that matches the predicate.

```
import static org.springframework.web.reactive.function.server.
RequestPredicates.*; RouterFunctions.route(GET("/echo"), request ->
ServerResponse.ok().body(fromValue(request.queryParam("name"))))
        .and(route(GET("/home"), request -> ServerResponse.ok().
        render("home")))
        .andRoute(POST("/users"), request -> ServerResponse.ok().
        build());
```

This example composes three route definitions into one; the incoming request will be handled by the first `HandlerFunction` that matches the `RequestPredicate`.

Suppose you need to compose multiple routes with the same prefix. Instead of repeating the URL path in every route, you can use `RouterFunctions.nest()` as follows:

```
RouterFunctions.nest(path("/api/users"),
    nest(accept(APPLICATION_JSON),
        route(GET("/{id}"), request -> ServerResponse.ok().build())
        .andRoute(method(HttpMethod.GET), request -> ServerResponse.ok().
        build())));
```

The code maps two URLs to their handler functions. GET /api/users returns all users and GET /api/users/{id} returns the user details for the given id. Instead of repeating the common path prefix /api/users, it uses nest() to compose the routes.

You can create a `RequestPredicate` using the `RequestPredicates` static methods, and you can also compose request predicates using `RequestPredicate` and (RequestPredicate) and RequestPredicate or (RequestPredicate).

```
RouterFunctions.route(path("/api/users").and(method(HttpMethod.GET)),
                    request -> ServerResponse.ok().build());
RouterFunctions.route(GET("/api/users").or(GET("/api/users/list")),
                    request -> ServerResponse.ok().build());
```

HandlerFilterFunction

If you have to compare annotation-based approaches to functional approaches, RouterFunction is similar to the @RequestMapping annotation and HandlerFunction is similar to the method annotated with @RequestMapping. The new functional web framework also provides HandlerFilterFunction, which is similar to the servlet Filter or @ControllerAdvice methods.

```
@FunctionalInterface
public interface HandlerFilterFunction<T extends ServerResponse, R extends
ServerResponse>
{
    Mono<R> filter(ServerRequest request, HandlerFunction<T> next);
    //other methods
}
```

For example, you can filter a route based on a user role using HandlerFilterFunction as follows:

```
RouterFunction<ServerResponse> route = route(DELETE("/api/users/{id}"),
request -> ok().build());
RouterFunction<ServerResponse> filteredRoute = route.filter((request,
next) -> {
   if (hasAdminRole()) {
      return next.handle(request);
   }
   else {
      return ServerResponse.status(UNAUTHORIZED).build();
   }
});
private boolean hasAdminRole()
{
      //logic to check current user has ADMIN role or not
}
```

When you make a request to the /api/users/{id} URL, the filter checks whether the user has the admin role or not and decides to execute the handler function or return an UNAUTHORIZED response.

Registering HandlerFunctions as Method References

Instead of defining the HandlerFunctions using inline lambdas, it would be better to define them as methods and use method references in the route configuration, as shown in Listing 11-4.

Listing 11-4. Registering HandlerFunction with Route Using Method References

```
@Component
class EchoHandler
{
    public Mono<ServerResponse> echo(ServerRequest request)
    {
        return ServerResponse.ok().body(fromValue(request.
        queryParam("name")));
    }
}
@SpringBootApplication
class Applications
{
    @Autowired
    EchoHandler echoHandler;
    @Bean
    public RouterFunction<ServerResponse> echoRouterFunction() {
        return RouterFunctions.route(GET("/echo"), echoHandler::echo);
    }
}
```

Now let's create the same endpoints you built in the earlier section using the functional programming model. Create a PostHandler class with methods to define HandlerFunctions for various operations and then configure RouterFunctions mapping routes to handle functions. See Listing 11-5.

Listing 11-5. PostHandler.java Using the Functional Programming Model

```java
import com.apress.demo.springblog.dto.PostDto;
import com.apress.demo.springblog.service.PostService;
import lombok.RequiredArgsConstructor;
import org.springframework.http.HttpStatus;
import org.springframework.http.MediaType;
import org.springframework.stereotype.Component;
import org.springframework.web.reactive.function.server.ServerRequest;
import org.springframework.web.reactive.function.server.ServerResponse;
import reactor.core.publisher.Flux;
import reactor.core.publisher.Mono;

import static org.springframework.web.reactive.function.BodyInserters.
fromValue;

@Component
@RequiredArgsConstructor
public class PostHandler {
    private final PostService postService;

    public Mono<ServerResponse> listPosts(ServerRequest serverRequest) {
        Flux<PostDto> allPosts = postService.findAllPosts();
        Mono<ServerResponse> notFound = ServerResponse.notFound().build();

        return ServerResponse.ok()
                .contentType(MediaType.APPLICATION_JSON)
                .body(allPosts, PostDto.class)
                .switchIfEmpty(notFound);
    }

    public Mono<ServerResponse> findPostBySlug(ServerRequest
    serverRequest) {
        String slug = serverRequest.pathVariable("slug");
        Mono<PostDto> postBySlug = postService.findBySlug(slug);
        Mono<ServerResponse> notFound = ServerResponse.notFound().build();
```

```java
    return postBySlug.flatMap(post -> ServerResponse.ok().
    contentType(MediaType.APPLICATION_JSON)
                    .body(fromValue(post)))
            .switchIfEmpty(notFound);
}

public Mono<ServerResponse> savePost(ServerRequest serverRequest) {
    Mono<PostDto> postDtoMono = serverRequest.bodyToMono(PostDto.class);
    Mono<ServerResponse> notFound = ServerResponse.notFound().build();

    return postDtoMono.flatMap(postDto ->
                    ServerResponse
                            .status(HttpStatus.CREATED)
                            .contentType(MediaType.APPLICATION_JSON)
                            .body(postService.save(postDto),
                            PostDto.class))
            .switchIfEmpty(notFound);
}

public Mono<ServerResponse> updatePost(ServerRequest serverRequest) {
    Mono<PostDto> postDtoMono = serverRequest.bodyToMono(PostDto.class);
    Mono<ServerResponse> notFound = ServerResponse.notFound().build();

    return postDtoMono.flatMap(postDto ->
                    ServerResponse
                            .status(HttpStatus.OK)
                            .contentType(MediaType.APPLICATION_JSON)
                            .body(postService.update(postDto),
                            PostDto.class))
            .switchIfEmpty(notFound);
}

public Mono<ServerResponse> deletePost(ServerRequest serverRequest) {
    String id = serverRequest.pathVariable("id");
    Mono<ServerResponse> notFound = ServerResponse.notFound().build();
    return ServerResponse
```

```
                .status(HttpStatus.NO_CONTENT)
                .build(postService.delete(id))
                .switchIfEmpty(notFound);
    }
}
```

Let's define the handler functions for CRUD operations as separate methods. Now you can configure router functions, as shown in Listing 11-6.

Listing 11-6. SpringblogApplication.java

```java
import com.apress.demo.springblog.controller.PostHandler;
import org.springframework.boot.SpringApplication;
import org.springframework.boot.autoconfigure.SpringBootApplication;
import org.springframework.context.annotation.Bean;
import org.springframework.http.HttpMethod;
import org.springframework.http.MediaType;
import org.springframework.web.reactive.function.server.RouterFunction;
import org.springframework.web.reactive.function.server.ServerResponse;

import static org.springframework.web.reactive.function.server.
RequestPredicates.*;
import static org.springframework.web.reactive.function.server.
RouterFunctions.nest;
import static org.springframework.web.reactive.function.server.
RouterFunctions.route;

@SpringBootApplication
public class SpringblogApplication {

    public static void main(String[] args) {
        SpringApplication.run(SpringblogApplication.class, args);
    }

    @Bean
    RouterFunction<ServerResponse> routes(PostHandler postHandler) {
        return
                nest(path("/api/posts"),
                        nest(accept(MediaType.APPLICATION_JSON),
```

```
route(GET("/{slug}"), postHandler::
findPostBySlug)
        .andRoute(method(HttpMethod.GET),
        postHandler::listPosts)
        .andRoute(DELETE("/{id}"),
        postHandler::deletePost)
        .andRoute(POST("/"), postHandler::
        savePost)
        .andRoute(PUT("/"), postHandler::
        updatePost)));

  }
}
```

You define the router configurations and register them as a `RouterFunction` bean. You can even mix the annotation-based and functional-based programming models in the same application.

By default, `spring-boot-starter-webflux` uses `reactor-netty` as the runtime engine. You can exclude `reactor-netty` and use another server that supports reactive non-blocking I/O, such as Undertow, Jetty, or Tomcat.

Note   For more details on WebFlux autoconfiguration, look at the configuration classes in the `org.springframework.boot.autoconfigure.web.reactive` package.

Working with Spring Data R2DBC

Until now, you have seen how to interact with the reactive applications using Reactive MongoDB as the database. Now let's see how to use Reactive Relational Database Connectivity (R2DBC), a specification to integrate SQL databases using reactive drivers.

You cannot use the traditional JDBC when working with reactive applications because the thread requesting the data from the database sits idle until you receive the response from the database.

With R2DBC, this is possible to work in a reactive way. Let's go ahead and implement this in your Spring blog application.

In Chapter 5, you saw that you could use `JdbcTemplate` to interact with the database using JDBC. With R2DBC, you can use the `R2dbcEntityTemplate` to interact with the database in a reactive way.

You will use H2 as the database for your Spring blog application. You can choose any of the databases that Spring Data R2DBC supports. Refer to the list here: `https://spring.io/projects/spring-data-r2dbc`.

To add Reactive H2 Driver and Spring Data R2DBC to your project, add the following dependencies to the `pom.xml` file:

```
<dependency>
    <groupId>io.r2dbc</groupId>
    <artifactId>r2dbc-h2</artifactId>
</dependency>
<dependency>
    <groupId>org.springframework.boot</groupId>
    <artifactId>spring-boot-starter-data-r2dbc</artifactId>
</dependency>
```

The next step is to make minor changes to your data model, the `Post` and `Comment` classes.

First of all, you no longer need MongoDB-related annotations like `@Document` and `@Field` in your `Post.java` class, so you can remove them.

Next, you must change the type of the ID field from String to an Integer (or) Long. Let's use the Long type for the id.

You no longer need to maintain the `List<Comment>` `commentList` variable inside the `Post` class because you will handle the relationship between `Post` and `Comment` objects through the database tables defined inside the `data.sql` file, similar to how you did in Chapter 5.

Listings 11-7 and 11-8 show the `Post.java` and `Comment.java` classes after the above-mentioned changes are applied.

Listing 11-7. Post.java Class

```
import com.apress.demo.springblog.validation.BlogPostTitleAlreadyExists;
import lombok.*;
import org.springframework.data.annotation.Id;
import java.time.LocalDateTime;
```

```
@Getter
@Setter
@AllArgsConstructor
@NoArgsConstructor
@Builder
@BlogPostTitleAlreadyExists
public class Post {
    @Id
    private Long id;
    @NonNull
    private String title;
    @NonNull
    private String description;
    private String body;
    private String slug;
    @NonNull
    private PostStatus postStatus;
    private LocalDateTime createdOn;
    private LocalDateTime updatedOn;
}
```

Listing 11-8. Comment.java Class

```
import lombok.*;
import java.time.LocalDateTime;

@Getter
@Setter
@AllArgsConstructor
@NoArgsConstructor
@Builder
public class Comment {
    private Long id;
    private String title;
    private String authorName;
    private String body;
```

```
    private LocalDateTime createdOn;
    private LocalDateTime updatedOn;
    private Post post;
}
```

Next, let's define the database tables you want to create inside the data.sql file. See Listing 11-9.

Listing 11-9. data.sql File

```
DROP TABLE IF EXISTS COMMENT;
DROP TABLE IF EXISTS POST;
CREATE TABLE POST
(
    ID int NOT NULL AUTO_INCREMENT,
    TITLE varchar(50) NOT NULL,
    DESCRIPTION varchar(500) NOT NULL,
    BODY LONGTEXT DEFAULT NULL,
    SLUG varchar(60) DEFAULT NULL,
    POST_STATUS varchar(50) NOT NULL,
    CREATED_ON datetime DEFAULT NULL,
    UPDATED_ON datetime DEFAULT NULL,
    PRIMARY KEY (ID)
);

CREATE TABLE COMMENT
(
    ID int NOT NULL AUTO_INCREMENT,
    POST_ID int NOT NULL,
    TITLE varchar(200) NOT NULL,
    AUTHOR_NAME varchar(200) NOT NULL,
    BODY LONGTEXT DEFAULT NULL,
    CREATED_ON datetime DEFAULT NULL,
    UPDATED_ON datetime DEFAULT NULL,
    PRIMARY KEY (ID),
    FOREIGN KEY (POST_ID) REFERENCES POST(ID)
);
```

One main difference here is that you changed the type of the POST_STATUS from ENUM in the previous chapters to a VARCHAR, as the R2DBC H2 driver does not support the enum types.

You don't need to make many changes in your `PostReactiveRepository.java` interface because you can use the same version you used for Reactive MongoDB. The main reason for this is that R2DBC also supports the `ReactiveCrudRepository` interface.

```
import com.apress.demo.springblog.domain.Post;
import org.springframework.data.repository.reactive.ReactiveCrudRepository;
import reactor.core.publisher.Mono;

public interface PostReactiveRepository extends
ReactiveCrudRepository<Post, Long> {
    Mono<Boolean> existsByTitle(String title);
    Mono<Post> findBySlug(String slug);
}
```

You may have to make some small changes across the `PostController.java`, `PostHandler.java`, `PostDto.java`, and `PostService.java` classes to migrate the id field from String to Long, but apart from that, there are not many changes you need to work with R2DBC.

So now, if you start the `SpringBlogApplication.java` and try to access the four CRUD endpoints, you should be able to persist and retrieve the data from the H2 database reactively.

Reactive WebClient

Spring provides `RestTemplate` to invoke RESTful service endpoints, which support message converters so that HTTP requests can be made using Java objects instead of manually preparing an input request body with JSON or XML.

Spring WebFlux provides `WebClient` as a reactive alternative to `RestTemplate`, which supports non-blocking. Instead of using `InputStream` and `OutputStream` for request processing, `WebClient` uses `Flux<DataBuffer>` as the request and the response body.

Listing 11-10 shows how, as a client, you can make a request to a reactive endpoint.

Listing 11-10. Invoking Reactive REST Endpoints Using WebClient

```
WebClient webClient = WebClient.create("http://localhost:"+port);
List<User> users = webClient.get().uri("/api/users")
                        .accept(MediaType.APPLICATION_JSON)
                        .exchangeToFlux()
                        .flatMap(response -> response.bodyToFlux
                        (User.class).collectList()).block();
```

The `webClient.get().uri("/api/users").exchange()` returns a `Mono<ClientResponse>` and `ClientResponse` provides various utility methods, like the `bodyToMono()`, `bodyToFlux()`, and `body(BodyExtractor)` methods to extract body content.

Testing Spring WebFlux Applications

The `spring-boot-starter-test` module provides `WebTestClient`, which can test reactive endpoints, and also the test slice `@WebFluxTest` to test the Spring WebFlux endpoints.

The `@WebFluxTest` annotation populates a Spring Test Context, which contains the relevant infrastructure and beans to run WebFlux application endpoints.

Listing 11-11 shows how to test the reactive REST endpoint `GET /api/posts` using `@WebFluxTest` and `WebTestClient`.

Listing 11-11. Testing Reactive Endpoints Using WebFluxTest

```
import com.apress.demo.springblog.controller.PostController;
import com.apress.demo.springblog.domain.PostStatus;
import com.apress.demo.springblog.dto.PostDto;
import com.apress.demo.springblog.service.PostService;
import org.junit.jupiter.api.Test;
import org.mockito.BDDMockito;
import org.springframework.beans.factory.annotation.Autowired;
import org.springframework.boot.test.autoconfigure.web.reactive.WebFluxTest;
import org.springframework.boot.test.mock.mockito.MockBean;
import org.springframework.test.web.reactive.server.WebTestClient;
import reactor.core.publisher.Flux;
```

```java
@WebFluxTest(controllers = PostController.class)
class PostControllerTest {
    @Autowired
    private WebTestClient webTestClient;
    @MockBean
    private PostService postService;

    @Test
    void testFindAllPosts() {
        PostDto post = new PostDto();
        post.setTitle("title");
        post.setBody("body");
        post.setDescription("description");
        post.setPostStatus(PostStatus.DRAFT);

        PostDto secondPost = new PostDto();
        secondPost.setTitle("title2");
        secondPost.setBody("body2");
        secondPost.setDescription("description2");
        secondPost.setPostStatus(PostStatus.DRAFT);

        BDDMockito.when(postService.findAllPosts()).thenReturn(Flux.
        just(post, secondPost));

        webTestClient.get().uri("/api/posts")
                .exchange()
                .expectStatus().isOk()
                .returnResult(PostDto.class);
    }
}
```

You can inject WebTestClient and use relative URLs for testing instead of providing complete URLs. Once the REST endpoint is invoked, you can assert the HTTP status and specify the class type to which the response body needs to be converted.

You can also perform JSON assertions on the response body by using JSON Path library assertions. You can invoke the GET /api/posts/ endpoint to retrieve a list of posts and assert the response JSON, as shown in Listing 11-12.

Listing 11-12. Performing JSON Assertions on WebTestClient Response Body

```
@Test
void testFindAllPosts() {
    PostDto post = new PostDto();
    post.setTitle("title");
    post.setBody("body");
    post.setDescription("description");
    post.setPostStatus(PostStatus.DRAFT);

    PostDto secondPost = new PostDto();
    secondPost.setTitle("title2");
    secondPost.setBody("body2");
    secondPost.setDescription("description2");
    secondPost.setPostStatus(PostStatus.DRAFT);

    BDDMockito.when(postService.findAllPosts()).thenReturn(Flux.just(post,
    secondPost));

    webTestClient.get().uri("/api/posts")
            .exchange()
            .expectStatus().isOk()
            .expectBody()
            .jsonPath("$.[0].title").isEqualTo("title")
            .jsonPath("$.[1].title").isEqualTo("title2");
}
```

This example asserts the response JSON using `jsonPath()` assertions provided by the JSON Path library. As the `/api/posts` endpoint returns a list of `PostDto` objects, it simply verifies the title fields of the first and second elements of the list. For more details on JSON Path, see `https://github.com/json-path/JsonPath`.

Note   You will learn more about testing Spring Boot applications in Chapter 14.

Summary

This chapter showed you how to build reactive web applications using the Spring WebFlux framework, which is a new module introduced in Spring Framework 5. You built a reactive application using the MongoDB reactive stream driver and WebFlux with annotation-based and functional-style programming models. In the next chapter, you learn how to secure traditional web applications and REST APIs using Spring Security.

CHAPTER 12

Securing Web Applications

Security is an essential aspect of software application design. It protects software from unauthorized access and misuse. Numerous threats are lurking around the Internet to steal users' information. Hence, you as a software engineer must understand how to develop secure applications.

There are two essential terms to understand when talking about security. *Authentication* refers to verifying the user's credentials by asking for the user's credentials. *Authorization* refers to verifying the user's ability to do a certain activity.

Spring Security is a powerful and flexible framework for securing Java-based web applications. Even though Spring Security is commonly used with Spring-based applications, you can also use it to secure non-Spring-based web applications.

This chapter explains how to use the Spring Boot Security Starter to secure your Spring Blog application and how to secure service layer components using method-level security. The chapter also explores implementing the OAuth2 protocol using Spring Security to secure the REST API.

Spring Security in Spring Boot Web Application

Spring Security is a framework for securing Java-based applications at various layers with great flexibility and customization. Spring Security provides authentication and authorization support against database authentication, LDAP, form authentication, JA-SIG central authentication service, Java Authentication and Authorization Service (JAAS), and many more. With minimal configuration, Spring Security has built-in support to block common attacks like CSRF, XSS, and session fixation.

© K. Siva Prasad Reddy, Sai Upadhyayula 2023
K. S. P. Reddy and S. Upadhyayula, *Beginning Spring Boot 3*, https://doi.org/10.1007/978-1-4842-8792-7_12

You can use Spring Security to secure the application at various layers, such as web URLs, service layer methods, and more. Spring Security from version 3.2 onward provides Java configuration support for security. Using Spring Security in a Spring Boot application became easier with its autoconfiguration features.

Adding the Spring Security Starter (`spring-boot-starter-security`) to a Spring Boot application will

- Enable HTTP basic security

- Enable a single user with the name "user" stored in an in-memory database

- Ignore paths for commonly used static resource locations (such as `/css/**`, `/js/**`, `/images/**`, etc.)

- Enable common low-level features such as XSS and CSRF protection, caching, and more

To get started, add the following dependency to your Spring blog application:

```
<dependency>
    <groupId>org.springframework.boot</groupId>
    <artifactId>spring-boot-starter-security</artifactId>
</dependency>
```

That's all you need to do to add basic security to your Spring blog application. Note the word "basic." When you start the application, you can see the following entry in the logs:

Using generated security password: b5dd65a5-b0e7-49d0-8f2b-eaa55abf0487 This generated password is for development use only. You must update your security configuration before running your application in production.

By default, Spring Boot provides a default username and password for you to use during the development phase. If you open your application at `http://localhost:8080`, the browser will navigate to a default login page, as shown in Figure 12-1.

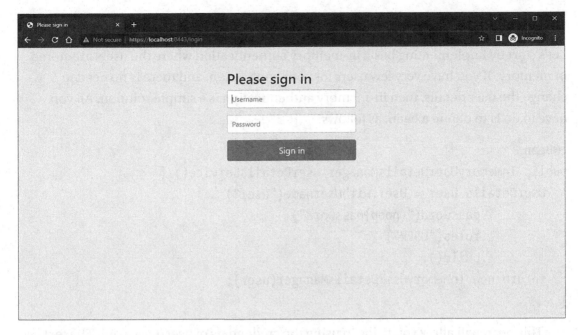

Figure 12-1. *Spring Security default login page*

Let's enter the credentials to access the application. The default user is **user,** and the password is autogenerated, one you can find in the logs, as mentioned.

You can change the default user credentials in `application.properties` as follows:

```
security.user.name=admin
security.user.password=secret
security.user.role=USER,ADMIN
```

That's nice for a quick demo. You may want to implement a more complex and mature security system like a registration feature where users can register before accessing the application and access resources where the user has necessary permissions. You may also want to introduce roles like ADMIN, USER, and such. Let's go ahead and implement them in your Spring blog application.

Implementing In-Memory Authentication

Let's start by implementing basic in-memory authentication where the users are stored in memory. If you have very few users for your application, and there is no need to change the user details, then in-memory authentication is a simple solution. All you have to do is to define a bean, as follows:

```
@Bean
public InMemoryUserDetailsManager userDetailsService() {
    UserDetails user = User.withUsername("user")
            .password("{noop}password")
            .roles("USER")
            .build();
    return new InMemoryUserDetailsManager(user);
}
```

This bean will allow you to log in using the credentials of user/password. The text {noop} before the password denotes that you are not encoding the password before storing it, but in real world applications you must encode passwords to avoid storing them in clear text. We will discuss this topic in the coming sections.

But this kind of authentication is not so flexible because it won't support registering new users, changing the user details, and such. You can create an implementation to store users in the database and authenticate those users with the help of the UserDetailsService interface from Spring Security. Let's see how to do that.

Implementing Custom User Authentication

As part of the custom user authentication, you will implement the UserDetailsService interface to read the users from the database instead of the memory.

The UserDetailsService interface exposes a single method called loadUserByUsername(). You just have to implement your class with your custom logic inside this method.

For that, you must to create the domain class User to store the user details like username, password, and roles, as shown in Listing 12-1.

You will use Spring Data JPA to persist the user information. You can also JDBC to store the details if you like, as shown in Listing 12-1.

Listing 12-1. User JPA Entity

```java
@Entity
@Table(name = "users")
@Getter
@Setter
@NoArgsConstructor
@AllArgsConstructor
@Builder
public class User implements UserDetails {
    @Id
    @GeneratedValue(strategy = GenerationType.IDENTITY)
    private Long id;
    @Column(unique = true, nullable = false)
    private String email;
    @Column(unique = true, nullable = false)
    private String userName;
    @Column(nullable = false)
    private String password;
    @Column(nullable = false)
    private String role;

    @Override
    public Collection<? extends GrantedAuthority> getAuthorities() {
        return List.of(new SimpleGrantedAuthority(role));
    }

    @Override
    public String getUsername() {
        return userName;
    }

    @Override
    public boolean isAccountNonExpired() {
        return true;
    }

    @Override
    public boolean isAccountNonLocked() {
```

```
        return true;
    }

    @Override
    public boolean isCredentialsNonExpired() {
        return true;
    }

    @Override
    public boolean isEnabled() {
        return true;
    }
}
```

The User class contains the necessary attributes like username, password, and role information. In addition, this class implements the UserDetails interface from Spring Security, which represents an Authenticated User object.

There are multiple methods like isEnabled(), isCredentialsNonExpired(), isAccountNonLocked(), and isAccountNonExpired() that are used at the time of authentication.

If any methods return false, the login will not be successful.

You also have the getAuthorities() method that returns the permissions of a given user.

Next, create the Spring Data JPA repository for the user entity, as shown in Listing 12-2.

Listing 12-2. Spring Data JPA Repository Interface UserRepository.java

```
public interface UserRepository extends JpaRepository<User, Integer>
{
    Optional<User> findByUserName(String userName);
}
```

The UserRepository interface defines a method named findByEmail() to look up the user by email.

Now let's implement the UserDetailsService called CustomUserDetailsService to read UserDetails from the database, as shown in Listing 12-3.

Listing 12-3. UserDetailsService Implementation

```
@Service
@Transactional
@RequiredArgsConstructor
public class CustomUserDetailsService implements UserDetailsService {
    private final UserRepository userRepository;

    @Override
    public UserDetails loadUserByUsername(String userName)
        throws UsernameNotFoundException {
    com.apress.demo.springblog.domain.User user = userRepository.
    findByUserName(userName)
            .orElseThrow(() -> new UsernameNotFoundException("Email " +
            userName + " not found"));
    return new org.springframework.security.core.userdetails.User(
            user.getEmail(),
            user.getPassword(),
            user.getAuthorities()
    );
    }
}
```

Inside the loadUserByUsername(), you query the database using the UserRepostiory to find the user by the username, and you encapsulate the user object with the User object from Spring Security, which is an implementation of the UserDetails interface.

The org.springframework.security.core.userdetails.User represents the authentication object, used internally by Spring Security.

Custom Spring Security Configuration

Until now you have worked with the default Spring Security settings that come with the Spring Boot Security Starter. To switch the default security configuration and provide your customized security configuration, you can create a configuration class with the @EnableWebSecurity annotation and create a bean of the type SecurityFilter Chain, as shown in Listing 12-4.

Listing 12-4. Customized Spring Security Configuration

```
@Configuration
@EnableWebSecurity
@RequiredArgsConstructor
public class WebSecurityConfig {
    @Bean
    public SecurityFilterChain defaultSecurityFilterChain(HttpSecurity http)
    throws Exception {
        http
                .authorizeRequests()
                .anyRequest().authenticated()
                .and()
                .formLogin();
        return http.build();
    }
}
```

This class defines two beans. One is of type `SecurityFilterChain`, which contains all the security configurations of your application. First, you make sure that all the requests to your Spring blog application are authenticated using the `authorizeRequests()`. `anyRequest().authenticated()` method calls. Then you inform Spring Security to use a form-based authentication using the `formLogin()` method.

If you want to use a custom login page, you can extend the `formLogin()` method call with the following method calls:

```
.formLogin()
.loginPage("/login")
.defaultSuccessUrl("/posts")
.failureUrl("/login?error")
.permitAll();
Spring Security will fetch the HTML from the path /login and display it
instead of the default login form.
```

When the login is successful, it will redirect to the default success URL /posts, and when the login fails, it will redirect to /login with an error request attribute.

The login page should be accessible for everyone, so for this reason, you add the method `permitAll()` to the method calls. If you do not add this method call, you will receive a 401 error when you try to access the login page.

You can see the code of the `login.html` file in Listing 12-5.

Listing 12-5. Login Page

```html
<!DOCTYPE html>
<html xmlns="http://www.w3.org/1999/xhtml"
    xmlns:th="http://www.thymeleaf.org">
<head>
   <title>SpringBoot Security</title>
</head>
<body>
<form action="login" th:action="@{/login}" method="post">
   <div th:if="${param.error}">
       <span>Invalid Email and Password.</span>
   </div>
   <input type="text" name="username" placeholder="Username" />
   <input type="password" name="password" placeholder="Password" />
   <button type="submit">LogIn</button>
</form>
</body>
</html>
```

Next, you need to add the following configuration inside the `WebConfig.java` class to tell Spring Security to use the `login.html` page as the custom login page instead of the default login page:

```java
@Override
public void addViewControllers(ViewControllerRegistry registry) {
   registry.addRedirectViewController("/", "/posts");
   registry.addViewController("/login").setViewName("login");
}
```

Implementing Logout Functionality

Spring Security also implements the logout functionality by default. All you have to do is define the following configuration inside the `defaultSecurityFilterChain` method.

```
.and()
.logout()
.logoutRequestMatcher(new AntPathRequestMatcher("/logout"))
.logoutSuccessUrl("/login?logout")
.permitAll();
```

This code triggers the logout functionality when it receives a request at the URL / logout. After the successful logout, the page will redirect to /login?logout.

Alright, now let's test whether your login and logout flow is working. But before that, you need some users in your database. Until you create the registration functionality, let's add initial test data to work with the login by implementing the `CommandLineRunner` interface to your Spring blog application main class and overriding the `run` method, as shown in Listing 12-6.

Listing 12-6. Initial Test Data in the SpringblogApplication.java Class

```java
@SpringBootApplication
public class SpringblogApplication implements CommandLineRunner {

    private final UserRepository userRepository;

    public SpringblogApplication(UserRepository userRepository) {
        this.userRepository = userRepository;
    }

    public static void main(String[] args) {
        SpringApplication.run(SpringblogApplication.class, args);
    }

    @Override
    public void run(String... args) throws Exception {
        if (userRepository.findAll().isEmpty()) {
            User user = User.builder()
                    .email("admin@gmail.com")
                    .userName("admin")
```

```
            .password("password")
            .role("ADMIN")
            .build();
        userRepository.save(user);
    }
  }
}
```

At the time of application startup, the `run` method will add the admin user to the database if no other users exist.

Now let's run the application and open the URL `http://localhost:8080`. You should see a basic HTML form, as shown in Figure 12-2.

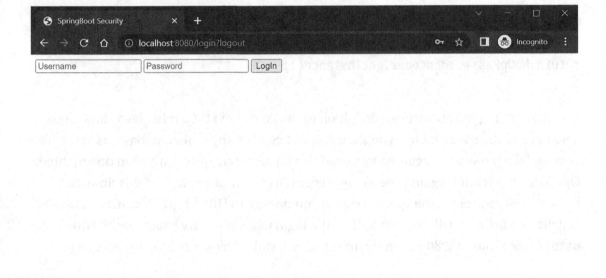

Figure 12-2. *Basic login page*

You may think this page looks far worse than the default Spring Security login page. I agree, but let's concentrate on the Spring Security functionality instead of styling the login page. I added the necessary styles to the login page and the blog application in general to the completed source code, which you can find in the GitHub repository.

Back to your application, if you type in the credentials you stored in your database, you will be greeted with the following error:

```
fixed java.lang.IllegalArgumentException: There is no PasswordEncoder
mapped for the id "null" error
```

Spring Security, by default, will expect your passwords to be stored in an encoded format. It will not allow you to store the passwords in clear text. In the previous section, when you stored the user details in-memory, you used a string {noop} to use the NoOpPasswordEncoder from Spring Security. So, to fix this issue, you must define a NoOpPasswordEncoder to temporarily allow the clear-text passwords. Please do not use this in your production applications! You will use the correct password encoding in the coming sections of this chapter.

```
@Bean
public static PasswordEncoder passwordEncoder() {
return NoOpPasswordEncoder.getInstance();
}
```

After adding the above bean definition to the WebSecurityConfig.java class, make sure to clear the users table if you are using a MySQL or any other database, as you have changed the password encoding format. If you are using h2, you don't need do anything. Open the application again, type in the credentials one more time, and this time the browser will redirect to the /posts page. If you now go to URL http://localhost:8080/ logout, the browser will redirect back to the login page. If you try to access the URL http://localhost:8080 one more time, you will still be redirected to the login page.

Implementing User Registration

Now, let's implement the user registration functionality in your Spring blog application. Create a new class called UserRegistrationController.java inside the controller package with the code shown in Listing 12-7.

Listing 12-7. User Registration Controller

```
@Controller
@RequestMapping("/user/register")
@RequiredArgsConstructor
```

```
public class UserRegistrationController {

    private final UserService userService;

    @GetMapping
    public String register() {
        return "register";
    }

    @PostMapping
    public String doRegister(@Valid UserForm userForm) {
        userService.registerUser(userForm);
        return "redirect:/login";
    }
}
```

This class is a standard Spring MVC Controller with the @Controller and @RequestMapping annotations.

The register() method handles the GET request and returns the register.html file as the response. When the user fills the necessary details and submits the form, the doRegister() method is invoked, which calls the registerUser() method inside the UserService, which performs the actual logic of storing the user inside the database. You can view the code of UserService class in Listing 12-8.

Listing 12-8. UserService Class

```
@Service
@RequiredArgsConstructor
@Transactional
public class UserService {
    private final UserRepository userRepository;

    public void registerUser(UserForm userForm) {
        User user = userForm.toUser(userForm);
        userRepository.save(user);
    }
}
```

The registerUser() method inside the UserService will first convert the UserForm object, which is a form representation of the User object, and save it to the database using the UserRepository.save() method.

This class has the @Transactional annotation, which creates a database transaction in the background when persisting the user entity to the database and then commits the transaction after successfully persisting the user entity. If there is any error during the save, the transaction will roll back, and the user information won't be saved to the database.

You can read the code for the UserForm.java class in Listing 12-9.

Listing 12-9. UserForm.java Class

```
@Data
@NoArgsConstructor
@AllArgsConstructor
@Builder
public class UserForm {
    @Email
    private String email;
    @NotBlank
    private String username;
    @NotBlank
    private String password;

    public User toUser(UserForm userForm) {
        User user = new User();
        user.setEmail(userForm.getEmail());
        user.setUserName(userForm.getUsername());
        user.setPassword(userForm.getPassword());
        user.setRole("USER");
        return user;
    }
}
```

The UserForm class contains all the fields coming from the web application. It also contains the bean validation annotations like @Email and @NotBlank to validate the incoming data.

Finally, let's create the `register.html` file under the `templates` directory and copy the code shown in Listing 12-10.

Listing 12-10. Registration Page

```
<!DOCTYPE html>
<html xmlns="http://www.w3.org/1999/xhtml"
    xmlns:th="http://www.thymeleaf.org">
<head>
   <title>SpringBoot Security</title>
</head>
<body>
<form action="login" th:action="@{/user/register}" method="post">
   <div th:if="${param.error}">
      <span>Invalid Email and Password.</span>
   </div>
   <input type="email" name="email" placeholder="Email"/>
   <input type="text" name="username" placeholder="Username"/>
   <input type="password" name="password" placeholder="Password"/>
   <button type="submit">Register</button>
</form>
</body>
</html>
```

Lastly, you must be able to access the `register.html` page without authentication. For this reason, you have to enhance your `defaultSecurityFilterChain()` method inside the `WebSecurityConfig` class with the following code:

```
http
       .authorizeRequests()
       .antMatchers("/user/register")
       .permitAll()
       .anyRequest()
       .authenticated()
```

The `antMatchers()` method allows you to define a matcher path like `/user/register`, and the `permitAll()` method allows you to access the path defined inside the `antMatchers()` method without authentication.

Start the application and open the URL `http://localhost:8080/user/register`. You should see the HTML page, and if you register, the user will be successfully saved into the database, and the page will be redirected to the `/login` path.

If you try to log in with your newly registered credentials, you should be able to login successfully.

As mentioned, Spring Security, by default, expects the password to be encoded using any of the standard password encoding mechanisms. Let's see how to do that in the next section.

Hashing Passwords Using PasswordEncoder

When storing passwords of users in a database, you must be very careful not to store them in plain text format. If, unfortunately, a hacker gets access to the database, they can find all the user's passwords in clear text, which is not so good.

Spring Security allows you to hash the passwords using industry-standard hashing algorithms before persisting to the database. It supports hashing algorithms like BCrypt and key-derivation functions like Scrypt, Pbkdf2, and Argon.

BCrypt is a widely used hashing algorithm to hash passwords, and Spring Security provides a class named `BCryptPasswordEncoder`, an implementation of the `PasswordEncoder` interface.

To be able to use this password encoder, you have to create a bean of the type `BCryptPasswordEncoder` in your `WebSecurityConfig` class, as follows:

```
@Bean
public PasswordEncoder passwordEncoder() {
    return new BCryptPasswordEncoder();
}
```

After defining this bean, inject the `PasswordEncoder` bean into the `SpringBlogApplication.java` class and replace the code with setting the password, as follows:

```
.password(passwordEncoder.encode("password"))
```

Refactor the `registerUser()` method in the `UserService.java` class to encode the password before saving the user to the database. You can view the code in Listing 12-11.

Listing 12-11. UserService.java Class with PasswordEncoder

```java
@Service
@RequiredArgsConstructor
@Transactional
public class UserService {
    private final UserRepository userRepository;
    private final PasswordEncoder passwordEncoder;

    public void registerUser(UserForm userForm) {
        User user = userForm.toUser(userForm);
        user.setPassword(passwordEncoder.encode(userForm.getPassword()));
        userRepository.save(user);
    }
}
```

Spring Security will now automatically decode the password at the time of authentication and check if it matches the password saved in the database.

If the password matches, then the authentication will be successful.

Implementing the Remember-Me Feature

Spring Security provides the Remember-Me feature so that applications can remember the identity of a user between sessions. To use the Remember-Me functionality, you just need to send the HTTP parameter remember-me.

```html
<form th:action="@{/login}" method="post">
    <input type="email" name="username"/>
    <input type="password" name="password" />
    <input type="checkbox" name="remember-me"> Remember Me
    <button type="submit">LogIn</button>
</form>
```

Spring Security provides the following two implementations of the Remember-Me feature out of the box:

- **Simple hash-based token as a cookie**: This approach creates a token by hashing the user identity information and setting it as a cookie on the client browser.

- **Persistent token**: This approach uses a persistent store like a relational database to store the tokens.

Simple Hash-Based Token as a Cookie

You can enable the Remember-Me feature in the Security configuration, which uses a hash-based token approach, as shown in Listing 12-12.

Listing 12-12. Spring Security Configuration Enabling Remember-Me

```
@Bean
public SecurityFilterChain defaultSecurityFilterChain(HttpSecurity http)
throws Exception {
    http
        .authorizeRequests()
            .antMatchers("/user/register")
            .permitAll()
            .anyRequest()
            .authenticated()
            .and()
        .formLogin()
            .loginPage("/login")
            .defaultSuccessUrl("/posts")
            .failureUrl("/login?error")
            .permitAll()
            .and()
        .logout()
            .logoutRequestMatcher(new AntPathRequestMatcher("/logout"))
            .logoutSuccessUrl("/login?logout")
            .permitAll()
```

```
        .and()
      .rememberMe();

    return http.build();
}
```

You add a single line of code to the existing configuration: rememberMe().

With this configuration, when you log in by selecting the Remember Me checkbox, a cookie will be set with remember-me and will contain the hash-based token as a value. If you close and reopen the browser and go to the application, you will be automatically authenticated. Note that the remember-me cookie is deleted when the user logs out.

This hash-based token as a cookie approach is implemented by Spring Security using org.springframework.security.web.authentication.rememberme.TokenBasedRememberMeServices.

The remember-me cookie token value is generated as follows:

```
base64(username + ":" + expirationTime + ":" + md5Hex(username + ":" +
expirationTime + ":" password + ":" + key))
```

The default expirationTime is two weeks (1209600 seconds) and key is a random generated string (UUID.randomUUID().toString()).

You can customize the cookie name, expiration time, and key as follows:

```
.rememberMe()
    .key("my-secure-key")
    .rememberMeCookieName("my-remember-me-cookie")
    .tokenValiditySeconds(24 * 60 * 60)
    .and()
```

With this customization, after successful authentication, it will create the remember-me cookie with the name my-remember-me-cookie. It will be valid for one day (24 * 60 * 60 seconds).

Caution   In this approach, the generated token contains the MD5 hashed password and is a potential security vulnerability if the cookie is captured.

Persistent Tokens

Spring Security provides another implementation of the Remember-Me feature that can be used to store the generated tokens in persistent storage such as a database. The persistent tokens approach is implemented using org.springframework.security. web.authentication.rememberme.PersistentTokenBasedRememberMeServices, which internally uses the PersistentTokenRepository interface to store the tokens.

Spring provides the following two implementations of PersistentTokenRepository out of the box:

- InMemoryTokenRepositoryImpl can be used to store tokens in-memory (not recommended for production use).

- JdbcTokenRepositoryImpl can be used to store tokens in a database.

The JdbcTokenRepositoryImpl stores the tokens in the persistent_logins table. See Listing 12-13.

Listing 12-13. persistent_logins Table

```
create table persistent_logins
(
    username varchar(64) not null,
    series varchar(64) primary key,
    token varchar(64) not null,
    last_used timestamp not null
);
```

Now you'll see how to configure Remember-Me functionality to use a relational database to store the tokens. See Listing 12-14.

Listing 12-14. Configuring Remember-Me Using Persistent Tokens

```
@Configuration
@EnableWebSecurity
@RequiredArgsConstructor
public class WebSecurityConfig {
```

```java
private final DataSource dataSource;

@Bean
public SecurityFilterChain defaultSecurityFilterChain(HttpSecurity http)
throws Exception {
    http
            .authorizeRequests()
            .antMatchers("/user/register")
            .permitAll()
            .anyRequest()
            .authenticated()
            .and()
            .formLogin()
            .loginPage("/login")
            .defaultSuccessUrl("/posts")
            .failureUrl("/login?error")
            .permitAll()
            .and()
            .logout()
            .logoutRequestMatcher(new AntPathRequestMatcher("/logout"))
            .logoutSuccessUrl("/login?logout")
            .permitAll()
            .and()
            .rememberMe()
            .rememberMeCookieName("my-remember-me-cookie")
            .tokenRepository(persistentTokenRepository())
            .tokenValiditySeconds(24 * 60 * 60);
    return http.build();
}

@Bean
public PasswordEncoder passwordEncoder() {
    return new BCryptPasswordEncoder();
}

PersistentTokenRepository persistentTokenRepository() {
    JdbcTokenRepositoryImpl tokenRepositoryImpl = new
    JdbcTokenRepositoryImpl();
```

```
    tokenRepositoryImpl.setDataSource(dataSource);
    return tokenRepositoryImpl;
  }
}
```

When successfully logging in with the Remember-Me checkbox selected, Spring Security will store the generated token in the `persistent_logins` table.

This approach generates a unique series value for the user and random token data to create a token and set it as a cookie. Every time the user logs in with the cookie, Spring Security will generate new random token data, but the series value will be intact for that user.

Cross-Site Request Forgery Protection

Cross-Site Request Forgery (CSRF) is an attack that lets users execute unwanted actions on an authenticated web application. Suppose you go to the `genuinesite.com` website and authenticate yourself. This website may set cookies on your browser, including an authentication token. Now, if you open the `malicioussite.com` website on the same browser but in a different tab, you can send a request from `malicioussite.com` to `genuinesite.com` with unwanted data. This data will send the request along with the cookies set by `genuinesite.com`.

Spring Security provides CSRF protection by default using the `CsrfFilter` class. The `CsrfFilter` will intercept all the requests, ignore the `GET`, `HEAD`, `TRACE`, and `OPTIONS` requests, and check whether a valid CSRF token is present for all the other requests (such as `POST`, `PUT`, `DELETE`, etc.). If the CSRF token is missing or contains an invalid token, it will throw `AccessDeniedException`.

You should send the state-changing requests (such as `POST`, `PUT`, `DELETE`, etc.) with the CSRF token as a hidden parameter in the request. You can manually insert the token as follows:

```
<form method="post" action="/users">
    ...
    ...
    <input
      type="hidden"
```

```
      th:name="${_csrf.parameterName}"
      th:value="${_csrf.token}" />
</form>
```

If you are using Spring Security and Thymeleaf, the CSRF token will be automatically included if the `<form>` has the `th:action` attribute and `method` is anything other than GET, HEAD, TRACE, or OPTIONS.

For your Spring blog application, the `csrf` field is automatically added. You can inspect the code for the `addPost.html` page, and you will see the hidden field for `csrf` token, as shown in Figure 12-3.

```
▼<body data-new-gr-c-s-check-loaded="14.10/3.0" data-gr-ext-installed>
   <h1>Welcome to Spring Blog</h1>
  ▼<form action="/posts" method="post">
     <input type="hidden" name="_csrf" value="1ce20159-f6da-4b43-abbc-1f5e921d9cce"> == $0
   ▼<div>
       <label for="title">Title</label>
       <input id="title" type="text" name="title" value>
     </div>
   ▼<div>
       <label for="description">Description</label>
       <input id="description" type="text" name="description" value>
```

Figure 12-3. Hidden CSRF token added in the HTML page

Note   If you use the `action` attribute instead of setting the `th:action` or `method` value to any of GET, HEAD, TRACE, or OPTIONS, the CSRF token won't be inserted automatically.

If you submit the form without a CSRF token or an invalid CSRF token, then `AccessDeniedException` will be thrown with the 403 HTTP status code.

Method-Level Security

You have learned how to secure web applications by protecting access to web URLs. But the service-layer methods that are supposed to be invoked only by authenticated users are still accessible without restriction if users have the Spring bean. You can use Spring not only for developing web applications but also for batch-processing applications, integration servers, and such, which doesn't provide a web interface. So, you may need to secure the methods access based on roles and permissions.

Spring Security provides method-level security using the @Secured annotation. It also supports the JSR-250 security annotation @RolesAllowed. From version 3.0, Spring Security has provided an expression-based security configuration using the @PreAuthorize and @PostAuthorize annotations, which provides more fine-grained control.

You can enable method-level security using the @EnableGlobalMethodSecurity annotation on any configuration class, as follows:

```
@EnableGlobalMethodSecurity(securedEnabled = true,
                            prePostEnabled=true,
                            jsr250Enabled=true)
public class WebSecurityConfig {
    ...
    ...
}
```

- secureEnabled: Defines whether @Secured is enabled

- prePostEnabled: Defines whether the pre/post annotations @PreAuthorize and @PostAuthorize are enabled

- jsr250Enabled: Defines whether the JSR-250 annotation @RolesAllowed is enabled

Once you enable method-level security, you can annotate the SpringMVC controller request-handling methods, service-layer methods, or any Spring components with @Secured, @PreAuthorize, or @RolesAllowed in order to define your security restrictions. See Listing 12-15.

Listing 12-15. SpringMVC REST Controller Using Method-Level Security Annotations

```
@PostMapping
@PreAuthorize("hasRole('ADMIN')")
public String addPost(@ModelAttribute("post") @Valid Post post, Errors errors) {
    if (errors.hasErrors()) {
        return "addPost";
    }
```

```
    postService.addPost(post);
    return "redirect:/posts";
}
```

Similarly, you can secure service-layer methods using the @Secured, @PreAuthorize, or @RolesAllowed annotations.

```
@Service
@Transactional
public class PostService
{
    @PreAuthorize("hasRole('ADMIN')")
    public void addPost(Post post)
    {
        ....
    }
}
```

You can also use the @Secured, @PreAuthorize, or @RolesAllowed annotations at the class level to apply security configuration to all methods in that class.

You can use the Spring Expression Language (SpEL) to define the security expressions as follows:

- hasRole(role): Returns true if the current user has the specified role

- hasAnyRole(role1,role2): Returns true if the current user has any of the supplied roles

- isAnonymous(): Returns true if the current user is an anonymous user

- isAuthenticated(): Returns true if the user is not anonymous

- isFullyAuthenticated(): Returns true if the user is not an anonymous or Remember-Me user

You can combine these expressions using the logical operators AND, OR, and NOT(!).

```
@PreAuthorize("hasRole('ADMIN') OR hasRole('USER')")
@PreAuthorize("isFullyAuthenticated() AND hasRole('ADMIN')")
@PreAuthorize("!isAnonymous()")
```

Although defining security restrictions using @Secured and @PreAuthorize looks similar, there are some minor differences to be noted.

The @Secured("ROLE_ADMIN") annotation is the same as @PreAuthorize ("hasRole('ROLE_ADMIN')"). The @Secured({"ROLE_USER", "ROLE_ADMIN") is considered as ROLE_USER OR ROLE_ADMIN, so you cannot express the AND condition using @Secured. You can define the same with @PreAuthorize("hasRole('ADMIN') OR hasRole('USER')"), which is easier to understand. You can express AND, OR, or NOT(!) as well.

```
@PreAuthorize("!isAnonymous() AND hasRole('ADMIN')")
```

Note   The @PreAuthorize annotation is more powerful compared to @Secured/@RolesAllowed, so it's better to use @PreAuthorize.

Securing Spring Boot REST APIs using OAuth2

Until now, you have learned how to secure Spring Boot web applications developed with Spring MVC using Spring Security by manually implementing the authentication and authorization logic. How can you secure a REST API?

If you are using a REST API, you cannot provide a UI to authenticate the users to access your application. You can use HTTP basic authentication, but this is not a secure way of authenticating. The password is usually encoded using Base-64 format; if any hacker somehow manages to access the password, it's straightforward to decode. Not only that, but once you give out the credentials to the clients, you cannot revoke access to that user unless you change the password.

There is a need for a more secure way to authorize your REST APIs, so to handle this, OAuth Framework was introduced.

What Is OAuth2.0?

The term OAuth stands for Open Authorization, and it's an industry-standard protocol that was developed for authorization between services or applications. This protocol is right now in version 2.0, which is why it's usually known as Oauth2.

For example, imagine you are developing an image editing application, and you are developing a feature to let users import pictures from their Google Photos, iCloud, or One Drive account into your application. For this, your application needs to access

240

the user's photos. In this case, the user cannot just hand over their Google/iCloud/One Drive credentials to your application because it is not secure. So how can a third-party client like your application access the user's pictures?

OAuth2.0 protocol was developed to address this problem. It's a standard way of providing authorization, which means permission for service A (in your case, the image editing application) to access Service B (a user's Google/iCloud account).

Now let's learn some OAuth2 terminologies:

- **Resource**: The first one is called a **resource** or a **protected resource**. In your image editing application, the resource is the image or picture stored inside the user's Google Photos account. So, anything that needs to be accessed by an external service and which needs authorization to access it is called a resource.

- **Resource owner**: As the name suggests, this means the owner of the resource. In this case, it would be the person who owns the Google Photos account.

- **Resource server**: The server that stores or hosts the resource. In your case, it's the Google Photos server that stores users' photos.

- **Client**: This is the application or service that wants to access the resource. In your case, it's the image editing application.

  You can have a couple of types of clients. A **public** client such as web applications and desktop or mobile applications is one that can be accessed publicly.

  You can also have **confidential** clients that are not exposed to the public. They can be a service or a CRON job running on a remote server.

  For each client, there are different ways of authorizing itself. After the authorization, each client will receive an access token, which can be used to access the resource from the **Resource Server**. The process of fetching this access token is called authorization flow or grant type.

- **Authorization Server**: Responsible for generating and providing access tokens to the client and verifying whether an access token is valid. You will use Spring's implementation of the Authorization Server (`https://spring.io/projects/spring-authorization-server`) in your Spring blog application to secure the REST API.

241

An access token is nothing but a unique identifier that is used for an application to authenticate incoming requests. Instead of sending the username and password for the authentication, you can send out the access tokens generated by the Authorization Server to your application (a Resource Server). In this way, you can make your REST APIs stateless.

OAuth Grant Types

A client can authorize itself and request an access token in different ways. You can use various grant types to fetch the access token based on multiple use cases. The most common OAuth grant types are listed below:

- Authorization Code

- PKCE

- Client Credentials

- Device Code

- Refresh Token

To learn more about the grant types, you can refer to this guide: `https://oauth.net/2/grant-types/`.

Authorization Code

Let's see how your fictional image editing application, discussed in the previous section, can access the user's pictures using the Authorization Code grant type.

1. The user tries to access their Google/iCloud account from the image editing application.

2. The client (the image editing application) redirects to a login page from the Authorization Server (Google/iCloud), along with a redirect URL.

3. The user enters the credentials, and upon successful login, the Authorization Server asks the user for consent to allow the client to access the images.

4. The user verifies the consent form and allows the client (the image editing application) to access the resource (the photos).

5. The Authorization Server redirects the page to the client's redirect URL from Step 2, along with an authorization code.

6. The client exchanges the authorization code for an access token from the Authorization Server.

7. The client requests the Resource Server for the images by sending an access token as part of the authorization header.

8. The Resource Server (Google/iCloud image servers) verifies whether the access token is valid or not and returns the required response to the client.

Refer to Figure 12-4 for reference.

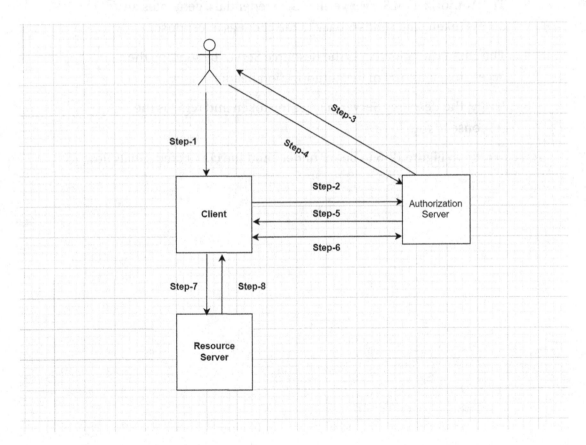

Figure 12-4. *Authorization code flow*

The authorization code flow is used when dealing with some kind of user interface where it's possible to authenticate using a web browser. But in the case of REST APIs, this is not feasible because the client wants to authenticate silently without filling out any login form. For this reason, you can use the Client Credentials grant type.

Client Credentials

In this grant type, the client will be first registered in the Authorization Server and get a client id and a client secret. Whenever the user wants to access the resource server, this is what the process looks like:

1. The user asks to fetch images from the Google/iCloud account.

2. The client requests the Authorization Server with the provided client ID and client secret.

3. The Authorization Server verifies the credentials, generates an access token, and sends it back to the client as a response.

4. The client can now access the Resource Server by sending the access token as part of the authorization header.

5. Lastly, the Resource Server verifies the token and returns the response to the client.

You can refer to Figure 12-5 to better understand the client credentials flow.

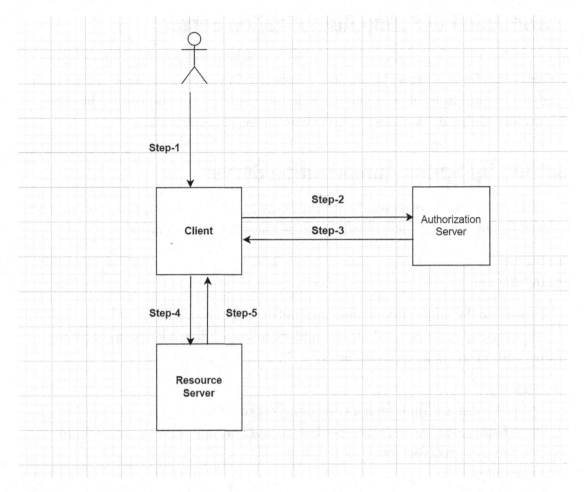

Figure 12-5. *Client credentials flow*

As you can see, fewer steps are involved while using the Client Credentials grant flow, as no manual user interaction is required.

Introduction to OIDC

OIDC stands for OpenID Connect, a protocol developed on top of the OAuth2 protocol. It allows the client to verify the identity of the user. You can learn more about it at `https://openid.net/connect/`.

An access token is used to verify if the particular user is authorized to access a given resource or not, but how do you know who is the user and the user details? For this reason, the Authorization Server will also issue an ID token using the OIDC protocol.

Introduction to Spring Authorization Server

Spring Team released a community-driven project called Spring Authorization Server (`https://spring.io/projects/spring-authorization-server`). Instead of relying on third-party vendors or software, you can maintain your Authorization Server by using this project. Let's see how to set this up in your Spring blog application.

Setting Up Spring Authorization Server

Create a new Spring Boot project from the website `https://start.spring.io`. You can name this project as auth-server and select the following dependencies:

```
Spring Web
Spring Security
```

Download the project to your machine and open it in your IDE.

After that, open the `pom.xml` file and add the following dependency to enable the Spring Authorization Server capabilities:

```
<dependency>
    <groupId>org.springframework.security</groupId>
    <artifactId>spring-security-oauth2-authorization-server</artifactId>
    <version>0.3.1</version>
</dependency>
```

Please note that as this project is still under active development, the version can change in the future, so make sure you refer to the latest version in the Maven repository at `https://mvnrepository.com/artifact/org.springframework.security/spring-security-oauth2-authorization-server` and use the latest version.

Also, please note that at the time of writing this book, the Spring Authorization Server does not yet support Spring Boot version 3.0. Hence, you will use the Spring Boot Starter parent version 2.7.2 in your examples. The examples in the GitHub repository will be updated when Spring Authorization Server supports Spring Boot 3.

Let's also add the Spring Data JPA and h2 dependencies to manage the users in the Authorization Server.

```
<dependency>
    <groupId>org.springframework.boot</groupId>
    <artifactId>spring-boot-starter-data-jpa</artifactId>
</dependency>
<dependency>
    <groupId>com.h2database</groupId>
    <artifactId>h2</artifactId>
    <scope>runtime</scope>
</dependency>
```

Go ahead and define the default Security Configuration settings for the Authorization Server to secure all the requests to your Spring Authorization Server.

```
@EnableWebSecurity
@Configuration
public class SecurityConfiguration {
    @Bean
    SecurityFilterChain defaultSecurityFilterChain(HttpSecurity http) throws
    Exception {
        http
                .authorizeRequests(authorizeRequests ->
                        authorizeRequests.anyRequest().authenticated()
                )
                .formLogin(Customizer.withDefaults());
        return http.build();
    }

    @Bean
    public PasswordEncoder passwordEncoder(){
        return new BCryptPasswordEncoder();
    }
}
```

This class defines a bean called defaultSecurityFilterChain(), which secures all the requests to your Spring Authorization Server by default. When the user wants to log in using the Authorization Server, it also provides a default form login page, as you saw at the beginning of this chapter.

To store the required user information in your Authorization Server, you need to define some domain classes to store the user data and the Spring Data JPA repositories to persist the data in the database, as shown in Listing 12-16.

Listing 12-16. User.java Class

```
package com.apress.auth.server.domain;

import lombok.*;
import org.springframework.security.core.GrantedAuthority;
import org.springframework.security.core.authority.SimpleGrantedAuthority;
import org.springframework.security.core.userdetails.UserDetails;

import javax.persistence.*;
import java.util.Collection;
import java.util.Collections;

@Entity
@Table(name = "users")
@Getter
@Setter
@NoArgsConstructor
@AllArgsConstructor
@Builder
public class User implements UserDetails {
    @Id
    @GeneratedValue(strategy = GenerationType.AUTO)
    private Long id;
    @Column(unique = true, nullable = false)
    private String email;
    @Column(unique = true, nullable = false)
    private String userName;
    @Column(nullable = false)
    private String password;
    @Column(nullable = false)
    private String role;
```

```java
@Override
public Collection<? extends GrantedAuthority> getAuthorities() {
    return Collections.singletonList(new SimpleGrantedAuthority(role));
}

@Override
public String getUsername() {
    return userName;
}

@Override
public boolean isAccountNonExpired() {
    return true;
}

@Override
public boolean isAccountNonLocked() {
    return true;
}

@Override
public boolean isCredentialsNonExpired() {
    return true;
}

@Override
public boolean isEnabled() {
    return true;
}
}
```

The User class is a simple Java class that extends the UserDetails interface and contains fields like userName, email, password, and role to store the user information. Let's also create the UserRepository interface that extends the JpaRepository interface from Spring Data JPA.

```java
@Repository
public interface UserRepository extends JpaRepository<User, Long> {
}
```

Now it's time to add some sample user data to your database. Add the necessary code inside the main `SpringBootApplication` class:

```
@SpringBootApplication
public class AuthServerApplication implements CommandLineRunner {

    private final UserRepository userRepository;
    private final PasswordEncoder passwordEncoder;

    public AuthServerApplication(UserRepository userRepository,
    PasswordEncoder passwordEncoder) {
        this.userRepository = userRepository;
        this.passwordEncoder = passwordEncoder;
    }

    public static void main(String[] args) {
        SpringApplication.run(AuthServerApplication.class, args);
    }

    @Override
    public void run(String... args) throws Exception {
        User user = User.builder()
                .email("admin@gmail.com")
                .userName("admin")
                .password(passwordEncoder.encode("password"))
                .role("ADMIN")
                .build();
        userRepository.save(user);
    }
}
```

By implementing the `CommandLineRunner` interface and overriding the `run()` method, you can seed your database with the sample data at the application startup.

Next, you need to update your Security Configuration class to look up the user information from the database whenever there is a login request with the user details. For this reason, you can create a bean called `UserDetailsService` inside the Security Configuration class to look up the user from the database by username.

```
@Bean
UserDetailsService userDetailsService(UserRepository userRepository) {
    return username -> userRepository.findByUsername(username)
            .orElseThrow(() -> new IllegalArgumentException("Cannot find user
            with username - " + username));
}
```

Now it's time to configure your Authorization Server. Create a new class called AuthServerConfiguration.java in a package called config, as shown in Listing 12-17.

Listing 12-17. AuthServerConfiguration.java Class

```
package com.apress.auth.server.config;

import com.nimbusds.jose.jwk.JWKSet;
import com.nimbusds.jose.jwk.RSAKey;
import com.nimbusds.jose.jwk.source.ImmutableJWKSet;
import com.nimbusds.jose.jwk.source.JWKSource;
import com.nimbusds.jose.proc.SecurityContext;
import org.springframework.beans.factory.annotation.Value;
import org.springframework.context.annotation.Bean;
import org.springframework.context.annotation.Configuration;
import org.springframework.core.Ordered;
import org.springframework.core.annotation.Order;
import org.springframework.security.config.annotation.web.builders.
HttpSecurity;
import org.springframework.security.config.annotation.web.configuration.
OAuth2AuthorizationServerConfiguration;
import org.springframework.security.crypto.password.PasswordEncoder;
import org.springframework.security.oauth2.core.AuthorizationGrantType;
import org.springframework.security.oauth2.core.ClientAuthenticationMethod;
import org.springframework.security.oauth2.core.oidc.OidcScopes;
import org.springframework.security.oauth2.server.authorization.client.
InMemoryRegisteredClientRepository;
import org.springframework.security.oauth2.server.authorization.client.
RegisteredClient;
```

251

```java
import org.springframework.security.oauth2.server.authorization.client.
RegisteredClientRepository;
import org.springframework.security.oauth2.server.authorization.config.
ClientSettings;
import org.springframework.security.oauth2.server.authorization.config.
ProviderSettings;
import org.springframework.security.oauth2.server.authorization.config.
TokenSettings;
import org.springframework.security.web.SecurityFilterChain;
import org.springframework.security.web.authentication.
LoginUrlAuthenticationEntryPoint;

import java.security.KeyPair;
import java.security.KeyPairGenerator;
import java.security.interfaces.RSAPrivateKey;
import java.security.interfaces.RSAPublicKey;
import java.time.Duration;
import java.util.UUID;

@Configuration
public class AuthServerConfiguration {

    private final PasswordEncoder passwordEncoder;

    public AuthServerConfiguration(PasswordEncoder passwordEncoder) {
        this.passwordEncoder = passwordEncoder;
    }

    @Bean
    @Order(Ordered.HIGHEST_PRECEDENCE)
    public SecurityFilterChain authorizationServerSecurityFilterChain(Http
    Security http) throws Exception {
        OAuth2AuthorizationServerConfiguration.applyDefaultSecurity(http);
        http
                .exceptionHandling(exceptions ->
                        exceptions.authenticationEntryPoint(new
                        LoginUrlAuthenticationEntryPoint("/login"))
                );
```

```
    return http.build();
}

@Bean
public RegisteredClientRepository registeredClientRepository() {
    RegisteredClient registeredClient = RegisteredClient.withId(UUID.
    randomUUID().toString())
            .clientId("springblog")
            .clientSecret(passwordEncoder.encode("secret"))
            .clientAuthenticationMethod(ClientAuthenticationMethod.CLIENT_
            SECRET_BASIC)
            .authorizationGrantType(AuthorizationGrantType.
            AUTHORIZATION_CODE)
            .authorizationGrantType(AuthorizationGrantType.REFRESH_TOKEN)
            .authorizationGrantType(AuthorizationGrantType.CLIENT_
            CREDENTIALS)
            .redirectUri("http://127.0.0.1:8080/login/oauth2/code/
            springblog-client-oidc")
            .redirectUri("http://127.0.0.1:8080/authorized")
            .scope(OidcScopes.OPENID)
            .scope("createBlogPost")
            .scope("updateBlogPost")
            .scope("deleteBlogPost")
            .clientSettings(ClientSettings.builder().requireAuthorization
            Consent(true).build())
            .build();

    // Save registered client in-memory
    return new InMemoryRegisteredClientRepository(registeredClient);
}

@Bean
public JWKSource<SecurityContext> jwkSource() {
    KeyPair keyPair = generateRsaKey();
    RSAPublicKey publicKey = (RSAPublicKey) keyPair.getPublic();
    RSAPrivateKey privateKey = (RSAPrivateKey) keyPair.getPrivate();
```

```
    RSAKey rsaKey = new RSAKey.Builder(publicKey)
            .privateKey(privateKey)
            .keyID(UUID.randomUUID().toString())
            .build();
    JWKSet jwkSet = new JWKSet(rsaKey);
    return new ImmutableJWKSet<>(jwkSet);
}

private static KeyPair generateRsaKey() {
    KeyPair keyPair;
    try {
        KeyPairGenerator keyPairGenerator = KeyPairGenerator.
        getInstance("RSA");
        keyPairGenerator.initialize(2048);
        keyPair = keyPairGenerator.generateKeyPair();
    } catch (Exception ex) {
        throw new IllegalStateException(ex);
    }
    return keyPair;
}

@Bean
public ProviderSettings providerSettings() {
    return ProviderSettings.builder().build();
}

@Bean
public TokenSettings tokenSettings() {
    return TokenSettings.builder()
            .accessTokenTimeToLive(Duration.ofMinutes(15L))
            .build();
}
}
```

- As the name suggests, this class defines the complete configuration for your Authorization Server.

- First, you create a bean of the type `SecurityFilterChain` that defines some default security configurations like securing all the requests to the Authorization Server and enabling different protocol endpoints.

- The `@Order` annotation with `HIGHEST_PRECEDENCE` ensures that if any other beans of the type `SecurityFilterChain` are defined inside your application, this bean will be picked up by Spring Boot due to the highest precedence.

- You can have a look at different protocol endpoints exposed by the Authorization Server at `https://docs.spring.io/spring-authorization-server/docs/current/reference/html/protocol-endpoints.html`.

- Next, you create a bean named `RegisteredClientRepository` that registers your Spring blog application client with `clientId - springblog` and `clientSecret - secret`.

- The client authentication method is set as `CLIENT_SECRET_POST` because you will send the `clientSecret` as part of the POST method body.

- This client can acquire an access token using an authorization code or a client credentials grant flow. If the token is expired, you can request a new token using the refresh token grant type instead of re-logging in. You can read more about the Refresh Token grant type at `https://oauth.net/2/grant-types/refresh-token/`

- Next, you define the redirect URLs the authorization server can redirect to after the successful authorization. The redirect URLs are applicable while using the Authorization Code grant type.

- You also define the scopes `createBlogPost`, `updateBlogPost`, and `deleteBlogPost` to define the actions your client can perform on the Post Resource.

- You also enable the user consent screen for your Spring blog application client.

- Since your authorization server generates JWT tokens, you must define a JSON web key (JWK) as a signing key. The `jwkSource` bean takes care of creating the necessary private and public key pairs and produces a JWK out of the key pair. The Authorization Server uses the private key to sign the token and the Resource Server uses the public key to verify the token.

- You have the `providerSettings` that creates a bean of type `ProviderSettings` used to configure the Spring Authorization Server. You can read more about it at `https://docs.spring.io/spring-authorization-server/docs/current/reference/html/configuration-model.html#configuring-provider-settings`.

- And you define the Token Time To Live as 15 minutes using the `tokenSettings` bean. This means your token will be active for 15 minutes after the Authorization Server generates it.

- Lastly, you define some properties in the `application.properties` file to change the default port of the authorization server to 9000 so that it won't clash with your Spring blog application running at 8080.

```
server.port=9000
```

Now go ahead and run the `AuthServerApplication` class, open the browser, and go to URL `http://localhost:9000`.

You should see a simple login screen. Fill in the username and password you added into your database (admin/password) and you should see a 404 error page.

That's fine because your Authorization Server is not exposing any endpoints or web pages by default.

Testing the Authorization Server Using Client Credentials

Go ahead and use the Client Credentials grant flow to request an access token.

To understand which URL to call to request an access token, you can refer to the Discovery Document provided by the Spring Authorization Server. You can access this by opening the URL `http://localhost:9000/.well-known/oauth-authorization-server`. This URL is a standard URL implemented by all Authorization Servers compliant with the OAuth 2.0 Framework. You should see the following response when you open this URL:

```
// 20220812061533
// http://localhost:9000/.well-known/oauth-authorization-server
{
  "issuer": "http://localhost:9000",
  "authorization_endpoint": "http://localhost:9000/oauth2/authorize",
  "token_endpoint": "http://localhost:9000/oauth2/token",
  "token_endpoint_auth_methods_supported": [
    "client_secret_basic",
    "client_secret_post",
    "client_secret_jwt",
    "private_key_jwt"
  ],
  "jwks_uri": "http://localhost:9000/oauth2/jwks",
  "response_types_supported": [
    "code"
  ],
  "grant_types_supported": [
    "authorization_code",
    "client_credentials",
    "refresh_token"
  ],
  "revocation_endpoint": "http://localhost:9000/oauth2/revoke",
  "revocation_endpoint_auth_methods_supported": [
    "client_secret_basic",
    "client_secret_post",
    "client_secret_jwt",
    "private_key_jwt"
  ],
  "introspection_endpoint": "http://localhost:9000/oauth2/introspect",
  "introspection_endpoint_auth_methods_supported": [
    "client_secret_basic",
    "client_secret_post",
    "client_secret_jwt",
    "private_key_jwt"
  ],
```

```
  "code_challenge_methods_supported": [
    "S256"
  ]
}
```

Here you can see all the different endpoints exposed by your Authorization Server. Now let's call the token_endpoint http://localhost:9000/oauth2/token to receive an access token.

```
curl --location --request POST 'http://localhost:9000/oauth2/token' \
--header 'Content-Type: application/x-www-form-urlencoded' \
--data-urlencode 'grant_type=client_credentials' \
--data-urlencode 'client_id=springblog' \
--data-urlencode 'client_secret=secret'
```

This request will return the following response:

```
{
    "access_token": "eyJraWQiOiJjNGY0Y2EyZCO5MjVkLTQzOTgtOGNlNi1lYjY5MDdiYT
    kwNjEiLCJhbGciOiJSUzI1NiJ9.eyJzdWIiOiJzcHJpbmdibG9nIiwiYXVkIjoic3ByaW5n
    YmxvZyIsIm5iZiI6MTY2MDI3NzQ5MCwic2NvcGUiOlsiY3JlYXRlQmxvZ1Bvc3QiLCJvcG
    VuaWQiLCJ1cGRhdGVCbG9nUG9zdCIsImRlbGV0ZUJsb2dQb3N0Il0sImlzcyI6Imh0dHA6X
    C9cL2xvY2FsaG9zdDo5MDAwIiwiZXhwIjoxNjYwMjc3NzkwLCJpYXQiOjE2NjAyNzcOOT
    B9.oEUbk5L5C7JrI2sOQl7pqt_KcMWuYBHNGy52sBMsmLKOiQmpcxmaAYRwN9mK9SRwgm
    EA-xAQAwpfQ54FZsD-GOhMbdOMwMDONjx1Hq3PmVOv-mTAHtk7gs6S7HW8K74xIV2dgSvSn
    2dkxAXzR979xrbbNgrVsHOZTSavnCpzzxFTqc1uOU-l9WVNOsro4tkTF8hkn-ay
    Pj-7lWP_1-kLBReNwth2SM7EPpA73UhaJu2UE4puUlyz4DKNeq5tPjOwLVl
    GVbcV7_gt_NMc_MIVtc2r4SkRN4hncCHptlWYTAOfiFX3CIjCJei_nkGubBBN7
    BtoxjSdIImXqOnkZo9SuA",
    "scope": "createBlogPost openid updateBlogPost deleteBlogPost",
    "token_type": "Bearer",
    "expires_in": 300
}
```

You received an access token in the JWT format (JSON web token), along with the scope you defined inside the AuthServerConfiguration class.

The token type is set as Bearer because usually the access token will be sent as part of the authorization HTTP header with the Bearer scheme.

Lastly, you have the expiration time as 300 seconds.

Now, if you open the website `https://jwt.io` and paste the JWT in the Encoded section (please note that you are doing this only for educational purposes; do not paste your access tokens anywhere for security reasons), you will see details about the client, like the `clientId - springblog`, the scope of the client, the issuer of the token, and the token's expiration time, as shown in Figure 12-6.

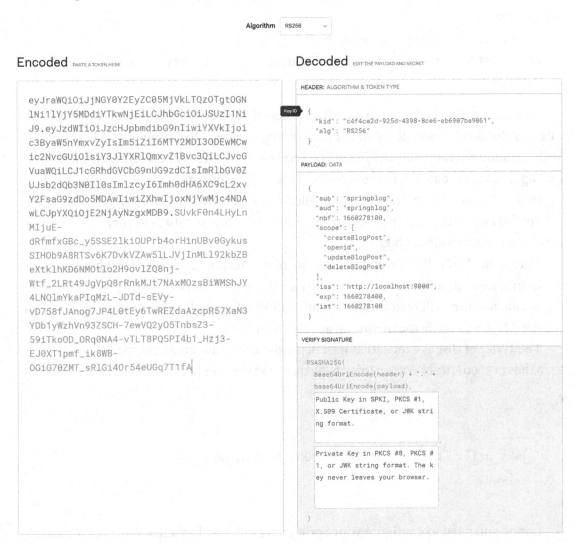

Figure 12-6. *JWT information*

Configuring the Resource Server

Alright, you configured the Authorization Server successfully. Now let's go ahead and set up the Resource Server: the Spring Blog REST API you developed in Chapter 11.

First, add the following dependency in the pom.xml file to enable the Resource Server capabilities in your REST API:

```
<dependency>
    <groupId>org.springframework.boot</groupId>
    <artifactId>spring-boot-starter-oauth2-resource-server</artifactId>
</dependency>
```

As you learned, the Resource Server contacts the Authorization Server to verify whether the access token is valid. For this reason, you need to define the URL of the Authorization Server inside the Resource Server. You can do that using the property spring.security.oauth2.resourceserver.jwt.jwk-set-uri.

Inside the application.properties file, define the following property:

spring.security.oauth2.resourceserver.jwt.jwk-set-uri=http://localhost:9000/oauth2/jwks

This is the JWKS (JSON web key set) URL of the Authorization Server, which contains the information about the keypair used to sign the access token.

Spring Security will read this information during the application startup to set up the required JWKS to verify the incoming access token.

The JWK Set URL is exposed as part of the discovery document http://localhost:9000/.well-known/oauth-authorization-server.

```
{

    .....
    jwks_uri": "http://localhost:9000/oauth2/jwks",
    ....
}
```

Lastly, you need to configure your Spring Blog REST API as a Resource Server. For that, let's create a class called SecurityConfig inside a package called config.

```
package com.apress.demo.springblog.config;

import org.springframework.context.annotation.Bean;
import org.springframework.context.annotation.Configuration;
import org.springframework.http.HttpMethod;
import org.springframework.security.config.annotation.web.builders.
HttpSecurity;
import org.springframework.security.config.annotation.web.configuration.
EnableWebSecurity;
import org.springframework.security.config.annotation.web.configurers.
oauth2.server.resource.OAuth2ResourceServerConfigurer;
import org.springframework.security.web.SecurityFilterChain;

@EnableWebSecurity
@Configuration
public class SecurityConfig {
    @Bean
    SecurityFilterChain defaultSecurityFilterChain(HttpSecurity http) throws
    Exception {
        http.authorizeRequests()
                .antMatchers(HttpMethod.POST, "/api/posts")
                .hasAuthority("SCOPE_createBlogPost")
                .antMatchers(HttpMethod.DELETE, "/api//posts")
                .hasAuthority("SCOPE_deleteIngredients")
                .and()
                .authorizeRequests()
                .anyRequest().authenticated()
                .and()
                .oauth2ResourceServer(OAuth2ResourceServerConfigurer::jwt);
        return http.build();
    }
}
```

You enable the Resource Server capabilities for your Spring blog application by calling the oauth2ResourceServer() method, which will read the incoming JWT, decode it, and verify it with the Authorization Server.

Now start the Spring blog application and test your implementation.

First, try to access the `listAllPosts()` endpoint at `http://localhost:8080/api/posts`.

```
curl --location --request GET 'http://localhost:8080/api/posts' \
```

You will get a 401 UnAuthorized Error, which means your Spring blog application is secured, which is good.

Now try to access the same endpoint using an access token. First, try to acquire a new access token from your Authorization Server.

```
curl --location --request POST 'http://localhost:9000/oauth2/token' \
--header 'Content-Type: application/x-www-form-urlencoded' \
--data-urlencode 'grant_type=client_credentials' \
--data-urlencode 'client_id=springblog' \
--data-urlencode 'client_secret=secret'
```

You should get the access token as a response from the Auth Server, copy the token, and make a call to the `listAllPosts()` endpoint again using the following command:

```
curl --location --request GET 'http://localhost:8080/api/posts' \
--header 'Authorization: Bearer <your-auth-token>'
```

Replace the text <your-auth-token> with the actual access token. Now you should see the response from the server for the `listAllPosts()` endpoint.

Testing the Authorization Server Using the Authorization Code Flow

In the previous sections, you learned how to request an access token from the Auth Server using the client credentials flow. Now, let's understand how to use the Authorization Code Flow grant type to request an access token. Let's configure your Spring blog application developed using Spring MVC and Thymeleaf as the client to request an access token from the Auth Server.

Add the following dependency in the `pom.xml` to enable Spring OAuth2 Client capabilities in your Spring MVC blog web application:

```
<dependency>
    <groupId>org.springframework.boot</groupId>
    <artifactId>spring-boot-starter-oauth2-client</artifactId>
</dependency>
```

Now define some security configurations for your application by creating a class called SecurityConfig.java in a package called config.

```
package com.apress.demo.springblog.config;

import org.springframework.context.annotation.Bean;
import org.springframework.context.annotation.Configuration;
import org.springframework.security.config.annotation.web.builders.
HttpSecurity;
import org.springframework.security.config.annotation.web.configuration.
EnableWebSecurity;
import org.springframework.security.web.SecurityFilterChain;

import static org.springframework.security.config.Customizer.withDefaults;

@Configuration
@EnableWebSecurity
public class SecurityConfig {
    @Bean
    SecurityFilterChain defaultSecurityFilterChain(HttpSecurity http) throws
    Exception {
        http
                .authorizeRequests(
                        authorizeRequests -> authorizeRequests.anyRequest().
                        authenticated()
                )
                .oauth2Login(
                        oauth2Login ->
                                oauth2Login.loginPage("/oauth2/authorization/
                                springblog"))
                .oauth2Client(withDefaults());
        return http.build();
    }
}
```

This configuration ensures that all requests to your application are secured. You enable the OAuth2 client capabilities in your application using the oauth2Client() method.

The `auth2Login.loginPage("/oauth2/authorization/springblog")` method will redirect to the login page of the Auth Server whenever an unauthenticated user tries to access your application.

And, lastly, you define the client properties inside the `application.properties` file like so:

```
spring.security.oauth2.client.registration.springblog.client-id=springblog
spring.security.oauth2.client.registration.springblog.client-secret=secret
spring.security.oauth2.client.registration.springblog.authorization-grant-type=authorization_code
spring.security.oauth2.client.registration.springblog.redirect-uri=http://127.0.0.1:8080/login/oauth2/code/springblog
spring.security.oauth2.client.registration.springblog.scope=createBlogPost,updateBlogPost,deleteBlogPost,openid

spring.security.oauth2.client.provider.springblog.issuer-uri=http://127.0.0.1:9000
```

These properties registers an OAuth2 Client called `springblog` with details like `client-id`, `client-secret`, `authorization-grant-type`, `redirect-uri`, and scope.

These are the same values you defined inside the Authorization Server.

Since you want to test the authorization code flow using this client, you defined the `authorization-grant-type` field as `authorization_code`. That's all you need to do to enable the OAuth2 Client capabilities. If you start the application and go to `http://localhost:8080,` you should see the login page shown in Figure 12-7, which is coming from the Authorization Server.

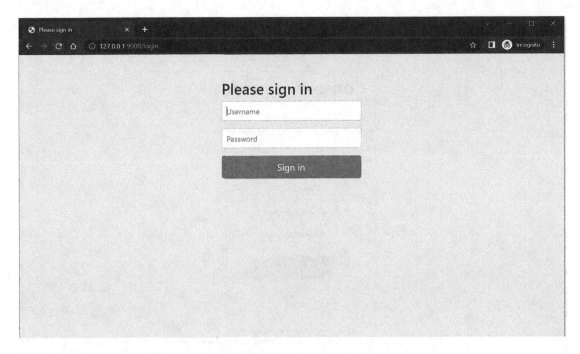

Figure 12-7. *Login page from the Authorization Server*

Once you log in using the sample user created in the Auth Server (admin/password), the page will be redirected to Consent screen, shown in Figure 12-6, where the server will ask you to review the permissions for the client and submit your approval.

You can select the permissions you want to grant the client and click the Submit Consent button, and after that you should be able to see the list of blog posts in your Spring blog application, as shown in Figure 12-8.

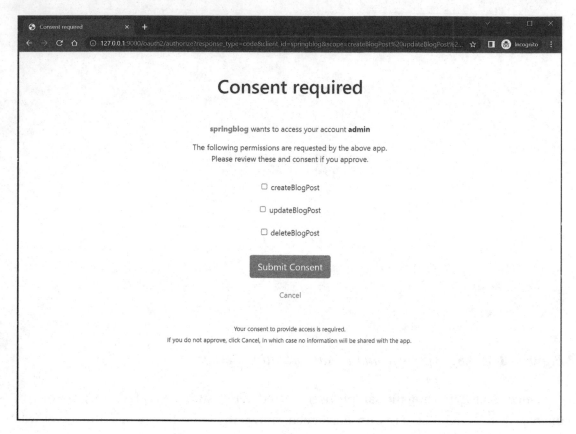

Figure 12-8. *Consent page from the Authorization Server*

Summary

This chapter explored how to secure traditional web applications built with SpringMVC and Thymeleaf using the Spring Security starter. Then you learned more about how to secure your Spring Boot application using OAuth2. You learned how to secure the REST APIs using the Client Credentials grant flow and the web applications using the Authorization Code grant flow.

In the next chapter, you will learn about Spring Boot Actuator.

## CHAPTER 13

Spring Boot Actuator

Spring Boot is an opinionated framework that autoconfigures various application components based on several criteria, like the starters you use, the properties configuration, and the active environment profile(s).

- Is there a way to know which components (which Spring beans) are automatically registered by Spring Boot?

- Is it possible to check all the configuration parameters for the currently running application?

- Can you determine which request URL will be handled by which controller?

- Can you get metrics on the application, such as memory usage, thread allocation, and such?

The answer to all these questions is yes. You can perform all these activities with the Spring Boot Actuator.

This chapter introduces the Spring Boot Actuator and explores the various Actuator endpoints that provide useful information about running Spring Boot applications. You will also learn how to secure Actuator endpoints, enable CORS for Actuator endpoints, and implement custom health checks and metrics. Finally, the chapter looks into using JMX to monitor your application using JConsole.

Introducing the Spring Boot Actuator

The Spring Boot Actuator module provides production-ready features such as monitoring, metrics, and health checks. The Spring Boot Actuator enables you to monitor the application using HTTP endpoints and JMX.

© K. Siva Prasad Reddy, Sai Upadhyayula 2023
K. S. P. Reddy and S. Upadhyayula, *Beginning Spring Boot 3*, https://doi.org/10.1007/978-1-4842-8792-7_13

Spring Boot provides a `spring-boot-starter-actuator` library to autoconfigure Actuator. As seen in this section, you can take advantage of Actuator's features to monitor a Spring Boot application.

To get started, add the following dependency to the `pom.xml` file:

```
<dependencies>
    <dependency>
        <groupId>org.springframework.boot</groupId>
        <artifactId>spring-boot-starter-actuator</artifactId>
    </dependency>
</dependencies>
```

After adding the dependency, start the application. You can see the console output displaying the request mapping provided by the Spring Boot Actuator.

```
... EndpointLinksResolver    : Exposing 1 endpoint(s) beneath base path
'/actuator'.....
```

Spring Boot exposes only one endpoint by default: `'/actuator'`. This endpoint provides an overview of all the other endpoints.

You can enable all the endpoints exposed by Actuator by adding the following property to the `application.properties` file:

```
management.endpoints.web.exposure.include= *
```

After adding the above endpoint, restart your application, and you can see the following output:

```
... EndpointLinksResolver    : Exposing 13 endpoint(s) beneath base path
'/actuator'.....
```

Spring Boot is now exposing a total of 13 endpoints instead of 1. In the next section, you will look at all the endpoints exposed by Spring Boot.

Exploring Actuator's Endpoints

The Actuator Starter autoconfigures the Actuator endpoints listed in Table 13-1 with the default settings.

Table 13-1. *Spring Boot Actuator Endpoints*

ID	Description
info	Displays arbitrary application info
health	Shows application basic health info for unauthenticated users and full details for authenticated users
beans	Shows a list of all Spring beans configured in the application
conditions	Provides information about the evaluation of conditions on configuration and auto-configuration classes
mappings	Displays a collated list of all @RequestMapping paths
configprops	Displays a collated list of all @ConfigurationProperties
metrics	Shows metrics information for the current application
env	Exposes properties from Spring's ConfigurableEnvironment
httptrace	Displays trace information (by default, the last 100 HTTP requests)
threaddump	Performs a thread dump
loggers	Shows and modifies the configuration of loggers in the application
Auditevents	Exposes audit events information for the current application
Flyway	Shows any Flyway database migrations that have been applied
liquibase	Shows any Liquibase database migrations that have been applied
shutdown	Allows the application to be gracefully shut down (not enabled by default)

Table 13-2 lists the additional Actuator endpoints that are available based on certain conditions.

Table 13-2. *Additional Spring Boot Actuator Endpoints for SpringMVC Applications*

ID	Description
docs	Displays documentation, including example requests and responses, for the Actuator's endpoints. Requires `spring-boot-actuator-docs` to be on the classpath.
heapdump	Returns a GZip-compressed `hprof` heap dump file
jolokia	Exposes JMX beans over HTTP (when `Jolokia` is on the classpath)
logfile	Returns the contents of the logfile (if the `logging.file` or `logging.path` properties have been set)
startup	Provides information about the application startup sequence
cache	Exposes available caches in the application
integrationGraph	Shows the Spring Integration Graph. Requires a dependency on `spring-integration-core`.

By default, Actuator endpoints run on the same HTTP port (`server.port`) with /actuator as the base path prefix.

In this section, you will explore several commonly used Actuator endpoints.

The /info Endpoint

If you added any information about the application in the `application.properties` file using the `info.app.*` properties, as shown in Figure 13-1, you can view it at the `http://localhost:8080/actuator/info` endpoint.

```
info.app.name=Beginning Spring Boot 3
info.app.description=This is a SpringBoot Demo app
info.app.version=1.0.0
```

Although you enabled all the Actuator endpoints, you can only view the response from the /info endpoint by adding the following property to the `application.properties` file:

```
management.info.env.enabled=true
```

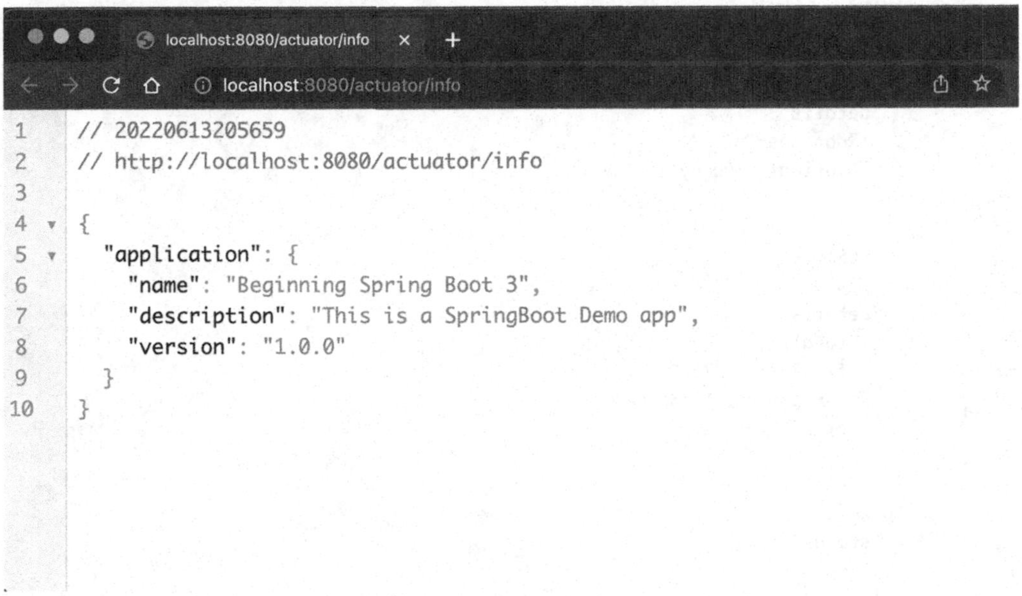

```
//  localhost:8080/actuator/info    ×    +

←  →  C  ⌂    ⓘ  localhost:8080/actuator/info                                    ⬆  ☆

 1      // 20220613205659
 2      // http://localhost:8080/actuator/info
 3
 4    ▾ {
 5    ▾   "application": {
 6          "name": "Beginning Spring Boot 3",
 7          "description": "This is a SpringBoot Demo app",
 8          "version": "1.0.0"
 9        }
10      }
```

Figure 13-1. *Spring Boot Actuator /info endpoint*

The /health Endpoint

The /health endpoint shows the health of the application, including the disk space, databases, and such.

By default, Actuator displays only the status of the application. You can display the rest of the attributes by adding the following property:

```
management.endpoint.health.show-details=always
```

Go to `http://localhost:8080/actuator/health` to check the application's health, as shown in Figure 13-2.

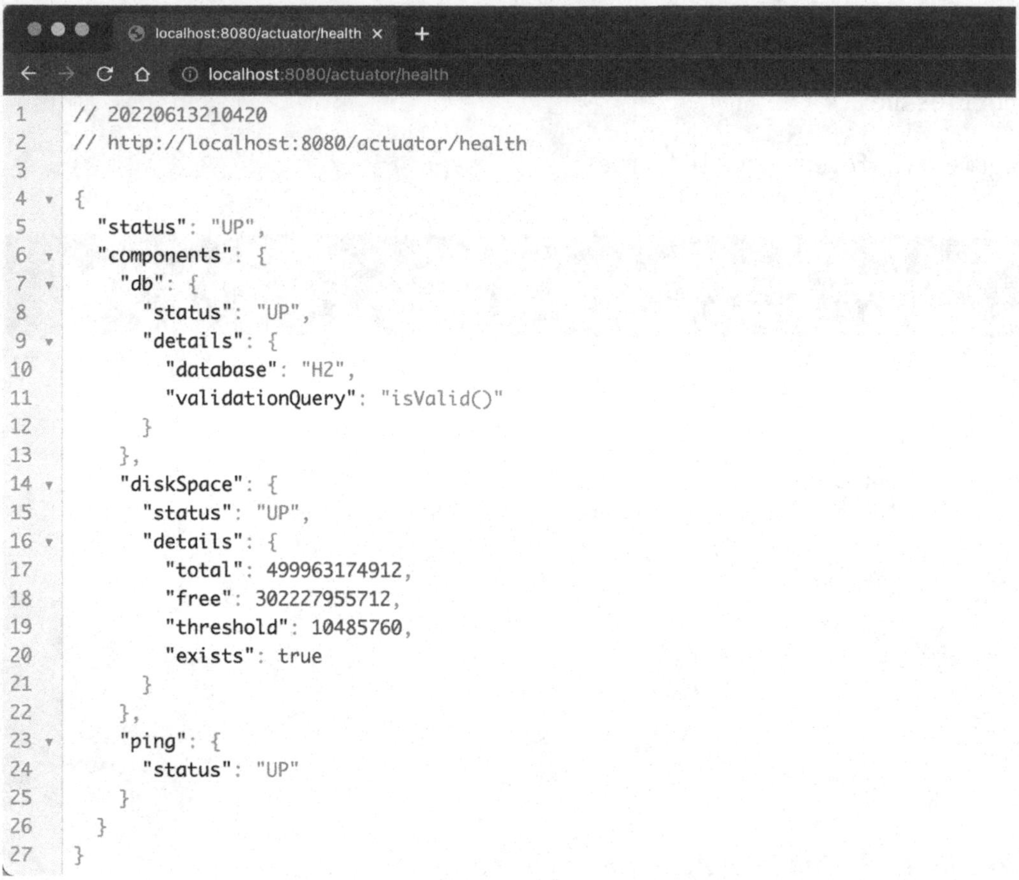

```
 1    // 20220613210420
 2    // http://localhost:8080/actuator/health
 3
 4  ▾ {
 5      "status": "UP",
 6  ▾    "components": {
 7  ▾      "db": {
 8          "status": "UP",
 9  ▾        "details": {
10            "database": "H2",
11            "validationQuery": "isValid()"
12          }
13        },
14  ▾      "diskSpace": {
15          "status": "UP",
16  ▾        "details": {
17            "total": 499963174912,
18            "free": 302227955712,
19            "threshold": 10485760,
20            "exists": true
21          }
22        },
23  ▾      "ping": {
24          "status": "UP"
25        }
26      }
27    }
```

Figure 13-2. *Spring Boot Actuator /health endpoint*

The /beans Endpoint

The /beans endpoint shows all the beans registered in your application, including the beans you explicitly configured and those autoconfigured by Spring Boot.

Point your browser to http://localhost:8080/actuator/beans. You should be able to see output similar to what's shown in Figure 13-3.

```
1    // 20220613211725
2    // http://localhost:8080/actuator/beans
3
4  ▼ {
5  ▼   "contexts": {
6  ▼     "application": {
7  ▼       "beans": {
8  ►         "spring.jpa-org.springframework.boot.autoconfigure.orm.jpa.JpaProperties":
     {↔},
19 ►         "endpointCachingOperationInvokerAdvisor": {↔},
31 ►         "defaultServletHandlerMapping": {↔},
42 ►         "metricsRestTemplateCustomizer": {↔},
56 ►         "applicationTaskExecutor": {↔},
68 ►         "persistenceExceptionTranslationPostProcessor": {↔},
79 ►         "management.health.db-
     org.springframework.boot.actuate.autoconfigure.jdbc.DataSourceHealthIndicatorPropert
     ies": {↔},
90 ►         "observationRegistryPostProcessor": {↔},
101►         "spring.data.web-
     org.springframework.boot.autoconfigure.data.web.SpringDataWebProperties": {↔},
112▼         "characterEncodingFilter": {
113▼           "aliases": [
114
```

Figure 13-3. *Spring Boot Actuator /beans endpoint*

The /conditions Endpoint

The /conditions endpoint shows the autoconfiguration report, categorized into positiveMatches and negativeMatches.

If you go to http://localhost:8080/actuator/conditions, you should see an autoconfiguration report similar to the one in Figure 13-4.

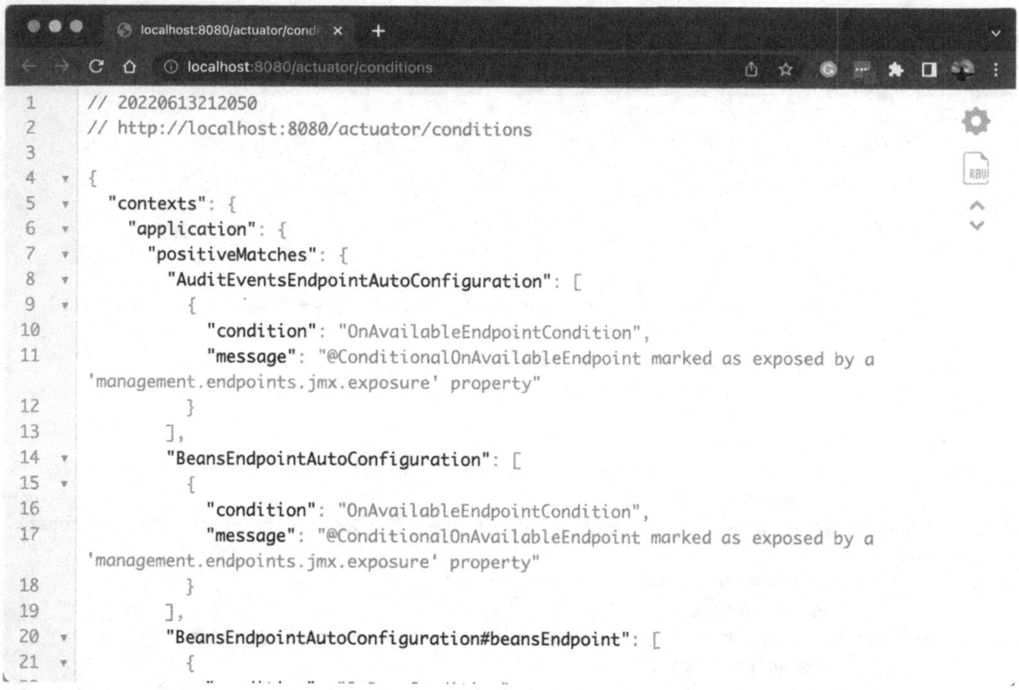

Figure 13-4. Spring Boot Actuator /conditions endpoint

The elements in positiveMatches are the conditions matched by various
@Conditional components.

For example:

```
DataSourceAutoConfiguration: [
    {
        condition: "OnClassCondition",
        message: "@ConditionalOnClass classes found: javax.sql.
        DataSource,org.springframework.jdbc.datasource.embedded.
        EmbeddedDatabase
]
```

Since this example added the data-jpa starter and H2 driver, the classes javax.sql.DataSource and org.springframework.jdbc.datasource. embedded.EmbeddedDatabaseType are found in the classpath and hence DataSourceAutoConfiguration becomes a positive match.

The elements in negativeMatches are the conditions not matched by various @Conditional components.

For example:

```
JooqAutoConfiguration: [
    {
        condition: "OnClassCondition",
        message: "required @ConditionalOnClass classes not found: org.jooq.
        DSLContext"
    }
]
```

As there aren't JOOQ libraries on the application classpath, @ConditionalOnClass could not find the org.jooq.DSLContext class so JooqAutoConfiguration became a negative match.

The /mappings Endpoint

The /mappings endpoint shows all the @RequestMapping paths declared in the application. This is very helpful for checking which request path will be handled by which controller method.

If you go to http://localhost:8080/actuator/mappings, you should see all the mappings shown in Figure 13-5.

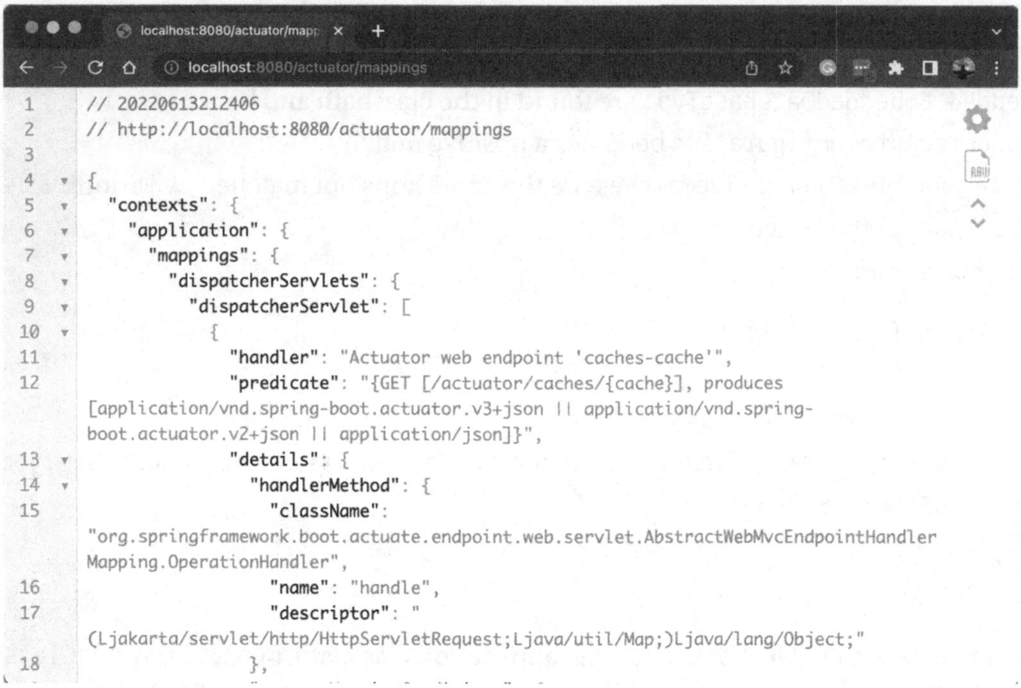

Figure 13-5. *Spring Boot Actuator /mappings endpoint*

The /configprops Endpoint

The /configprops offers all the configuration properties defined by the @ConfigurationProperties beans, including your configuration properties defined in the application.properties or YAML files.

If you go to http://localhost:8080/actuator/configprops, you should see all the configuration properties shown in Figure 13-6.

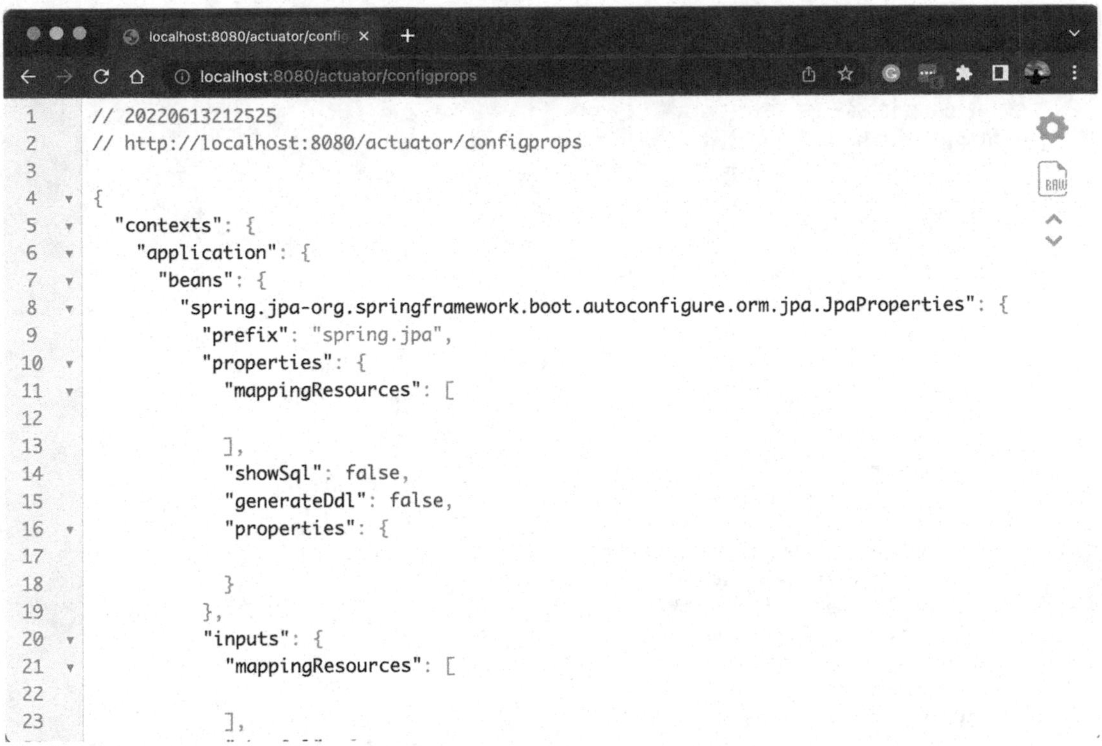

Figure 13-6. *Spring Boot Actuator /configprops endpoint*

The /metrics Endpoint

The /metrics endpoint shows various metrics about the current application, such as how much memory it is using, how much memory is free, the size of the heap used, the number of threads used, and so on.

If you go to http://localhost:8080/actuator/metrics, you should see all the configuration properties shown in Figure 13-7.

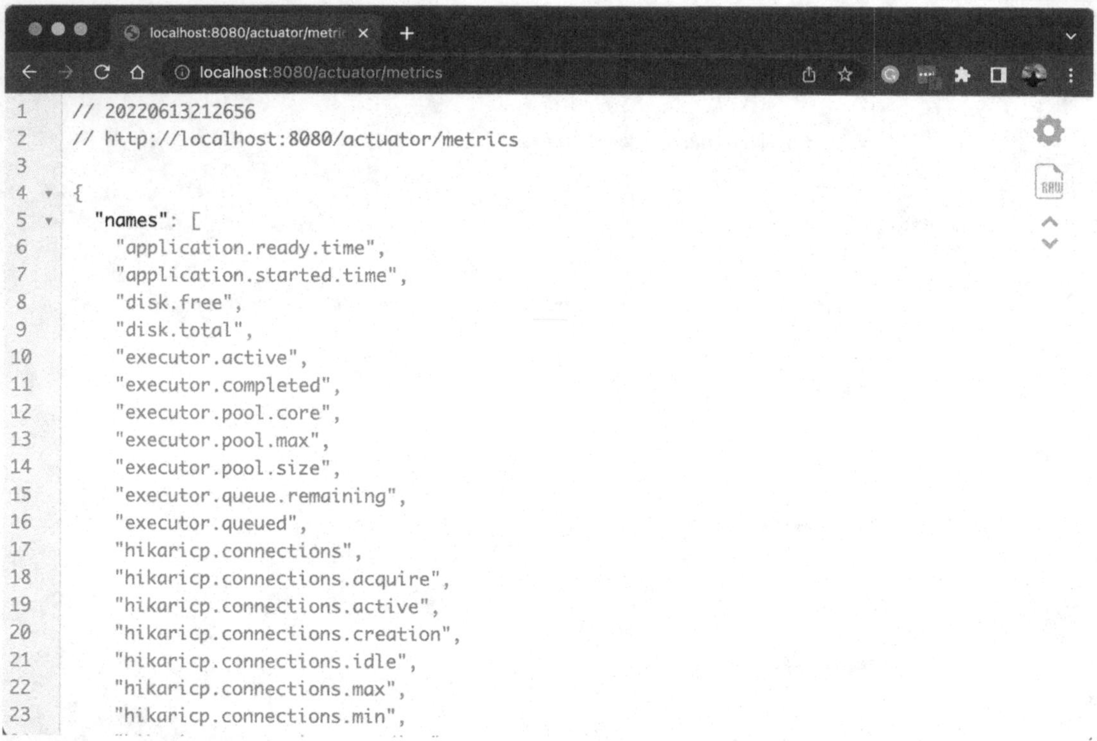

```
1    // 20220613212656
2    // http://localhost:8080/actuator/metrics
3
4  ▼ {
5  ▼    "names": [
6          "application.ready.time",
7          "application.started.time",
8          "disk.free",
9          "disk.total",
10         "executor.active",
11         "executor.completed",
12         "executor.pool.core",
13         "executor.pool.max",
14         "executor.pool.size",
15         "executor.queue.remaining",
16         "executor.queued",
17         "hikaricp.connections",
18         "hikaricp.connections.acquire",
19         "hikaricp.connections.active",
20         "hikaricp.connections.creation",
21         "hikaricp.connections.idle",
22         "hikaricp.connections.max",
23         "hikaricp.connections.min",
```

Figure 13-7. *Spring Boot Actuator /metrics endpoint*

The /env Endpoint

The /env endpoint exposes all the properties from the Spring's
ConfigurableEnvironment interface, such as a list of active profiles, application
properties, system environment variables, and such.

If you go to http://localhost:8080/actuator/env, you should be able to see all the
environment details shown in Figure 13-8.

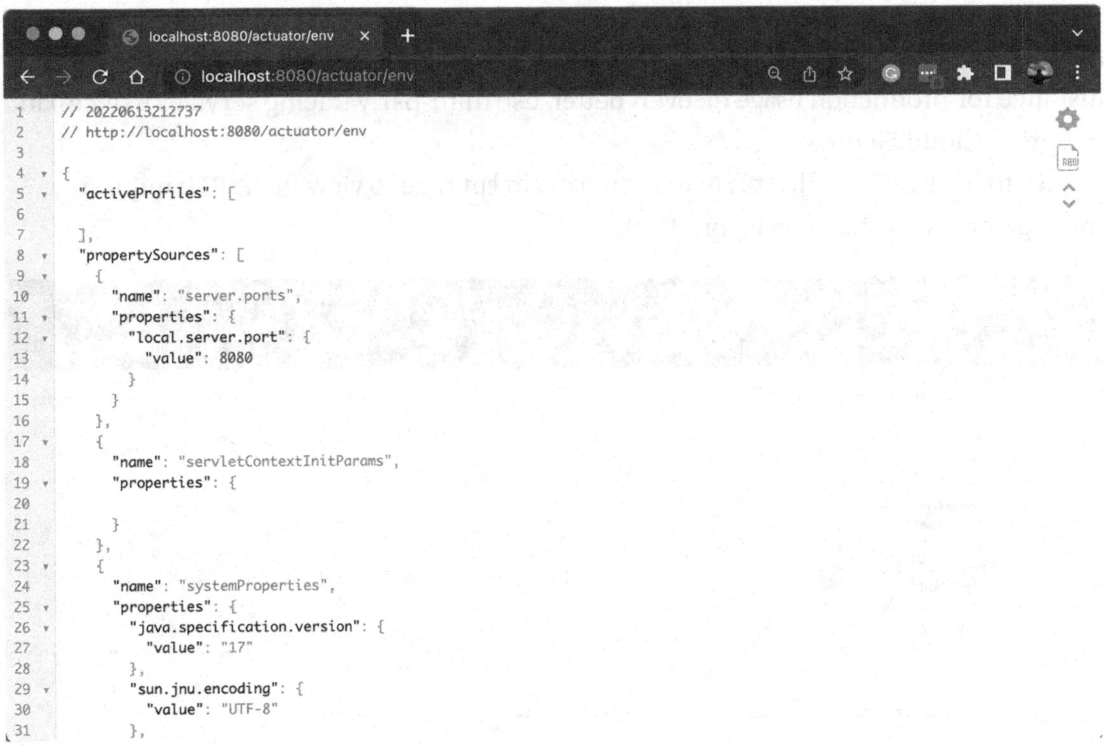

Figure 13-8. *Spring Boot Actuator /env endpoint*

The /httptrace Endpoint

The /httptrace endpoint shows the tracing information of the last few HTTP requests, which is very helpful for debugging the request/response details like headers and cookies.

To enable /httptrace endpoint, add the following property:

```
management.trace.http.enabled=true
```

Not only that, you have to define a bean called as HttpTraceRepository to be able to access the trace information.

```
@Bean
public HttpTraceRepository httpTraceRepository() {
    return new InMemoryHttpTraceRepository();
}
```

Here you are using an instance of `InMemoryHttpTraceRepository` for the bean for the local development, but it's recommended to create your own `HttpTraceRepository` instance for production usage or, even better, use third-party tracing services like Zipkin or Spring Cloud Sleuth.

Go to `http://localhost:8080/actuator/httptrace` to view the HTTP request tracing details, as shown in Figure 13-9.

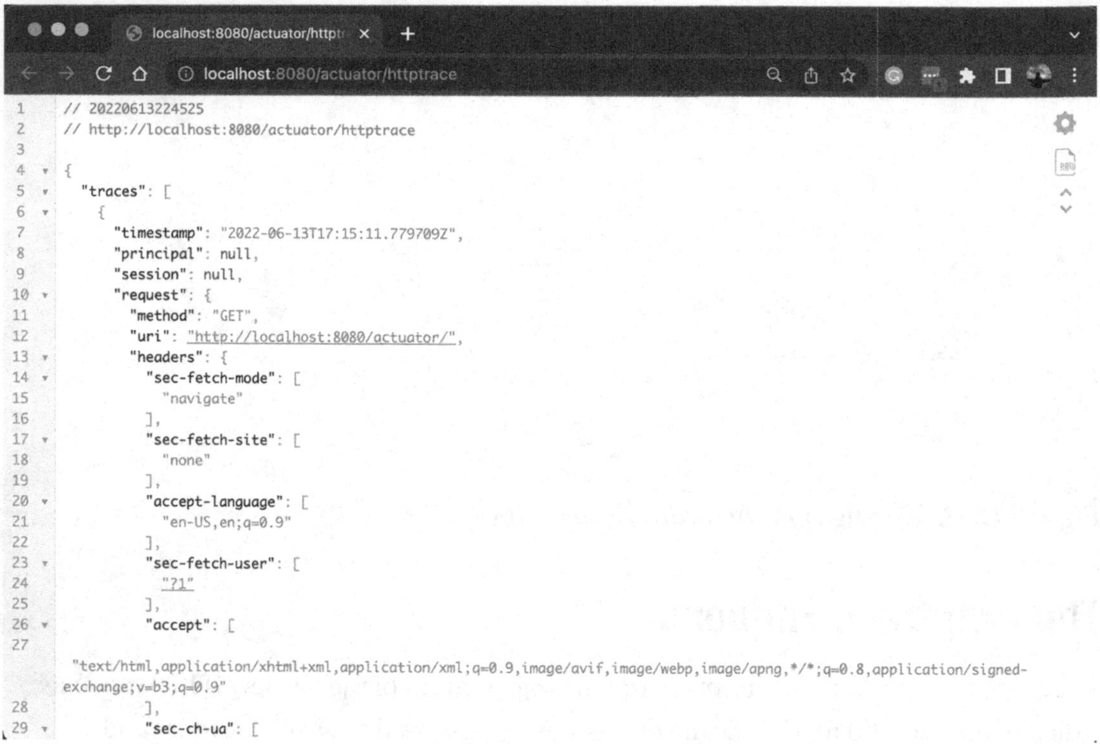

Figure 13-9. *Spring Boot Actuator /httptrace endpoint*

The /threaddump Endpoint

You can view your application's thread dump with the runnings threads details and the JVM stack trace using the /threaddump endpoint, which is enabled by default through the `management.endpoints.web.exposure.include=*` endpoint, but you can toggle this on or off using the following property:

```
management.endpoint.threaddump.enabled=true
management.endpoint.threaddump.enabled=false
```

You can get the thread dump details at `http://localhost:8080/actuator/`
`threaddump` endpoint. See Figure 13-10.

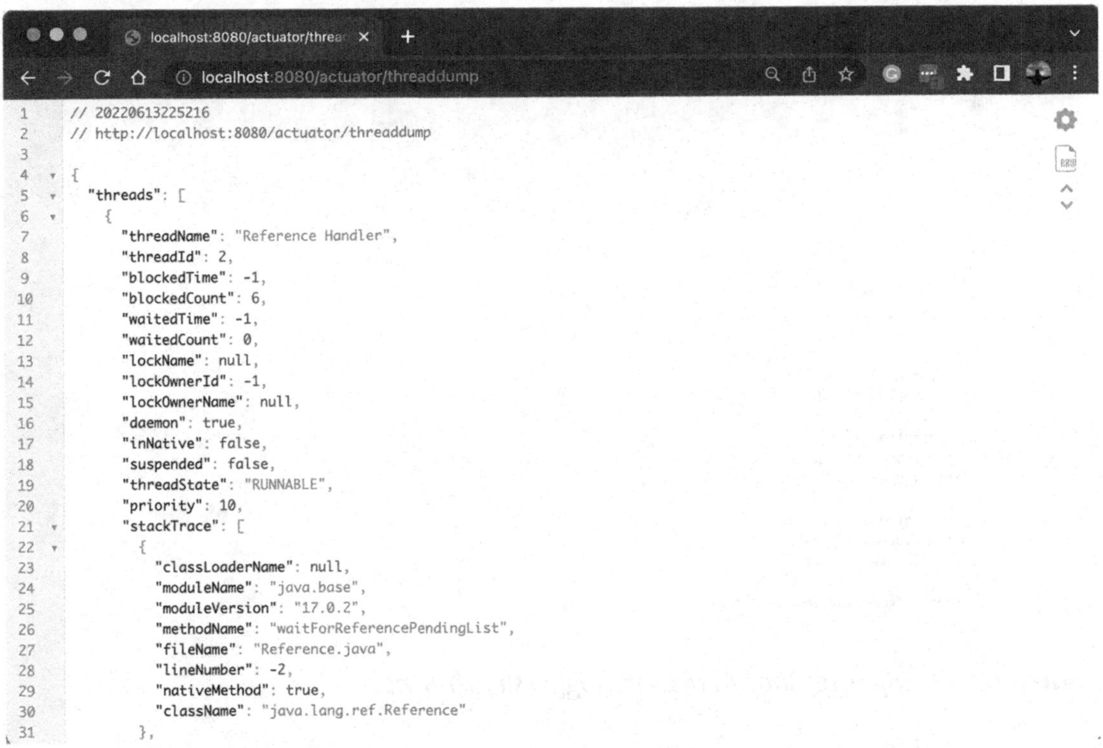

Figure 13-10. *Spring Boot Actuator /threaddump endpoint*

The /loggers Endpoint

The `/loggers` endpoint allows you to view and configure the log levels of your
application at runtime. You can view the logging levels of all loggers at `http://`
`localhost:8080/actuator/loggers`, as shown in Figure 13-11.

```
1    // 20220613230526
2    // http://localhost:8080/actuator/loggers
3
4  ▼  {
5  ▼    "levels": [
6        "OFF",
7        "ERROR",
8        "WARN",
9        "INFO",
10       "DEBUG",
11       "TRACE"
12     ],
13 ▼   "loggers": {
14 ▼     "ROOT": {
15         "configuredLevel": "INFO",
16         "effectiveLevel": "INFO"
17       },
18 ▼     "_org": {
19         "configuredLevel": null,
20         "effectiveLevel": "INFO"
21       },
22 ▼     "_org.springframework": {
23         "configuredLevel": null,
24         "effectiveLevel": "INFO"
25       },
26 ▼     "_org.springframework.web": {
27         "configuredLevel": null,
28         "effectiveLevel": "INFO"
29       },
30 ▼     "_org.springframework.web.servlet": {
31         "configuredLevel": null,
```

Figure 13-11. *Spring Boot Actuator /loggers endpoint*

You can view the logging level of a specific logger at http://localhost:8080/
actuator/{loggerName}. For example, if you want to view the logging level of the
com.apress.demo logger, go to http://localhost:8080/actuator/loggers/com.
apress.demo.

```
{
configuredLevel: null,
effectiveLevel: "INFO"
}
```

You can update the logging level of a logger at runtime by issuing a POST request to
http://localhost:8080/actuator/{loggerName}. Suppose you want to change the
logging level of com.apress.demo to DEBUG. You can send a POST request to the http://
localhost:8080/actuator/loggers/com.apress.demo URL with the following request
body JSON:

```
{
    configuredLevel: "DEBUG"
}
> curl -i -X POST -H 'Content-Type: application/json' -d
'{"configuredLevel": "DEBUG"}' http://localhost:8080/actuator/loggers/com.
apress.demo
```

Now, if you again check the logging level of the com.apress.demo logger by issuing a
GET request to http://localhost:8080/actuator/loggers/com.apress.demo, you will
see the updated logging configuration.

```
{
    configuredLevel: "DEBUG",
    effectiveLevel: "DEBUG"
}
```

The /logfile Endpoint

If you enabled file-based logging by setting logging.file or logging.path or using
the native file configuration files (logback.xml, log4j.properties, etc.), you can use
the /logfile endpoint to view the log file content. Go to http://localhost:8080/
actuator/logfile, as shown in Figure 13-12.

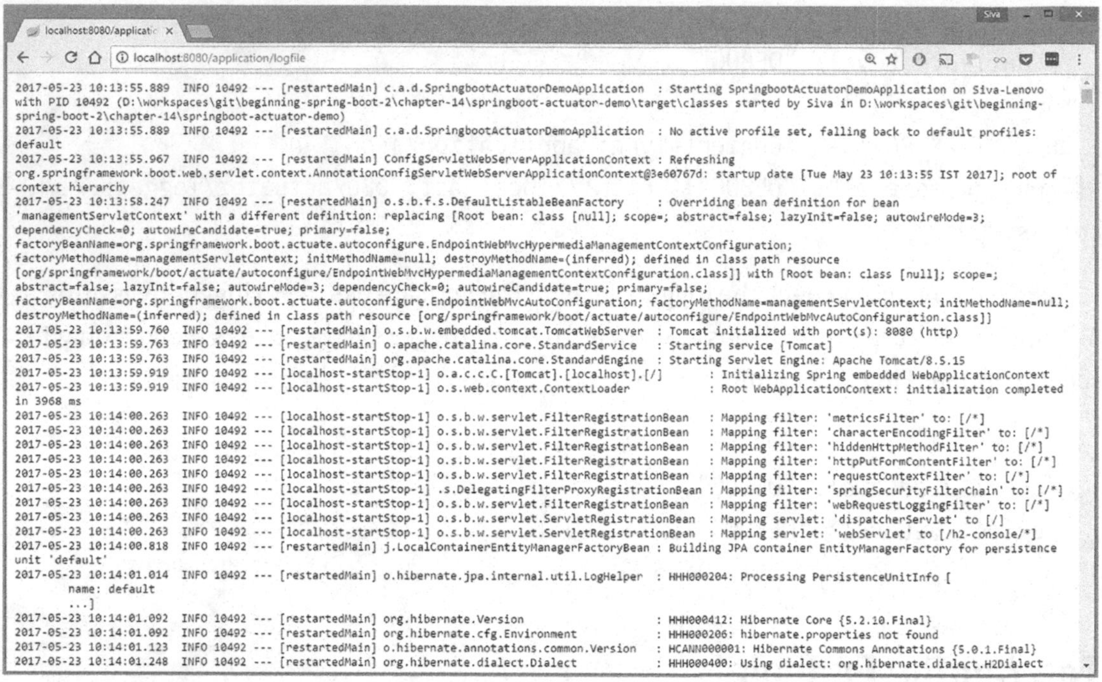

Figure 13-12. *Spring Boot Actuator /logfile endpoint*

The /shutdown Endpoint

The /shutdown endpoint can be used to gracefully shut down the application, which is not enabled by default. You can enable this endpoint by adding the following property to application.properties:

management.endpoint.shutdown.enabled=true

After adding this property, you can send the HTTP POST method to http:// localhost:8080/actuator/shutdown to invoke the /shutdown endpoint.

Once the /shutdown endpoint is invoked successfully, you should see the following message:

```
{
    "message": "Shutting down, bye..."
}
```

Note   Be careful about enabling or shutting down an endpoint. Enable or shut down an endpoint only when it is absolutely required, and be sure to protect the endpoint with the appropriate security configuration.

Customizing Actuator Endpoints

By default, the Spring Boot Actuator endpoints run on the same port and the default management context-path is `"/actuator"`. You can customize these properties using the following properties:

```
management.endpoints.web.base-path=/management
```

With this customization, you can access Actuator endpoints at `http://localhost:8080/management/` as the base path. The `/health` endpoint becomes `http://localhost:8080/management/health`.

You can change endpoint IDs, sensitivity, and enabled values using the `management.endpoints.web.path-mapping.{endpointName}.*` properties.

```
management.endpoints.web.path-mapping.beans=mybeans
```

With these customizations, you can access the `/beans` endpoint at `http://localhost:8080/actuator/mybeans`.

You can also selectively enable/disable an endpoint using the `endpoints.{endpoint}.enabled` property.

```
management.trace.http.enabled=false
management.endpoint.shutdown.enabled=true
```

You can enable/disable all endpoints using the `endpoints.enabled` property and selectively override for specific endpoints. For example, if you want to disable all endpoints except `/info`, then configure as follows:

```
management.endpoints.enabled-by-default=false
management.info.env.enabled=true
```

If you don't want to expose the endpoints over HTTP, you can disable this option by adding the following property:

```
management.server.port=-1
```

Securing Actuator Endpoints

By default, all sensitive endpoints are secured and only authenticated users who have the `ACTUATOR` role can access those endpoints. You can change the `ACTUATOR` role name to something else, say `SUPERADMIN`, by setting the following property:

```
management.security.roles=SUPERADMIN
```

If you have the Spring Boot Security Starter on the classpath, the Actuator endpoints will be secured by Spring Security.

Add the Security Starter dependency to `pom.xml`.

```
<dependency>
    <groupId>org.springframework.boot</groupId>
    <artifactId>spring-boot-starter-security</artifactId>
</dependency>
```

Instead of using the default user credentials, you can configure the security user credential in `application.properties`, as follows:

```
security.user.name=admin
security.user.password=secret
security.user.role=USER,ADMIN,ACTUATOR
```

Now if you try to access an endpoint, say `http://localhost:8080/application/beans`, you will be prompted to enter credentials.

But most likely you will be using a custom Spring Security configuration backed by a data store for user credentials, so you can configure Actuator endpoints for security as needed.

Implementing Custom Health Indicators

Spring Boot provides the following `HealthIndicator` implementations out of the box. They are autoconfigured by default.

- `CassandraHealthIndicator`

- `DiskSpaceHealthIndicator`

- `DataSourceHealthIndicator`

- ElasticsearchHealthIndicator

- JmsHealthIndicator

- MailHealthIndicator

- MongoHealthIndicator

- RabbitHealthIndicator

- RedisHealthIndicator

- SolrHealthIndicator

In addition to these, you can implement your own HealthIndicators based on your application health check needs.

Suppose you need to download some feed data from a remote server on a regular interval basis and there is an endpoint to invoke for checking the server reachability.

To implement a custom HealthIndicator, you need to register a Spring bean that implements the HealthIndicator interface. You can implement a HealthIndicator to ping the feed server, as shown in Listing 13-1.

Listing 13-1. Implementing a Custom HealthIndicator

```
import java.util.Date;
import org.springframework.boot.actuate.health.Health;
import org.springframework.boot.actuate.health.HealthIndicator;
import org.springframework.stereotype.Component;
import org.springframework.web.client.RestClientException;
import org.springframework.web.client.RestTemplate;
@Component
public class FeedServerHealthIndicator implements HealthIndicator
{
    @Override
    public Health health() {
        RestTemplate restTemplate = new RestTemplate();
        String url = "http://feedserver.com/ping";
        try {
            String resp = restTemplate.getForObject(url, String.class);
            if("OK".equalsIgnoreCase(resp)){
```

```
                        return Health.up().
                                build();
                } else {
                    return Health.down()
                            .withDetail("ping_url", url)
                            .withDetail("ping_time", new Date())
                            .build();
                }
        } catch (RestClientException e) {
            return Health.down(e)
                    .withDetail("ping_url", url)
                    .withDetail("ping_time", new Date())
                    .build();
        }
    }
}
```

Now, when you go to the http://localhost:8080/actuator/health URL and the feed server is not reachable, you will see the following response:

```
{
    status: "DOWN",
    feedServer: {
        status: "DOWN",
        error: "org.springframework.web.client.HttpClientErrorException:
        410 Gone",
        ping_url: "http://feedserver.com/ping",
        ping_time: 1495777475435
    },
    diskSpace: {
        status: "UP",
        total: 340650881024,
        free: 260343615488,
        threshold: 10485760
    },
    db: {
```

```
        status: "UP",
        database: "H2",
        hello: 1
    }
}
```

Having health checks for various application components and integration points will help you monitor the overall application health.

Capturing Custom Application Metrics

You have already seen how you can use Actuator's /metrics endpoint to view various application metrics, such as memory, heap, thread pool, and datasource information.

In addition, you can define your own application metrics using Micrometer (https://micrometer.io/), a vendor-neutral application metrics facade that enables you to publish the metrics to different monitoring systems supported by Spring Boot like Prometheus, Datadog, New Relic, and Graphite. You can find the list of supported monitoring systems at https://docs.spring.io/spring-boot/docs/current/reference/htmlsingle/#actuator.metrics.export.

Based on the monitoring system, you can add different dependencies to your project like micrometer-registry-prometheus if you want to integrate with Prometheus, micrometer-registry-datadog if you want to integrate with Datadog, and so on. The dependency to integrate Prometheus looks like this:

```
<dependency>
        <groupId>io.micrometer</groupId>
        <artifactId>micrometer-registry-prometheus</artifactId>
        <version>1.9.1</version>
</dependency>
```

You can register your metrics using the MeterRegistry class. Once you inject the MeterRegistry class into your required class, you can use the counter() method to register the metric into the monitoring system of your choice.

For example, imagine that you have a class called LoginService in place and you want to capture the metrics for successful and failed login attempts. You can use MeterRegistry class to capture those metrics, as shown in Listing 13-2.

Listing 13-2. Using MeterRegistry to record Login Metrics

```
import io.micrometer.core.instrument.MeterRegistry;
import org.springframework.stereotype.Service;

@Service
public class LoginService {
   private final MeterRegistry meterRegistry;
   public LoginService(MeterRegistry meterRegistry) {
       this.meterRegistry = meterRegistry;
   }
   public boolean login(String email, String password) {
       if ("admin@gmail.com".equalsIgnoreCase(email) && "admin".
       equals(password)) {
           meterRegistry.counter("login-counter",
                   "success", email).increment();
           return true;
       } else {
           meterRegistry.counter("login-counter",
                    "failure", email).increment();
           return false;
       }
   }
}
```

Inside the login method, you use the counter() of the MeterRegistry class to define a metric called "Login Counter" and with a tag either "success" or "failure."

You use the increment() method to increase the counter for each metric. On either a successful or failed login attempt, the corresponding counter will be increased.

You can view the custom metrics by going to http://localhost:8080/actuator/metrics/login-counter.

```
{
  "name": "login-counter",
  "measurements": [ { "statistic": "COUNT", "value": 10.0 }
  ],
  "availableTags": [
```

```
    {
      "tag": "success",
      "values": [ "admin@gmail.com"]
    },
    {
      "tag": "failure",
      "values": [ "admin@gmail.com"]
    }
  ]
}
```

In this response, you can observe that under the "measurements" object you can check how many times your custom metric was triggered and was registered.

Under the "availableTags" object, you can check the different values registered for each metric. You can also search the metrics based on tags and the value associated with the tag. For example, if you want to check how many times the user performed a successful login for a given email address, you can simply go to http://localhost:8080/actuator/metrics/login-counter?tag=success:admin@gmail.com.

```
{
    "name": "login-counter",
    "measurements": [
        {
            "statistic": "COUNT",
            "value": 3.0
        }
    ],
    "availableTags": []
}
```

According to this output, for the email address admin@gmail.com there are three successful login attempts.

CORS Support for Actuator Endpoints

To access the Actuator endpoints from other origins, you need to enable CORS support for them. CORS support is disabled by default and you need to set the `endpoints.cors.allowed-origins` property to enable it.

```
management.endpoints.cors.allowed-origins=http://remoteserver.com
management.endpoints.cors.allowed-methods=GET,POST
```

You can add other CORS properties using the `management.endpoints.cors.*` properties.

Monitoring and Management Over JMX

By default, Spring Boot exposes Actuator endpoints as JMX MBeans under the `org.springframework.boot` domain. You can use JConsole, which comes with JDK, to view JMX MBeans.

Run JConsole from `C:\\Program Files\\Java\\jdk17\\bin\\jconsole.exe`. Select the Spring Boot application `main` class and click Connect. If you see a dialog box that says "Secure Connection Failed. Retry Insecurely?", click Insecure Connection.

By default, you will be on the Overview tab. Click the MBeans tab. Now expand the `org.springframework.boot` domain where you'll find Actuator endpoints exported as MBeans. See Figure 13-13.

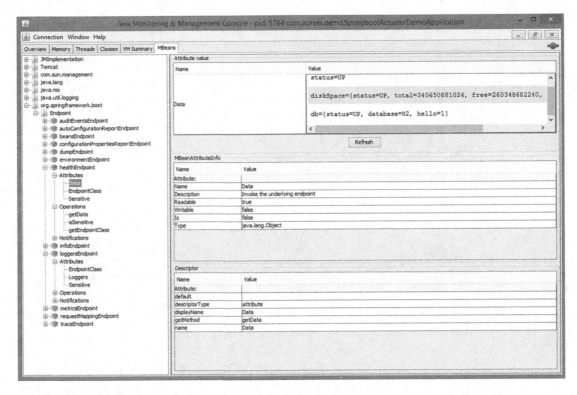

Figure 13-13. *Spring Boot Actuator JMX monitoring*

You can customize the domain name by using the endpoints.jmx.domain property.

```
spring.jmx.unique-names=true
management.endpoints.jmx.domain=mydomain
```

You can disable exposing endpoints over JMX by setting management.endpoints.
jmx.exposure.exclude=*.

Summary

In this chapter, you explored the Spring Boot Actuator, which includes very helpful
production support features. You learned about the various endpoints, including how to
customize them and how to invoke them over HTTP and JMX. In the next chapter, you
will learn how to test Spring Boot applications.

CHAPTER 14

Testing Spring Boot Applications

Testing is an essential part of software development. It helps developers verify the correctness of the functionality. JUnit and TestNG are two of the most popular testing libraries used in Java projects.

Test-driven development (TDD) is a popular development practice where you write tests first and write just enough production code to pass the tests. You write various tests, such as unit, integration, and performance tests. Unit tests focus on testing one component in isolation, whereas integration tests verify a feature's behavior, which can involve multiple components. While doing unit tests, you may have to mock the behavior of dependent components such as third-party web service classes and database method invocations. There are mocking libraries, like Mockito, PowerMock, and jMock, for mocking the object's behavior.

The dependency injection (DI) design pattern encourages programming to practice and write testable code. With dependency injection, you can inject mock implementations for testing and actual implementations for production. Spring is a dependency injection container at its core, providing excellent support for testing various parts of an application.

This chapter will teach you how to test Spring components in Spring Boot applications. You will take a detailed look at how to test slices of applications, such as web components (regular MVC controllers, REST API endpoints), Spring data repositories, and secured controller/service methods using the @WebMvcTest, @DataJpaTest, and the @JdbcTest annotations.

© K. Siva Prasad Reddy, Sai Upadhyayula 2023
K. S. P. Reddy and S. Upadhyayula, *Beginning Spring Boot 3*, https://doi.org/10.1007/978-1-4842-8792-7_14

Testing Spring Boot Applications

One of the key reasons for the popularity of the Spring Framework is its excellent support for testing. Spring provides `SpringExtension`, a custom JUnit extension helping to load the Spring `ApplicationContext` by using `@ContextConfiguration` `(classes=AppConfig.class)`.

A typical Spring unit/integration test is shown in Listing 14-1.

Listing 14-1. Typical Spring JUnit Test

```
@ExtendWith(SpringExtension.class)
@ContextConfiguration(classes=AppConfig.class)
public class PostServiceTests
{
    @Autowired
    PostService userService;
    @Test
    public void should_load_all_posts()
    {
        List<PostDto> posts = postService.getAllPosts();
        assertNotNull(posts);
        assertEquals(10, posts.size());
    }
}
```

A Spring Boot application is also nothing but a Spring application so you can use all of Spring's testing features in your Spring Boot applications.

However, some Spring Boot features, like loading external properties and logging, are available only if you create `ApplicationContext` using the `SpringApplication` class, which you'll typically use in your entry point class. These additional Spring Boot features won't be available if you use `@ContextConfiguration`.

```
@SpringBootApplication
public class SpringbootTestingDemoApplication
{
```

```
public static void main(String[] args)
{
    SpringApplication.run(SpringbootTestingDemoApplication.class, args);
}
}
```

Spring Boot provides the @SpringBootTest annotation, which uses SpringApplication behind the scenes to load ApplicationContext so that all the Spring Boot features will be available. See Listing 14-2.

Listing 14-2. Typical Spring Boot JUnit Test

```
@SpringBootTest
public class SpringbootTestingDemoApplicationTests
{
    @Autowired
    PostService postService;
    @Test
    public void should_load_all_posts()
    {
        ...
        ...
    }
}
```

For @SpringBootTest, you can pass Spring configuration classes, Spring bean definition XML files, and more, but in Spring Boot applications, you typically use the entry point class.

The Spring Boot Test Starter spring-boot-starter-test pulls in the JUnit, Spring Test, and Spring Boot Test modules, along with the following most commonly used mocking and asserting libraries:

- **Mockito**: A Java mocking framework found at http://site. mockito.org/

- **Hamcrest**: A matcher/predicates library for data assertion found at http://hamcrest.org/JavaHamcrest/

- **AssertJ**: A fluent assertion library found at `https://joel-costigliola.github.io/assertj/`

- **JSONassert**: An assertion library for JSON found at `https://github.com/skyscreamer/JSONassert`

- **JsonPath**: XPath for JSON found at `https://github.com/json-path/JsonPath`

Now you'll see how to create a simple Spring Boot web application with a simple REST endpoint.

```
<dependencies>
    <dependency>
        <groupId>org.springframework.boot</groupId>
        <artifactId>spring-boot-starter-web</artifactId>
    </dependency>
    <dependency>
        <groupId>org.springframework.boot</groupId>
        <artifactId>spring-boot-starter-test</artifactId>
        <scope>test</scope>
    </dependency>
</dependencies>
```

First, create an entry point class called `Application.java`, as follows:

```
@SpringBootApplication
public class Application
{
    public static void main(String[] args)
    {
        SpringApplication.run(Application.class, args);
    }
}
```

Listing 14-3 shows how to create a simple REST endpoint called `/ping`.

Listing 14-3. Spring REST Controller

```
@RestController
public class PingController
{
    @GetMapping("/ping")
    public String ping()
    {
        return "OK";
    }
}
```

If you run the application, you can invoke the REST endpoint `http://localhost:8080/ping`, which gives the response `"OK"`. You can write a test for the `/ping` endpoint. See Listing 14-4.

Listing 14-4. Testing Spring REST Endpoint Using TestRestTemplate

```
import static org.assertj.core.api.Assertions.assertThat;
import org.junit.jupiter.api.Test;
import org.springframework.beans.factory.annotation.Autowired;
import org.springframework.boot.test.context.SpringBootTest;
import org.springframework.boot.test.context.SpringBootTest.WebEnvironment;
import org.springframework.boot.test.web.client.TestRestTemplate;
import org.springframework.http.HttpStatus;
import org.springframework.http.ResponseEntity;
@SpringBootTest(webEnvironment=WebEnvironment.RANDOM_PORT)
class PingControllerTests {
    @Autowired
    TestRestTemplate restTemplate;

    @Test
    void testPing() {
        ResponseEntity<String> respEntity =
                restTemplate.getForEntity("/ping", String.class);
        assertThat(respEntity.getStatusCode()).isEqualTo(HttpStatus.OK);
        assertThat(respEntity.getBody()).isEqualTo("OK");
    }
}
```

Since you need to test the REST endpoint, you start the embedded servlet container by specifying the webEnvironment attribute of @SpringBootTest.

The default webEnvironment value is WebEnvironment.MOCK, which doesn't start an embedded servlet container.

You can use various webEnvironment values based on how you want to run the tests.

- MOCK (default): Loads a WebApplicationContext and provides a mock servlet environment. It will not start an embedded servlet container. If servlet APIs are not on your classpath, this mode will fall back to creating a regular non-web ApplicationContext.

- RANDOM_PORT: Loads a ServletWebServerApplicationContext and starts an embedded servlet container listening on a random available port

- DEFINED_PORT: Loads a ServletWebServerApplicationContext and starts an embedded servlet container listening on a defined port (server.port)

- NONE: Loads an ApplicationContext using SpringApplication but does not provide a servlet environment

The TestRestTemplate bean will be registered automatically only when @SpringBootTest is started with an embedded servlet container.

While running the integration tests that start the embedded servlet containers, it is better to use WebEnvironment.RANDOM_PORT so that it won't conflict with other running applications, especially in continuous integration (CI) environments where multiple builds run in parallel.

You can specify which configuration classes to use to build ApplicationContext by using the classes attribute of the @SpringBootTest annotation. If you don't determine any classes, it will automatically search for nested @Configuration classes and fall back to searching for @SpringBootConfiguration classes. The @SpringBootApplication is annotated with @SpringBootConfiguration so that @SpringBootTest will pick up the application's entry point class.

Testing with Mock Implementations

While performing unit testing, you may want to mock calls to external services like database interactions and web service invocations. You can create mock implementations for tests and actual implementations used in production.

Say you have an EmployeeRepository file that talks to the database and gets employee data, as shown in Listing 14-5.

Listing 14-5. EmployeeRepository.java

```java
public interface EmployeeRepository
{
    List<Employee> findAllEmployees();
}
```

Suppose you have EmployeeService, which depends on EmployeeRepository, with getMaxSalariedEmployee() and a few other employee-related methods. See Listing 14-6.

Listing 14-6. EmployeeService.java

```java
@Service
public class EmployeeService
{
    private EmployeeRepository employeeRepository;

    public EmployeeService(EmployeeRepository employeeRepository)
    {
      this.employeeRepository = employeeRepository;
    }
    public Employee getMaxSalariedEmployee()
    {
        Employee emp = null;
        List<Employee> emps = employeeRepository.findAllEmployees();
        //loop through emps and find max salaried emp
        return emp;
    }
}
```

Now you can create a mock `EmployeeRepository` file for testing, as shown in Listing 14-7.

Listing 14-7. MockEmployeeRepository.java

```java
@Repository
@Profile("test")
public class MockEmployeeRepository implements EmployeeRepository
{
    public List<Employee> findAllEmployees()
    {
        return Arrays.asList(
            new Employee(1, "A", 50000),
            new Employee(2, "B", 75000),
            new Employee(3, "C", 43000)
        );
    }
}
```

Now you'll create a real implementation of `EmployeeRepository` for production, as shown in Listing 14-8.

Listing 14-8. JdbcEmployeeRepository.java

```java
@Service
@Profile("production")
public class JdbcEmployeeRepository implements EmployeeRepository
{
    private JdbcTemplate jdbcTemplate;

    public JdbcEmployeeRepository(JdbcTemplate jdbcTemplate) {
            this.jdbcTemplate = jdbcTemplate;
    }
    public List<Employee> findAllEmployees()
    {
        return jdbcTemplate.query(...);
    }
}
```

You can use the @ActiveProfiles annotation to specify which profiles to use so that Spring Boot will activate only the beans associated with those profiles. See Listing 14-9.

Listing 14-9. Testing with Mock Implementation Using Profiles

```
@ActiveProfiles("test")
@SpringBootTest
public class ApplicationTests
{
    @Autowired
    EmployeeService employeeService;
    @Test
    public void test_getMaxSalariedEmployee()
    {
        Employee emp = employeeService.getMaxSalariedEmployee();
        assertNotNull(emp);
        assertEquals(2, emp.getId());
        assertEquals("B", emp.getName());
        assertEquals(75000, emp.getSalary());
    }
}
```

Since you have enabled the test profile, MockEmployeeRepository will be injected into EmployeeService. You can activate the production profile while running the application in production as follows:

```
java -jar myapp.jar -Dspring.profiles.active=production
```

While running the main application, Spring Boot will use the production profile and JdbcEmployeeRepository will be injected into EmployeeService.

In addition, providing mock implementations for every use case can be tedious. You can use mocking libraries to create mock objects without actually creating classes. The next section looks into how to unit test using the popular mocking library Mockito.

Testing with Mockito

Mockito is a popular Java mocking framework that can be used along with JUnit. Mockito lets you write tests by mocking the external dependencies with the desired behavior.

For example, assume you are invoking some external web service and want to retry the invocation three times when it fails due to communication failures. To test the retry behavior, that external web service should throw an exception that may not be in your control. You can use Mockito to simulate this behavior to test the retry functionality.

Suppose you import user data from a third party using a web service, as shown in Listing 14-10.

Listing 14-10. UsersImporter.java

```
@Service
public class UsersImporter
{
    public List<User> importUsers() throws
    UserImportServiceCommunicationFailure
    {
        List<User> users = new ArrayList<>();
        //get users by invoking some web service
        //if any exception occurs throw UserImportService
          CommunicationFailure
        //dummy data
        users.add(new User());
        users.add(new User());
        users.add(new User());
        return users;
    }
}
```

UserService uses UsersImporter to get user data and retries three times if a UserImportServiceCommunicationFailure occurs. See Listing 14-11.

Listing 14-11. UsersImportService.java

```
@Service
@Transactional
public class UsersImportService
{
    private Logger logger = LoggerFactory.getLogger(UserService.class);
    private UsersImporter usersImporter;
```

```java
    public UsersImportService(UsersImporter usersImporter)
    {
        this.usersImporter = usersImporter;
    }
    public UsersImportResponse importUsers()
    {
        int retryCount = 0;
        int maxRetryCount = 3;
        for (int i = 0; i < maxRetryCount; i++)
        {
            try
            {
                List<User> importUsers = usersImporter.importUsers();
                logger.info("Import Users: "+importUsers);
                break;
            } catch (UserImportServiceCommunicationFailure e)
            {
                retryCount++;
                logger.error("Error: "+e.getMessage());
            }
        }
        if(retryCount >= maxRetryCount)
            return new UsersImportResponse(retryCount, "FAILURE");
        else
            return new UsersImportResponse(0, "SUCCESS");
    }
}
public class UsersImportResponse
{
    private int retryCount;
    private String status;
    //setters & getters
}
```

This code invokes the usersImporter.importUsers() method and, if it throws
UserImportServiceCommunicationFailure, it retries three times.

If you want to test if usersImporter.importUsers() returns the result without getting an exception, then UsersImportResponse(0, "SUCCESS") should be returned; otherwise, UsersImportResponse(3, "FAILURE") should be returned.

You can use @Mock to create a mock object and @InjectMocks to inject the dependencies with mocks. You can use @ExtendWith(MockitoExtension. class) to initialize the mock objects or trigger the mock object initialization using MockitoAnnotations.initMocks(this) in the JUnit @Before method. See Listing 14-12.

Listing 14-12. Testing Using Mockito Mock Objects

```
import static org.assertj.core.api.Assertions.assertThat;
import static org.mockito.BDDMockito.*;
import org.junit.jupiter.api.Test;
import org.junit.jupiter.api.extension.ExtendWith;
import org.mockito.InjectMocks;
import org.mockito.Mock;
import org.mockito.junit.jupiter.MockitoExtension;
import com.apress.demo.model.UsersImportResponse;
@ExtendWith(MockitoExtension.class)
class UsersImportServiceMockitoTest {
    @Mock
    private UsersImporter usersImporter;
    @InjectMocks
    private UsersImportService usersImportService;
    @Test
    void should_import_users() {
        UsersImportResponse response = usersImportService.importUsers();
        assertThat(response.getRetryCount()).isEqualTo(0);
        assertThat(response.getStatus()).isEqualTo("SUCCESS");
    }
    @Test
    void should_retry_3times_when_UserImportServiceCommunicationFailure_
    occured() {
        given(usersImporter.importUsers()).willThrow(new
        UserImportServiceCommunicationFailure());
```

```
UsersImportResponse response = usersImportService.
importUsers();
assertThat(response.getRetryCount()).isEqualTo(3);
assertThat(response.getStatus()).isEqualTo("FAILURE");
    }
}
```

Here you are simulating the failure condition while importing users using the web service as follows:

```
given(usersImporter.importUsers()).willThrow(new
UserImportServiceCommunicationFailure());
```

So, when you call userService.importUsers() and the mock usersImporter object throws UserImportServiceCommunicationFailure, it will retry three times. Similarly, you can use Mockito to simulate any behavior to meet these test cases.

Spring Boot provides the @MockBean annotation that can be used to define a new Mockito mock bean or replace a Spring bean with a mock bean and inject that into their dependent beans. Mock beans will be automatically reset after each test method. See Listing 14-13.

Listing 14-13. Testing Using Spring Boot's @MockBean Mocks

```
import static org.assertj.core.api.Assertions.assertThat;
import static org.mockito.BDDMockito.*;
import org.junit.jupiter.api.Test;
import org.springframework.beans.factory.annotation.Autowired;
import org.springframework.boot.test.context.SpringBootTest;
import org.springframework.boot.test.mock.mockito.MockBean;
import com.apress.demo.exceptions.UserImportServiceCommunicationFailure;
import com.apress.demo.model.UsersImportResponse;
@ExtendWith(MockitoExtension.class)
class UsersImportServiceMockitoTest {
    @MockBean
    private UsersImporter usersImporter;
    @Autowired
    private UsersImportService usersImportService;
    @Test
```

```
    void should_import_users() {
            UsersImportResponse response = usersImportService.importUsers();
            assertThat(response.getRetryCount()).isEqualTo(0);
            assertThat(response.getStatus()).isEqualTo("SUCCESS");
    }
    @Test
    void should_retry_3times_when_UserImportServiceCommunicationFailure_
    occured() {
            given(usersImporter.importUsers()).willThrow(new
            UserImportServiceCommunicationFailure());
            UsersImportResponse response = usersImportService.
            importUsers();
            assertThat(response.getRetryCount()).isEqualTo(3);
            assertThat(response.getStatus()).isEqualTo("FAILURE");
    }
}
```

Spring Boot will create a Mockito mock object for UsersImporter and inject it into the UsersImportService bean.

Testing Slices of Application Using @*Test Annotations

While testing various application components, you may want to load a subset of the Spring ApplicationContext beans related to the subject under test (SUT). For example, when testing a SpringMVC controller, you may want to load only the MVC layer components and provide mock service-layer beans as dependencies.

Spring Boot provides annotations like @WebMvcTest, @DataJpaTest, @DataMongoTest, @JdbcTest, and @JsonTest to test slices of the application.

Testing SpringMVC Controllers Using @WebMvcTest

Spring Boot provides the @WebMvcTest annotation, which will autoconfigure SpringMVC infrastructure components and load only @Controller, @ControllerAdvice, @JsonComponent, Filter, WebMvcConfigurer, and HandlerMethodArgumentResolver components. Other Spring beans (annotated with @Component, @Service, @Repository, etc.) will not be scanned using this annotation.

Let's return to your Spring blog application and see how to write tests for your Spring MVC controllers. Listing 14-14 shows how to write a test for the PostController class that uses Spring MVC and Thymeleaf using the @WebMvcTest.

Listing 14-14. Testing SpringMVC Controller Using MockMvc

```
package com.apress.demo.springblog;

import com.apress.demo.springblog.domain.Post;
import com.apress.demo.springblog.service.PostService;
import org.junit.jupiter.api.Test;
import org.mockito.BDDMockito;
import org.springframework.beans.factory.annotation.Autowired;
import org.springframework.boot.test.autoconfigure.web.servlet.WebMvcTest;
import org.springframework.boot.test.mock.mockito.MockBean;
import org.springframework.http.MediaType;
import org.springframework.test.web.servlet.MockMvc;
import org.springframework.test.web.servlet.request.MockMvcRequestBuilders;
import org.springframework.test.web.servlet.result.MockMvcResultMatchers;

import java.util.Arrays;

import static org.hamcrest.Matchers.hasSize;

@WebMvcTest(controllers = PostControllerTest.class)
class PostControllerTest {
    @Autowired
    private MockMvc mvc;
    @MockBean
    private PostService postService;

    @Test
    public void testFindAllPosts() throws Exception {
        Post post = new Post();
        post.setId(1);
        post.setTitle("Test");
        post.setDescription("Test");
```

```
    Post secondPost = new Post();
    secondPost.setId(2);
    secondPost.setTitle("Test 1");
    secondPost.setDescription("Test 1");
    BDDMockito.given(postService.findAllPosts()).willReturn(Arrays.
    asList(post, secondPost));

    this.mvc.perform(MockMvcRequestBuilders.get("/posts")
                .accept(MediaType.TEXT_HTML))
        .andExpect(MockMvcResultMatchers.status().isOk())
        .andExpect(MockMvcResultMatchers.view().name("post"))
        .andExpect(MockMvcResultMatchers.model().attribute("posts",
        hasSize(2)));
    }
}
```

In this test, you annotate the test with @WebMvcTest(controllers =
PostController.class) by explicitly specifying which controller you are testing. As
@WebMvcTest doesn't load other regular Spring beans and PostController depends
on PostService, you provided a mock bean using the @MockBean annotation. The
@WebMvcTest autoconfigures MockMvc, which helps to test controllers without starting an
actual servlet container.

In this test method, you set the expected behavior on postService.findAllPosts()
to return a list of two Post objects. Then you issue a GET request to the "/posts"
endpoint and assert various things in response. The first assertion is to check whether
the HTTP Response's status is OK.

In the following assertion, you check if the name of the view returned is "post", and in
the last assertion, you verify if the post Model Attribute has a size of 2, representing the
number of objects you expect as the response.

Testing SpringMVC REST Controllers Using @WebMvcTest

Similar to how you can test SpringMVC controllers, you can also test REST controllers.
You can write assertions on response data using JsonPath or JSONAssert libraries.

Go ahead and write a test for your PostController that serves the REST API, as
shown in Listing 14-15.

Listing 14-15. Testing SpringMVC REST Controller Using MockMvc

```
package com.apress.demo.springblog;

import com.apress.demo.springblog.controller.PostController;
import com.apress.demo.springblog.dto.PostDto;
import com.apress.demo.springblog.service.PostService;
import org.hamcrest.Matchers;
import org.junit.jupiter.api.Test;
import org.mockito.BDDMockito;
import org.springframework.beans.factory.annotation.Autowired;
import org.springframework.boot.test.autoconfigure.web.servlet.WebMvcTest;
import org.springframework.boot.test.mock.mockito.MockBean;
import org.springframework.http.MediaType;
import org.springframework.test.web.servlet.MockMvc;
import org.springframework.test.web.servlet.request.MockMvcRequestBuilders;
import org.springframework.test.web.servlet.result.MockMvcResultMatchers;

@WebMvcTest(controllers = PostController.class)
class PostRestControllerTest {
    @Autowired
    private MockMvc mvc;
    @MockBean
    private PostService postService;

    @Test
    public void testFindPostBySlug() throws Exception {
        PostDto post = new PostDto();
        post.setId(1L);
        post.setTitle("Test");
        post.setDescription("Test");
        post.setSlug("Test");

        BDDMockito.given(postService.findBySlug("Test")).willReturn(post);

        this.mvc.perform(MockMvcRequestBuilders.get("/api/posts/Test")
                    .accept(MediaType.APPLICATION_JSON))
            .andExpect(MockMvcResultMatchers.status().isOk())
```

```
                    .andExpect(MockMvcResultMatchers.jsonPath("$.id",
                    Matchers.is(1)))
                    .andExpect(MockMvcResultMatchers.jsonPath("$.title",
                    Matchers.is("Test")))
                    .andExpect(MockMvcResultMatchers.jsonPath("$.description",
                    Matchers.is("Test")));
    }
}
```

You test the `PostController` REST API endpoint `"/api/posts/{slug}"` in the same way you tested the `findAllPosts()` endpoint in `PostController` from Spring MVC.

The main difference is in the assertions. In this test class, you use the JSON `Path` assertions using the `MockMvcResultMatchers.jsonPath` method to verify the returned JSON response data.

Testing Persistence Layer Components Using @DataJpaTest and @JdbcTest

You might want to test the persistence layer components of your application, which doesn't require loading many components like controllers, security configuration, and so on. Spring Boot provides the `@DataJpaTest` and `@JdbcTest` annotations to test the Spring beans, which talk to relational databases.

Spring Boot provides the `@DataJpaTest` annotation to test the persistence layer components that will autoconfigure in-memory embedded databases and scan for `@Entity` classes and Spring Data JPA repositories. The `@DataJpaTest` annotation doesn't load other Spring beans (`@Components`, `@Controller`, `@Service`, and annotated beans) into `ApplicationContext`.

Now you'll see how to test the Spring Data JPA repositories in your Spring blog application. Let's create a test for the `PostRepository.java` class using the `@DataJpaTest` annotation. See Listing 14-16.

Listing 14-16. Testing Spring Data JPA Repositories Using @DataJpaTest

```
package com.apress.demo.springblog;

import com.apress.demo.springblog.domain.Post;
import com.apress.demo.springblog.repository.PostRepository;
```

```java
import org.junit.jupiter.api.*;
import org.junit.jupiter.api.TestInstance;
import org.springframework.beans.factory.annotation.Autowired;
import org.springframework.boot.test.autoconfigure.orm.jpa.DataJpaTest;

import java.util.Optional;

@DataJpaTest
public class PostRepositoryTest {
    @Autowired
    private PostRepository postRepository;

    @BeforeEach
    public void setup() {
        Post post = new Post();
        post.setId(1L);
        post.setTitle("Test");
        post.setDescription("Test");
        post.setSlug("test");
        postRepository.save(post);
    }

    @Test
    public void testPostBySlug() {
        Optional<Post> postOptional = postRepository.findBySlug("test");
        Assertions.assertTrue(postOptional.isPresent());
        Assertions.assertEquals(1L, postOptional.get().getId());
        Assertions.assertEquals("Test", postOptional.get().getTitle());
    }
}
```

When you run PostRepositoryTest, Spring Boot will autoconfigure the H2 in-memory embedded database (as you have the H2 database driver in the classpath) and run the tests.

You initialize the test data inside the setup() method of the Test class, which will be executed before each test.

If you want to run the tests against the actual registered database, you can annotate the test with @AutoConfigureTestDatabase(replace=Replace.NONE), which will use the registered DataSource instead of an in-memory data source. You can use Replace.AUTO_ CONFIGURED to replace autoconfigured DataSource and use Replace.ANY (the default) to replace any datasource bean that's autoconfigured or explicitly defined.

The @DataJpaTest tests are transactional and rolled back at the end of each test by default. You can disable this default rollback behavior for a single test or for an entire test class by annotating with @Transactional(propagation = Propagation.NOT_ SUPPORTED). See Listing 14-17.

Listing 14-17. @DataJpaTest with Custom Transactional Behavior

```
@DataJpaTest
@TestInstance(TestInstance.Lifecycle.PER_CLASS)
public class PostRepositoryTest {

    @Autowired
    private PostRepository postRepository;

    @BeforeAll
    public void setup() {
        Post post = new Post();
        post.setId(1L);
        post.setTitle("Test");
        post.setDescription("Test");
        post.setSlug("test");

        postRepository.save(post);
    }

    @Test
    public void testPostBySlug() {
        Optional<Post> postOptional = postRepository.findBySlug("test");
        Assertions.assertTrue(postOptional.isPresent());
        Assertions.assertEquals(1L, postOptional.get().getId());
        Assertions.assertEquals("Test", postOptional.get().getTitle());
    }
}
```

```java
@Test
@Transactional(propagation = Propagation.NOT_SUPPORTED)
public void testCreatePost() {
    Post post = new Post();
    post.setId(2L);
    post.setTitle("Test 1");
    post.setDescription("Test 1");
    post.setSlug("test 1");
    post.setComments(null);
    postRepository.save(post);

    Optional<Post> byTest1Slug = postRepository.findBySlug("test 1");
    Assertions.assertTrue(byTest1Slug.isPresent());
}

@Test
public void testUpdatePost() {
    Post post = new Post();
    post.setId(1L);
    post.setTitle("Test Updated");
    post.setDescription("Test Updated");
    post.setSlug("test updated");
    post.setComments(null);
    postRepository.save(post);

    Optional<Post> byTest1Slug = postRepository.findBySlug("test updated");
    Assertions.assertTrue(byTest1Slug.isPresent());
}

}
```

When the testCreatePost() test method runs, the changes will not be rolled back, whereas the database changes made in testUpdateUser() will be automatically rolled back. In the above test, the @TestInstance(TestInstance.Lifecycle.PER_CLASS) ensures that the test instance is created only once per Test class, whereas by default the test instance will be created for each Test method in Junit Jupiter. This will lead to state sharing between the tests, which is bad and makes your tests flaky and unreliable, so use this option very rarely.

You may also observe that the above test fails when you add the Propogation.NOT_ SUPPORTED option when the orphanRemoval = true attribute is added to the comments field inside the Post class. Just remove this attribute to make the test work normally.

The @DataJpaTest annotation also autoconfigures TestEntityManager, which is an alternative to the JPA EntityManager to be used in JPA tests. See Listing 14-18.

Listing 14-18. @DataJpaTest Using TestEntityManager

```
@DataJpaTest
public class PostRepositoryTestUsingTestEntityManager {

    @Autowired
    private PostRepository postRepository;
    @Autowired
    private TestEntityManager entityManager;

    @Test
    public void testPostBySlug() {

        Post post = new Post();
        post.setTitle("Test");
        post.setDescription("Test");
        post.setSlug("test");
        post.setComments(null);

        postRepository.save(post);
        Long id = entityManager.persistAndGetId(post, Long.class);

        Optional<Post> postOptional = postRepository.findById(id);
        Assertions.assertTrue(postOptional.isPresent());
        Assertions.assertEquals(1L, postOptional.get().getId());
        Assertions.assertEquals("Test", postOptional.get().getTitle());
    }
}
```

The TestEntityManager provides some convenient methods like persistAndGetId(), persistAndFlush(), and persistFlushFind(), which are useful in tests.

Similar to the @DataJpaTest annotation, you can use @JdbcTest as discussed in Chapter 5 to test plain JDBC-related methods using JdbcTemplate. The @JdbcTest annotation also autoconfigures in-memory embedded databases and runs the tests in a transactional manner.

Like @DataJpaTest and @JdbcTest, Spring Boot provides other annotations like @DataMongoTest, @DataNeo4jTest, @JooqTest, @JsonTest, and @DataLdapTest to test slices of an application.

Testing Persistence Layer Using TestContainers

In the previous section, you learned how to test your persistence layer by using an in-memory database like H2. Ideally, you want to test your persistence logic against a real database like MySQL, PostgreSQL, or any other relational database of your choice.

But the challenge in accomplishing this is the availability of the database while running the tests. In a real-world project, your test suite will run on a CI server like Jenkins where it's not so easy to install a real database each time you run your tests.

To address this challenge, you can use a Java library called TestContainers. According to the TestContainers website, "Testcontainers is a Java library that supports JUnit tests, providing lightweight, throwaway instances of common databases, Selenium web browsers, or anything else that can run in Docker container." See www.testcontainers.org/.

To work with TestContainers, you need to have Docker installed on your machine as a prerequisite.

After that, add the following dependency to the pom.xml file:

```
<dependency>
    <groupId>org.testcontainers</groupId>
    <artifactId>testcontainers</artifactId>
    <version>1.17.2</version>
    <scope>test</scope>
</dependency>
<dependency>
    <groupId>org.testcontainers</groupId>
    <artifactId>junit-jupiter</artifactId>
    <version>1.17.2</version>
```

```
        <scope>test</scope>
</dependency>
<dependency>
        <groupId>org.testcontainers</groupId>
        <artifactId>mysql</artifactId>
        <version>1.17.2</version>
        <scope>test</scope>
</dependency>
```

Please check the latest version available on Maven Central.

To avoid adding the same version number for multiple test container dependencies, you can add the Bill of Materials or a BOM dependency to the dependencyManagement section of the pom.xml file.

Now you can add the dependencies without specifying the version, like so:

```
<dependency>
        <groupId>org.testcontainers</groupId>
        <artifactId>testcontainers</artifactId>
        <scope>test</scope>
</dependency>
<dependency>
        <groupId>org.testcontainers</groupId>
        <artifactId>junit-jupiter</artifactId>
        <scope>test</scope>
</dependency>
<dependency>
        <groupId>org.testcontainers</groupId>
        <artifactId>mysql</artifactId>
        <scope>test</scope>
</dependency>
```

After adding these dependencies, you can add the @TestContainers annotation on top of the UserRepositoryTest class to enable the support for TestContainers in your test. This annotation is coming from the junit-jupiter test containers dependency. Add the following code to the test class to initialize the MySQL docker container during the test start-up:

```
@Container
MySQLContainer mySQLContainer = new MySQLContainer("mysql:8.0.29")
        .withDatabaseName("test-db")
        .withUsername("testuser")
        .withPassword("pass");
```

Listing 14-19 shows the test with the TestContainers support.

Listing 14-19. DataJpaTest using TestContainers Support

```
package com.apress.demo.springblog;

import com.apress.demo.springblog.domain.Post;
import com.apress.demo.springblog.repository.PostRepository;
import org.junit.jupiter.api.Assertions;
import org.junit.jupiter.api.Test;
import org.springframework.beans.factory.annotation.Autowired;
import org.springframework.boot.test.autoconfigure.jdbc.
AutoConfigureTestDatabase;
import org.springframework.boot.test.autoconfigure.orm.jpa.DataJpaTest;
import org.springframework.test.context.DynamicPropertyRegistry;
import org.springframework.test.context.DynamicPropertySource;
import org.testcontainers.containers.MySQLContainer;
import org.testcontainers.junit.jupiter.Container;
import org.testcontainers.junit.jupiter.Testcontainers;

import java.util.Optional;

@Testcontainers
@DataJpaTest
@AutoConfigureTestDatabase(replace = AutoConfigureTestDatabase.
Replace.NONE)
public class PostRepositoryTCTest {
    @Container
    static MySQLContainer mySQLContainer = new MySQLContainer
    ("mysql:8.0.29");
```

```java
@Autowired
private PostRepository postRepository;

@DynamicPropertySource
static void overrideProperties(DynamicPropertyRegistry registry) {
    registry.add("spring.datasource.url", mySQLContainer::getJdbcUrl);
    registry.add("spring.datasource.username", mySQLContainer::
    getUsername);
    registry.add("spring.datasource.password", mySQLContainer::
    getPassword);
}

@Test
public void testPostBySlug() {
    setup();
    Optional<Post> postOptional = postRepository.findBySlug("test");
    Assertions.assertTrue(postOptional.isPresent());
    Assertions.assertEquals(1L, postOptional.get().getId());
    Assertions.assertEquals("Test", postOptional.get().getTitle());
}

private void setup() {
    Post post = new Post();
    post.setId(1L);
    post.setTitle("Test");
    post.setDescription("Test");
    post.setSlug("test");

    postRepository.save(post);
}
}
```

When you add the @TestContainers and @Container annotations, TestContainers will automatically start and stop the required containers during the startup and teardown phase of the tests.

The datasource properties like `spring.datasource.url`, `spring.datasource.username` and `spring.datasource.password` are passed during the initialization of the test dynamically by using the @DynamicPropertySource annotation.

You can also do the initialization and destruction of the containers manually by initializing the containers without the @Container annotation, and then calling the container.start() and container.stop() methods manually. Here is an example of how to start and stop the containers manually:

```
@DataJpaTest
@AutoConfigureTestDatabase(replace = AutoConfigureTestDatabase.
Replace.NONE)
public class PostRepositoryTCManualStartupTest {
    static MySQLContainer<?> mysqlContainer =
            new MySQLContainer<>(DockerImageName.parse("mysql:8.0.29"));

    @Autowired
    private PostRepository postRepository;

    @BeforeAll
    static void beforeAll() {
        mysqlContainer.start();
    }

    @AfterAll
    static void afterAll() {
        mysqlContainer.stop();
    }

    @DynamicPropertySource
    static void overrideProperties(DynamicPropertyRegistry registry) {
        registry.add("spring.datasource.url", mysqlContainer::getJdbcUrl);
        registry.add("spring.datasource.username", mysqlContainer::
        getUsername);
        registry.add("spring.datasource.password", mysqlContainer::
        getPassword);
    }

    @Test
    public void testPostBySlug() {
        setup();
        Optional<Post> postOptional = postRepository.findBySlug("test");
        Assertions.assertTrue(postOptional.isPresent());
```

```
        Assertions.assertEquals(1L, postOptional.get().getId());
        Assertions.assertEquals("Test", postOptional.get().getTitle());
    }

    private void setup() {
        Post post = new Post();
        post.setId(1L);
        post.setTitle("Test");
        post.setDescription("Test");
        post.setSlug("test");

        postRepository.save(post);
    }
}
```

Reusing the Containers

If you have multiple tests in your test suite, which are dependent on an external system like a database, your tests will start and stop the containers multiple times, leading to higher test execution time. To get over this issue, TestContainers allows you to reuse the existing containers, which helps you with shorter test execution times.

To enable the reuse of containers, follow these steps:

- Add the `.withReuse(true)` method while initializing the container.

- Add the property `testcontainers.reuse.enable=true` to the `testcontainer.properties` file. You must create the file under the home directory of your system.

Singleton Container Pattern

The Singleton Container Pattern provides another way to reuse the containers. You can manually start a container once before the test execution and reuse the same container for subsequent test classes.

```
public abstract class BaseTest {
    static final MySQLContainer<?> MY_SQL_CONTAINER;

    static {
```

```
    MY_SQL_CONTAINER = new MySQLContainer<>(DockerImageName.
    parse("mysql:8.0.29"));
    MY_SQL_CONTAINER.start();
}

@DynamicPropertySource
static void overrideProperties(DynamicPropertyRegistry registry) {
    registry.add("spring.datasource.url", MY_SQL_CONTAINER::getJdbcUrl);
    registry.add("spring.datasource.username", MY_SQL_
    CONTAINER::getUsername);
    registry.add("spring.datasource.password", MY_SQL_
    CONTAINER::getPassword);
}
}
```

Here you created an abstract class called BaseTest, which contains the logic to initialize the container inside a static initializer block manually. The container will be reused for all the tests which inherit the BaseTest class.

Summary

In this chapter, you learned various techniques to test Spring Boot applications. You looked at testing controllers, REST API endpoints, and service-layer methods. Using the Spring Security test module, you also learned how to test secured methods and REST endpoints. You learned how to test the persistence layer using an actual database with the help of the TestContainers library. In the next chapter, you will look at how to create your own Spring Boot Starter.

## CHAPTER 15

GraphQL with Spring Boot

In the previous chapters, you saw how to implement a RESTful API using Spring Boot. This chapter will teach you how to work with GraphQL using Spring Boot.

Introduction to GraphQL

First, let's understand GraphQL and why you need it. GraphQL is a query language that gives you the power to ask exactly what you want as a response from the server and nothing more. When you are already building REST APIs, it's pretty common that some kind of front end like a single page application built with a framework like React, Vue, or Angular or a mobile application will consume this data. As the application grows in size, there will also be new requirements that require your clients to display the data in different shapes and formats. Also, if you want to access multiple resources at once, you must make multiple API calls to the server, leading to slower response times for the application.

Also, suppose you are working with mobile applications. In this case, you must be very careful when defining the required payload, as a typical mobile application cannot handle the same payload as the web browser. For this reason, you may want to set up different endpoints for mobile and normal web users.

GraphQL provides a solution for all these problems by providing a query language where you can mention exactly what you want for a given request from the server. Not only that, but you can also query multiple resources in a single query call. This will be very useful if your front-end application displays multiple kinds of data on a single screen.

You can learn more about GraphQL at `https://graphql.org/`.

You can use a sample query for your Spring Blog application to display all blog posts.

```
query {
```

© K. Siva Prasad Reddy, Sai Upadhyayula 2023
K. S. P. Reddy and S. Upadhyayula, *Beginning Spring Boot 3*, https://doi.org/10.1007/978-1-4842-8792-7_15

```
        allPosts {
            id, title, body, content
        }
    }
```

In this query, you request a method called `allPosts` to return the Post data. Instead of returning the information about all fields, you request exactly four fields: `id, title, body,` and `content`.

In this way, GraphQL provides a very easy-to-use query language. If you want to create, update, or delete data using GraphQL, you must send a Mutation query to the server that looks like the following:

```
mutation {
      createPost(
            postInput: {title: "Spring Boot11", description: "Spring
            Boot11", body: "Spring Boot11",
            slug: "spring_boot11", postStatus: "DRAFT"}
      ) {
          id
          title
          body
      }
    }
```

In this query, you request the `createPost` method on the server, which accepts the required fields as input, and in the response, you can mention exactly which fields you need.

```
    {
        "data": {
            "createPost": {
                "id": "2",
                "title": "Spring Boot11",
                "body": "Spring Boot11"
            }
        }
    }
```

You can also run multiple queries at a time. The following snippet shows two queries, one to read all posts and another to read a post by title:

```
query {
    allPosts {
        id,
        title,
        body
    }
    onePost(title: "Spring Boot1") {
            id
    }
}
```

This query will return the following response:

```
{
  "data": {
    "allPosts": [
      {
        "id": "1",
        "title": "Spring Boot1",
        "body": "Spring Boot1"
      },
      {
        "id": "2",
        "title": "Spring Boot11",
        "body": "Spring Boot11"
      }
    ],
    "onePost": {
      "id": "1"
    }
  }
}
```

Working with GraphQL and Spring Boot

Spring Team released a new module under the Spring Framework project called Spring for GraphQL. It's built on top of the GraphQL Java library, a Java implementation of GraphQL.

Spring for GraphQL provides an additional layer on top of the GraphQL Java library by providing different kinds of `ServerTransport` mechanisms to access the GraphQL Java engine. You can access the GraphQL Java engine via the following three means:

1. HTTP

2. WebSocket

3. RSocket

To work with GraphQL and Spring Boot, let's add the following dependencies to the Spring Blog project. You can find the starter code for this chapter in the GitHub repository.

```
<dependency>
    <groupId>org.springframework.boot</groupId>
    <artifactId>spring-boot-starter-graphql</artifactId>
</dependency>
<dependency>
    <groupId>org.springframework</groupId>
    <artifactId>spring-webflux</artifactId>
    <scope>test</scope>
</dependency>
<dependency>
    <groupId>org.springframework.graphql</groupId>
    <artifactId>spring-graphql-test</artifactId>
    <scope>test</scope>
</dependency>
```

The first dependency, `spring-boot-starter-graphql`, enables Graphql support for your Spring Boot application and auto-configures all the required beans. It also adds a client called GraphiQL UI, which helps you run queries from the browser against your Spring Boot application. Next, the `spring-webflux` and `spring-graphql-test` dependencies to enable testing support for the Graphql endpoints.

After adding the above dependencies, the next step you are going to do is to create a Graphql schema file inside the `src/main/resources` folder.

In the previous section, you saw how different queries look, but how do you know what fields are available for a resource to request? You simply define a schema document in GraphQL, which lists all the different types of queries a client can make to the server, and as part of the schema, it will also list all the fields the server will expose.

Go ahead and create a file called `schema.graphqls` inside the `src/main/resources` folder.

```
type Query {
    allPosts: [PostPayload]
    onePost(title: String): PostPayload
}

type Mutation {
    createPost(postInput: PostInput): PostPayload,
    updatePost(postInput: PostInput): PostPayload
    deletePost(title: String): String
}
input PostInput {
    id: ID
    title: String
    description: String
    body: String
    slug: String
    postStatus: String
}

type PostPayload {
    id: ID
    title: String
    description: String
    body: String
    slug: String
    postStatus: String
}
```

Make sure to install the required plugins in your favorite IDE to enable features like auto-completion while working with GraphQL schema files.

In the above schema document, you can observe two types available: a Query type and a Mutation type.

You can use a Query type when you simply want to query the data from the server.

A Mutation type is used when you want to mutate the data in the server, which means performing operations like Create, Update, and Delete.

In the above query, you define the queries for the Query and Mutation types by using the `PostInput` object as an input, which means all the mutation operations will take `PostInput` as the input object (i.e., DTO in your application).

You also define an object called `PostPayload`, which acts as the output type. In GraphQL, you cannot define a single object as both input and output type.

Each field inside the object can be of type String, ID, Int, Float, or Boolean. If you want to define any other custom data type, like date, you must set it up manually.

Creating a GraphQL Controller

Go ahead and create a class called `PostGraphQLController` under the `controller` folder. This class contains the familiar `@Controller` annotation, which defines it as a normal Spring bean. There is no need to add the `@RequestMapping` annotation for this class because you will use a dedicated mapping annotation called `@SchemaMapping` when working with GraphQL.

If you want to write an endpoint to read all the posts, the code is as follows:

```
@SchemaMapping(typeName = "Query", value = "allPosts")
public List<PostInput> findAllPosts() {
    return postService.findAllPosts();
}
```

Using the `@SchemaMapping` annotation, you define the required `typeName` as either Query or Mutation, and for the value, you can provide the name of the operation defined inside the schema document.

The `@SchemaMapping` annotation is similar to the `@RequestMapping` annotation when working with RESTful-based APIs. There are specialized annotations like `@GetMapping` and `@PostMapping` while working with RESTful APIs. In the GraphQL world, there are annotations like `@QueryMapping` and `@MutationMapping`.

Listing 15-1 contains the complete code for the PostGraphQLController.java class.

Listing 15-1. PostGraphQLController.java

```java
package com.apress.demo.springblog.controller;

import com.apress.demo.springblog.dto.PostInput;
import com.apress.demo.springblog.service.PostService;
import lombok.RequiredArgsConstructor;
import org.springframework.graphql.data.method.annotation.Argument;
import org.springframework.graphql.data.method.annotation.MutationMapping;
import org.springframework.graphql.data.method.annotation.QueryMapping;
import org.springframework.stereotype.Controller;

import java.util.List;

@Controller
@RequiredArgsConstructor
public class PostGraphqlController {
    private final PostService postService;

    @QueryMapping
    public List<PostInput> allPosts() {
        return postService.findAllPosts();
    }

    @QueryMapping
    public PostInput onePost(@Argument String title) {
        return postService.findOnePost(title);
    }

    @MutationMapping
    public PostInput createPost(@Argument PostInput postInput) {
        return postService.createPost(postInput);
    }

    @MutationMapping
    public PostInput updatePost(@Argument PostInput postInput) {
        return postService.updatePost(postInput);
    }
```

```
@MutationMapping
public String deletePost(@Argument String title) {
    postService.deletePost(title);
    return title;
}
}
```

You have the @Argument annotation that reads the method argument you will receive as part of the request. If you do not add that annotation, Spring Boot will not understand the request and will throw an exception.

Since you are using a Service layer, all the business logic is stored inside the PostService.java class, so all you have to do is add a separate controller class to work with GraphQL in your Spring Boot application.

Enabling GraphiQL UI Client

Before you test your implementation, let's add the below property to your application. properties file to enable the GraphiQL UI client, which provides a nice UI to run your queries and work with GraphQL:

```
spring.graphql.graphiql.enabled=true
```

Once you start the application, open the browser and go to the URL http:// localhost:8080/graphiql. You can see the expected output in Figure 15-1.

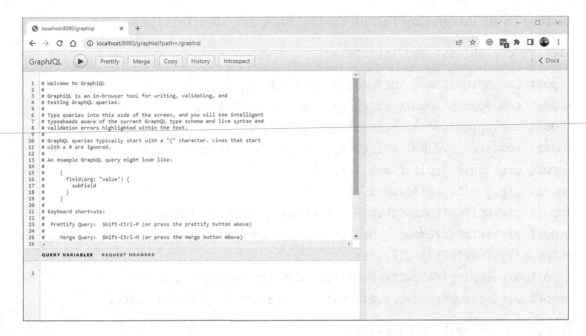

Figure 15-1. *GraphiQL UI client*

The GraphiQL client provides an editor where you can type in the GraphQL queries and request your Spring Boot application. You can test out the queries you defined in the first section to understand how to work with GraphQL.

Testing Support in Spring for GraphQL

Spring for GraphQL supports testing GraphQL requests over HTTP, WebSocket, and RSocket. To enable this support, you must add the `spring-graphql-test` dependency to your `pom.xml` file, which you already did.

Spring for GraphQL provides an interface called `GraphQLTester`, which provides multiple implementations like `HttpGraphQLTester` for HTTP communication, `WebsocketGraphQLTester` for WebSockets, and `RSocketGraphQLTester` for RSocket.

Let's see how to write an integration test that spins up a Spring Boot application context and makes requests to the server using the `HttpGraphQLTester` class, as shown in Listing 15-2.

Listing 15-2. Integration Test for SpringblogApplicationTests.java

```java
package com.apress.demo.springblog;

import com.apress.demo.springblog.domain.Post;
import com.apress.demo.springblog.domain.PostStatus;
import com.apress.demo.springblog.dto.PostInput;
import com.apress.demo.springblog.repository.PostRepository;
import org.junit.jupiter.api.BeforeEach;
import org.junit.jupiter.api.Test;
import org.springframework.beans.factory.annotation.Autowired;
import org.springframework.boot.test.autoconfigure.graphql.tester.
AutoConfigureHttpGraphQlTester;
import org.springframework.boot.test.context.SpringBootTest;
import org.springframework.graphql.test.tester.HttpGraphQlTester;

import java.time.LocalDateTime;

import static org.junit.jupiter.api.Assertions.assertEquals;
import static org.junit.jupiter.api.Assertions.assertFalse;

@SpringBootTest(webEnvironment = SpringBootTest.WebEnvironment.RANDOM_PORT)
@AutoConfigureHttpGraphQlTester
class SpringblogApplicationTests {

    @Autowired
    private HttpGraphQlTester httpGraphQlTester;

    @Autowired
    private PostRepository postRepository;

    @BeforeEach
    public void setup() {
        // Setup clean Test Data
        postRepository.deleteAll();
        Post post = new Post(1L, "Title", "Description", "Body", "title",
                PostStatus.DRAFT, LocalDateTime.now(), LocalDateTime.
                now(), null);
        postRepository.save(post);
    }
```

```java
@Test
void shouldFindAllPosts() {

    // language=GraphQL
    String document = """
            query {
                allPosts {
                    id,
                    title,
                    body
                }
            }
        """;

    httpGraphQlTester.document(document)
        .execute()
        .path("allPosts")
        .entityList(PostInput.class)
        .hasSize(1);
}

@Test
void shouldFindOnePost() {
    // language=GraphQL
    String document = """
            query {
                onePost(title: "Title") {
                    id
                    title
                    body
                }
            }
        """;

    PostInput expectedPost = new PostInput(1L, "Title", "Content",
    "Body", "title", PostStatus.DRAFT);
```

335

```java
httpGraphQlTester.document(document)
        .execute()
        .path("onePost")
        .entity(PostInput.class)
        .satisfies(postDto -> {
            assertEquals(expectedPost.getTitle(), postDto.getTitle());
            assertEquals(expectedPost.getBody(), postDto.getBody());
        });
}

@Test
void shouldCreatePost() {
    // language=GraphQL
    String document = """
            mutation {
           createPost(
            postInput: { title: "Spring Boot11", description: "Spring
            Boot11", body: "Spring Boot11",\s
            slug: "spring_boot11", postStatus: "DRAFT" }
                    ) {
                        id
                        title
                        body
                    }

                    }
        """;

    PostInput expectedPost = new PostInput(2L, "Spring Boot11", "Spring
Boot11", "Spring Boot11",
        "spring_boot11", PostStatus.DRAFT);

    httpGraphQlTester.document(document)
            .execute()
            .path("createPost")
            .entity(PostInput.class)
```

```java
        .satisfies(postDto -> {
          assertEquals(expectedPost.getTitle(), postDto.getTitle());
          assertEquals(expectedPost.getBody(), postDto.getBody());
        });
}

@Test
void shouldUpdatePost() {
    // language=GraphQL
    String document = """
            mutation {
               updatePost(postInput: {id:1,title: "Title 1",
               description: "GraphQL Spring Boot Updated", body: "Spring
               Boot11",slug: "spring_boot11",
               postStatus: "DRAFT" }) {
                  id
                  title
                  body
               }
            }
            """;

    PostInput expectedPost = new PostInput(1L, "Title 1", "GraphQL Spring
    Boot Updated", "Spring Boot11",
            null, PostStatus.DRAFT);

    httpGraphQlTester.document(document)
        .execute()
        .path("updatePost")
        .entity(PostInput.class)
        .satisfies(postDto -> {
          assertEquals(expectedPost.getTitle(), postDto.getTitle());
          assertEquals(expectedPost.getBody(), postDto.getBody());
        });
}
```

```java
@Test
void shouldDeletePost() {
    // language=GraphQL
    String document = """
            mutation {
                deletePost(title: "Title")
            }
            """;

    httpGraphQlTester.document(document)
            .execute()
            .path("deletePost")
            .entity(String.class)
            .satisfies(title -> assertEquals("Title", title));

    assertFalse(postRepository.findByTitle("Title").isPresent());
}

}
```

- First is the `SpringBootTest` annotation, which spins up the whole application context and loads all the necessary beans required to run the application.

- The `@AutoConfigureHttpGraphQlTester` annotation, as the name suggests, auto-configures the `HTTPGraphQLTester`, `WebTestClient`, and `MockMvc` classes, which are useful when working with Spring Webflux and Spring MVC-based applications. Since you are working with a Spring MVC-based application, a `MockMvc` class instance will be auto-configured for you in the test.

- Next, you inject the `HttpGraphQlTester` bean into your test class to make HTTP requests to your Spring Boot back end.

- In the `setup()` method, you set up the initial test data for each test run by deleting the existing data and adding the new post information to the database.

- If you are using IntelliJ and have installed the GraphQL plugin, you can add the comment `//language=GraphQL` to enable GraphQL query auto-completion inside the test methods.

- In the `shouldFIndAllPosts()` test method, you define the query you want to execute using the multi-line string. You then pass the query to the `httpGraphQlTester` object, which executes your query and verifies whether a single post is coming as a response from the request.

- Similarly, you have test methods for the Read, Update, and Delete operations. As you can see in the `shouldCreatePost()` and `shouldUpdatePost()` methods, you can define custom assertions inside the `satisfies()` method from `httpGraphQlTester` object.

Summary

In this chapter, you learned about GraphQL and the advantages of using it. You developed a simple API that serves the GraphQL requests and integration tests using the Spring for GraphQL project. In the next chapter, you will learn how to build and run your Spring Boot applications natively using the Spring Native project.

CHAPTER 16

Deploying Spring Boot Applications

Spring Boot supports embedded servlet containers, which makes deploying applications much easier because you don't need an external application server setup. You can simply package your Spring Boot application as a JAR module and run it using the `java -jar` command. However, you need to consider a few things while running applications in a production environment.

You can use profiles to externalize configuration properties per environment and run your application, activating desired profiles. But you don't want to specify sensitive data in configuration properties and commit it in the source code. Spring Boot provides various mechanisms to override the configuration properties when starting the application.

Containerization technologies like Docker have become popular for running applications in both development and production environments. In complex applications, you may need to run multiple services like databases, search engines, and log monitoring tools. You can use Docker to spin up multiple containers with all the required services without installing them locally.

In this chapter, you'll look into how to run Spring Boot applications in production mode and override configuration properties. You will also look at deploying Spring Boot applications on the Heroku cloud platform. Finally, you will learn about running Spring Boot applications on Docker containers.

© K. Siva Prasad Reddy, Sai Upadhyayula 2023
K. S. P. Reddy and S. Upadhyayula, *Beginning Spring Boot 3*, https://doi.org/10.1007/978-1-4842-8792-7_16

Running Spring Boot Applications in Production Mode

Spring Boot applications with JAR-type packaging are self-contained applications that can run quickly and don't require any external application server setup. Once the application is packaged as a JAR, run the application as follows:

```
java -jar app.jar
```

As discussed in Chapter 3, you can have multiple profile configuration files, such as `application-qa.properties` and `application-prod.properties`, and you can activate the desired profiles using the `spring.profiles.active` system property. Suppose you configured the datasource properties in the `dev` and `prod` profile configuration files, as shown in Listing 16-1.

Listing 16-1. src/main/resources/application-dev.properties

```
spring.datasource.driver-class-name=com.mysql.jdbc.Driver
spring.datasource.url=jdbc:mysql://localhost:3306/myapp
spring.datasource.username=root
spring.datasource.password=admin
```

Listing 16-2 shows how to configure your local MySQL server properties for the `dev` profile.

Listing 16-2. src/main/resources/application-prod.properties

```
spring.datasource.driver-class-name=com.mysql.jdbc.Driver
spring.datasource.url=jdbc:mysql://prodmysqlsrv:3306/myapp
spring.datasource.username=appuser
spring.datasource.password=S3*(Hi)@32vi
```

The Listing 16-2 configuration points to remote MySQL server properties for the `prod` profile.

Now you can run the application in production by activating the `prod` profile as follows:

```
java -jar -Dspring.profiles.active=prod app.jar
```

Suppose you have Spring components that should be activated only when running in a cloud environment. In that case, you can activate multiple profiles by specifying a comma-separated list of profile names.

```
java -jar -Dspring.profiles.active=prod,cloud app.jar
```

By activating the `prod` and `cloud` profiles, Spring Boot will activate all the default profile components (i.e., components not associated with any specific environment) and components associated with the `prod` and `cloud` profiles. But you don't want to configure sensitive information like actual production server credentials in these properties files and commit them to version control systems.

Spring Boot allows you to override the configuration parameters in various ways. You can override the properties using system properties as follows:

```
java -jar -Dserver.port=8585 app.jar
```

By specifying system properties, even if you configure the `server.port` property in the `application-*.properties`, files will be overridden with `server.port=8585,` and the application will start on port 8585. Specifying a long list of properties like this can be cumbersome, so Spring Boot provides another mechanism to override the properties.

You can load the properties from multiple locations. `SpringApplication` will load properties from the `application-*.properties` files in the following locations:

- A classpath `/config` package
- The classpath root
- The current directory
- A `/config` subdirectory of the current directory
- Immediate child directories of the `/config` subdirectory

The properties defined in the top location take precedence over those defined in lower locations.

Suppose you have the `app.jar` in the `/home/appserver/app1.0/` directory from which you run the application using the `java -jar` command.

You can create an `application-prod.properties` file in the `/home/appserver/app1.0/config` directory, which overrides the properties defined in the `application-prod.properties` file in the classpath. You can configure all the default properties in the `src/main/resources/application-*.properties` files and override them using the `config/application-*properties` file while running the application.

Note that you should not commit the `config/application-*.properties` files into version control systems because they contain sensitive configuration details.

Spring Boot also supports running applications as native executable services on Unix-based systems or as a Windows service. For more information on installing Spring Boot applications as services, read `http://docs.spring.io/spring-boot/docs/ current/reference/htmlsingle/#deployment-install`.

Deploying Spring Boot Application on Heroku

Heroku (`www.heroku.com/`) is a Platform as a Service (PaaS) that enables developers to build and run applications in the cloud. Heroku supports various programming languages including Ruby, Java, NodeJS, Python, PHP, Scala, and Go.

This section teaches how to deploy a Spring Boot application on Heroku. First, familiarize yourself with Heroku by reading the "Getting Started on Heroku with Java" guide at `https://devcenter.heroku.com/articles/getting-started-with- java#introduction`.

Create an account on Heroku and install the Heroku command line interface based on your operating system.

You can create an application using the `heroku create` command, which will automatically create a GIT remote (called `heroku`) and associate it with your local GIT repository.

Another option is to host your application code on a GitHub repository and link that repository to your Heroku application. This chapter follows the second approach.

1. Create a repository on GitHub.

    Create an account on GitHub, if you don't have one, and create a repository named `springboot-heroku-demo`. I created a repository at `https://github.com/SaiUpadhyayula/springboot- heroku-demo`.

2. Create a Spring Boot application.

    You will create a simple Spring Boot application with the Web and Data-JPA starters. You will use the Postgres database, which is a free add-on for your application. See Listing 16-3.

Listing 16-3. pom.xml

```xml
<?xml version="1.0" encoding="UTF-8"?>
<project xmlns="http://maven.apache.org/POM/4.0.0" xmlns:xsi="http://www.
w3.org/2001/XMLSchema-instance"
xsi:schemaLocation="http://maven.apache.org/POM/4.0.0 https://maven.apache.
org/xsd/maven-4.0.0.xsd">
  <modelVersion>4.0.0</modelVersion>
  <parent>
     <groupId>org.springframework.boot</groupId>
     <artifactId>spring-boot-starter-parent</artifactId>
     <version>3.0.0-SNAPSHOT</version>
     <relativePath/> <!-- lookup parent from repository -->
  </parent>
  <groupId>com.apress</groupId>
  <artifactId>springboot-heroku-demo</artifactId>
  <version>0.0.1-SNAPSHOT</version>
  <name>springboot-heroku-demo</name>
  <description>Demo project for Spring Boot</description>
  <properties>
     <java.version>17</java.version>
  </properties>
  <dependencies>
     <dependency>
        <groupId>org.springframework.boot</groupId>
        <artifactId>spring-boot-starter-data-jpa</artifactId>
     </dependency>
     <dependency>
        <groupId>org.springframework.boot</groupId>
        <artifactId>spring-boot-starter-thymeleaf</artifactId>
     </dependency>
     <dependency>
        <groupId>org.springframework.boot</groupId>
        <artifactId>spring-boot-starter-web</artifactId>
     </dependency>
```

```xml
    <dependency>
        <groupId>com.h2database</groupId>
        <artifactId>h2</artifactId>
        <scope>runtime</scope>
    </dependency>
    <dependency>
        <groupId>org.postgresql</groupId>
        <artifactId>postgresql</artifactId>
        <scope>runtime</scope>
    </dependency>
    <dependency>
        <groupId>org.springframework.boot</groupId>
        <artifactId>spring-boot-starter-test</artifactId>
        <scope>test</scope>
    </dependency>
</dependencies>

<build>
    <plugins>
        <plugin>
            <groupId>org.springframework.boot</groupId>
            <artifactId>spring-boot-maven-plugin</artifactId>
        </plugin>
    </plugins>
</build>
<repositories>
    <repository>
        <id>spring-milestones</id>
        <name>Spring Milestones</name>
        <url>https://repo.spring.io/milestone</url>
        <snapshots>
            <enabled>false</enabled>
        </snapshots>
    </repository>
    <repository>
        <id>spring-snapshots</id>
```

```
            <name>Spring Snapshots</name>
            <url>https://repo.spring.io/snapshot</url>
            <releases>
                <enabled>false</enabled>
            </releases>
        </repository>
    </repositories>
    <pluginRepositories>
        <pluginRepository>
            <id>spring-milestones</id>
            <name>Spring Milestones</name>
            <url>https://repo.spring.io/milestone</url>
            <snapshots>
                <enabled>false</enabled>
            </snapshots>
        </pluginRepository>
        <pluginRepository>
            <id>spring-snapshots</id>
            <name>Spring Snapshots</name>
            <url>https://repo.spring.io/snapshot</url>
            <releases>
                <enabled>false</enabled>
            </releases>
        </pluginRepository>
    </pluginRepositories>
</project>
```

3. Create a JPA entity and a Spring Data repository.

    Now create a simple JPA entity called User and a Spring Data
    JPA repository called UserRepository, as shown in Listings 16-4
    and 16-5.

Listing 16-4. User.java

```
@Entity
@Table(name="USERS")
public class User
{
    @Id
    @GeneratedValue(strategy = GenerationType.IDENTITY)
    private long id;
    private String name;
    //setters & getters
}
```

Listing 16-5. UserRepository.java

```
@Repository
public interface UserRepository extends JpaRepository<User, Long>
{
}
```

4. Configure the datasource properties.

Since you have the H2 database driver in the classpath, if you don't configure any datasource properties, Spring Boot will create an in-memory datasource. While running the application locally, you can configure datasource properties by pointing to your local Postgres database in src/main/resources/application-dev. properties, as shown in Listing 16-6.

Listing 16-6. src/main/resources/application-dev.properties

```
spring.datasource.url=jdbc:postgresql://localhost:5432/demodb
spring.datasource.driver-class-name=org.postgresql.Driver
spring.datasource.username=postgres
spring.datasource.password=secret123
spring.datasource.tomcat.max-active=10
spring.datasource.tomcat.max-idle=5
spring.datasource.tomcat.min-idle=2
```

```
spring.datasource.tomcat.initial-size=5
spring.datasource.tomcat.remove-abandoned=true
spring.jpa.hibernate.ddl-auto=update
```

But when deploying on Heroku, you must use the Postgres database provided by the Heroku platform. Configure the datasource properties in `src/main/resources/application-heroku.properties`, as shown in Listing 16-7, and enable the heroku profile.

Listing 16-7. src/main/resources/application-heroku.properties

```
spring.datasource.url=${JDBC_DATABASE_URL}
spring.datasource.driver-class-name=org.postgresql.Driver
spring.datasource.tomcat.max-active=10
spring.datasource.tomcat.max-idle=5
spring.datasource.tomcat.min-idle=2
spring.datasource.tomcat.initial-size=5
spring.datasource.tomcat.remove-abandoned=true
spring.jpa.hibernate.ddl-auto=update
```

JDBC_DATABASE_URL is an environment variable that's generated dynamically by pointing to the Postgres database server. You can check the value of the JDBC_DATABASE_URL environment variable by running the following command:

```
heroku run echo \$JDBC_DATABASE_URL
```

5. Initialize the database with sample data. This example uses a SQL script to populate sample user data, as shown in Listing 16-8.

Listing 16-8. src/main/resources/data.sql

```
delete from users;
insert into users(id,name) values (1, 'Admin');
insert into users(id,name) values (2, 'Test');
```

6. Create a controller to display the users.

    Listing 16-9 shows how to create a SpringMVC request handler
    method to display a list of users.

Listing 16-9. HomeController.java

```java
@Controller
public class HomeController
{
    private UserRepository repository;
    @Autowired
    public HomeController(UserRepository repository) {
        this.repository = repository;
    }
    @GetMapping("/")
    public String home(Model model) {
        List<User> users = repository.findAll();
        model.addAttribute("users", users);
        return "home";
    }
}
```

7. Create a Thymeleaf view to render the users list, as shown in
    Listing 16-10.

Listing 16-10. src/main/resources/templates/home.html

```html
<!DOCTYPE HTML>
<html xmlns:th="http://www.thymeleaf.org">
<head>
    <title>SpringBoot Heroku Demo</title>
</head>
<body>
    <table>
        <thead>
            <tr>
                <th>List of Users</th>
```

```
            </tr>
        </thead>
        <tbody>
            <tr th:each="user : ${users}">
                <td th:text="${user.name}">user name</td>
            </tr>
        </tbody>
    </table>
</body>
</html>
```

8. Create a `Procfile`.

   In order to run an application on Heroku, you need to create a
   `Procfile` in the root directory of the project. The `Procfile` is a
   text file that declares what command should be executed to start
   your application. Add the command shown in Listing 16-11 in the
   `Procfile` to run your Spring Boot application.

Listing 16-11. Procfile in Project Root Directory

```
web java -Dserver.port=$PORT -Dspring.profiles.active=heroku
$JAVA_OPTS -jar target/springboot-heroku-demo.jar
```

> Note that the code configures the `server.port` property as a
> system property using -Dserver.port=$PORT, where the $PORT
> value is provided by Heroku dynamically. The code enables
> the heroku profile by specifying the -Dspring.profiles.
> active=heroku system property.

Now that you have the application code ready, you must create an application on
Heroku and link to the GitHub repository.

Go to www.heroku.com/ and log in with your credentials. After a successful login,
you will be redirected to the dashboard. On the dashboard page, you can click the New
button on the top-right corner and select Create New App. There you can provide the
app name and select the region where your application should be available.

If you don't provide an app name, Heroku will generate a random name. Enter the application name and click Create New App; it will take you to the application's Deploy configuration screen.

Click the Resources tab and search for Postgres Add-on. Add the Heroku Postgres database. Click the Deploy tab and click GitHub in the Deployment Method section.

Once you have connected your Heroku account to GitHub successfully, search for the GitHub repository you want to connect and click Connect.

Now you can click Deploy Branch to deploy your application on Heroku. You can also enable automatic deployment of your application whenever you push changes to the GitHub repository by clicking the Enable Automatic Deploys button.

Once the application is deployed, you can click the Open App button in the top-right corner, which will open your application home page in a new tab. If something goes wrong or you want to check the logs, choose More > View Logs. You can also view logs from the terminal by running the following command:

```
heroku logs --tail --app <application_name>
```

To learn more about the Heroku platform, visit `https://devcenter.heroku.com/`.

Running a Spring Boot Application on Docker

Docker (`www.docker.com/`) is an open source platform for packaging and running applications. Docker is popular because it enables quick packaging and runs the application in lightweight containers with the required dependencies installed and configured.

First, you should familiarize yourself with some Docker terminology.

- A *Docker image* is a blueprint from which you can create a container. For example, there is a Docker Ubuntu image from which you can create a container and perform actions like on any Ubuntu OS.

- A *Docker container* is an instance of a Docker image that can be started, stopped, paused, and restarted. Each Docker container is assigned a unique identifier.

- A *Docker host* is the host operating system from which you spin up the Docker containers.

- A *Docker hub* is a cloud-based registry service that hosts plenty of free Docker images that you can use. You can also build your image and publish them.

You can create Docker containers using various commands, but you can also use a Dockerfile. A Dockerfile contains the instructions on building the Docker image so that you can easily repeat the image-building process on any machine.

Installing Docker

Docker is a rapidly evolving technology so the installation process may change over time. I strongly recommend you refer to the official Docker installation documentation at https://docs.docker.com/engine/install/ to install Docker based on your operating system. Once Docker is installed, you can determine whether the installation is successful by running the following command:

```
sudo docker info
```

If the installation is successful, you should be able to see various details about Docker.

Listing 16-12 shows a sample `Dockerfile`.

Listing 16-12. Sample Dockerfile

```
# Base image is Ubuntu
FROM ubuntu:22.10
# Author: Siva
MAINTAINER Siva <sivaprasadreddy.k@gmail.com>
# Install apache2 package
RUN apt-get update && apt-get install -y apache2 && apt-get clean
# run command on startup
CMD ["echo", "Dockerfile demo"]
```

This file creates a base image called `ubuntu:22.10` by using the `FROM` command. You can optionally provide author details using the `MAINTAINER` command.

Next, the code runs the commands to install the `apache2` web server using the `RUN` command, which will be executed during the image-building time.

Finally, the code runs the echo command with the Dockerfile demo argument using the CMD command. You can use the CMD command to specify which command should be executed when you launch the container. You can override the CMD command while launching the container by specifying the command as an argument to the docker run command.

You should have only one CMD command in a Dockerfile. Even if you specify multiple CMD commands, Docker will consider only the last one.

You can use the docker build command to build an image from Dockerfile and tag it with a name using the -t flag. Run the following command from the same directory as the Dockerfile:

```
sudo docker build -t my-apache2 .
```

Note the dot at the end of the command. This indicates the location of Dockerfile, which is the current directory.

You can use the docker images command to list all available images locally.

Now you can launch a container from the my-apache2 image by using the docker run command as follows:

```
sudo docker run my-apache2
```

This command should print Dockerfile demo on the console.

You can use the sudo docker ps command to display the running container details.

Now that you have a basic understanding of how to work with Docker, you will see how to package and run a Spring Boot application in a Docker container in the next section.

Running a Spring Boot Application in a Docker Container

You will use the application you built for deploying Spring Boot on Heroku in the previous section. Create Dockerfile in the root of the project, as follows:

```
FROM openjdk:17.0.2-jdk
ADD target/springboot-heroku-demo.jar app.jar
RUN bash -c 'touch /app.jar'
ENTRYPOINT ["java","-Djava.security.egd=file:/dev/./urandom","-jar","/
app.jar"]
```

This code uses openjdk:17.0.2-jdk as the base image. It copies target/ springboot-heroku-demo.jar into the target image with the name app.jar. Finally, it invokes the java -jar app.jar command using ENTRYPOINT.

Before building the Docker image, you first need to build the application.

```
springboot-heroku-demo> mvn clean package
```

Now you can run the docker build command as follows:

```
docker build -t sivaprasadreddy/springboot-heroku-demo .
```

Here, you are tagging the image with the name sivaprasadreddy/springboot-heroku-demo. Since you haven't activated any profiles, the default profile will be active and the application will use the H2 in-memory database.

Now launch the container from the sivaprasadreddy/springboot-heroku-demo image, as follows.

```
docker run -d \
            --name springboot-heroku-demo \
            -p 80:8080 \
            sivaprasadreddy/springboot-heroku-demo
```

You are running the container by giving it the name springboot-heroku-demo and exposing the container's port 8080 on the Docker host machine at port 80.

Now you'll see how to launch a Postgres database in one Docker container and then launch the application in another container using the Postgres database from the first container.

You can launch a Postgres database container by using the postgres image, as follows:

```
docker run --name demo-postgres \
        -e POSTGRES_DB=demodb  \
        -e POSTGRES_USER=postgres \
        -e POSTGRES_PASSWORD=secret123 \
        -d postgres
```

This code launches a postgres container in detached mode by using the -d flag and gives it the name demo-postgres. It also specifies the database name, username, and password as environment variables by using -e flags.

Now you create the Docker profile configuration file `application-docker.properties`, as follows:

```
spring.datasource.driver-class-name=org.postgresql.Driver
spring.datasource.url=jdbc:postgresql://${POSTGRES_PORT_5432_TCP_
ADDR}:${POSTGRES_PORT_5432_TCP_PORT}/demodb
spring.datasource.username=${POSTGRES_ENV_POSTGRES_USER}
spring.datasource.password=${POSTGRES_ENV_POSTGRES_PASSWORD}
spring.jpa.hibernate.ddl-auto=update
```

You can modify the `Dockerfile` to run the application by activating the `docker` profile.

```
FROM openjdk:17.0.2-jdk
ADD target/springboot-heroku-demo.jar app.jar
RUN bash -c 'touch /app.jar'
ENTRYPOINT ["java","-Djava.security.egd=file:/dev/./urandom","-Dspring.
profiles.active=docker","-jar","/app.jar"]
```

Note that the code specifies `-Dspring.profiles.active=docker` to activate the docker profile so that the application will use the Postgres database running in another Docker container instead of using the H2 in-memory database.

Now build the project using the `mvn clean package` command and build your application Docker image.

```
docker build -t sivaprasadreddy/springboot-heroku-demo .
```

Before launching your container, you need to delete the existing container. You can remove the existing container as follows:

```
sudo docker rm springboot-heroku-demo
```

You need to link the application's Docker container with the `demo-postgres` Docker container in order to be able to use the Postgres database from the application.

Launch the application container using the following command:

```
docker run -d \
        --name springboot-heroku-demo \
        --link demo-postgres:postgres \
        -p 80:8080 \
        sivaprasadreddy/springboot-heroku-demo
```

Note that you linked the `demo-postgres` container using the `--link` flag and gave it an alias called `postgres`. Now the application is running in one container and is talking to the Postgres database running in another container.

Creating Layered Docker Images

The Docker image created above has some disadvantages. It is unnecessarily large because it contains the full JDK of OpenJDK 17 and other tools that are part of the JDK. But you only need the Java Runtime Environment to run your application, so you can only pull in the JRE used to run your Spring Boot application.

Next, Spring Boot provides the option to create optimized Docker images by enabling the layering of the Docker image. Docker images, in general, are built in the form of layers. With the present setup, you are creating one big layer, which will be rebuilt for each small change in your Spring Boot application.

For this reason, you can divide your Spring Boot application image into different layers, where the first layer contains the files that are changed the least (example files are related to the libraries) and the last layer contains the files that are changed frequently (example files include the application code).

Spring Boot will package your application into different folders like the following:

- `dependencies`: This folder contains all the application's dependencies.

- `spring-boot-loader`: This folder contains classes that understand how to start your Spring Boot Application.

- `snapshot-dependencies`: This folder contains snapshot dependencies if there are any.

- `application`: This folder contains all the classes that are part of the application.

Most of the changes happen in the `application` folder, so you can create a layer for each folder to create an optimized docker image.

You can find the updated Docker image as part of Listing 16-13.

Listing 16-13. Updated Dockerfile

```
# Stage 1
FROM eclipse-temurin:17-jre-focal as builder
WORKDIR extracted
ADD ./target/*.jar app.jar
RUN java -Djarmode=layertools -jar app.jar extract

#Stage 2
FROM eclipse-temurin:17-jre-focal
WORKDIR application
COPY --from=builder extracted/dependencies/ ./
COPY --from=builder extracted/spring-boot-loader/ ./
COPY --from=builder extracted/snapshot-dependencies/ ./
COPY --from=builder extracted/application/ ./
EXPOSE 8080
ENTRYPOINT ["java", "org.springframework.boot.loader.JarLauncher"]
```

You are using a multi-stage build in Docker to define different stages while creating the Docker image. In the first stage, as mentioned, you replace the OpenJDK 17 with a JRE 17 base image, and you extract the folders inside the JAR by using the `extract` command and passing the `jarmode` as `layertools`.

In the next stage, you copy all the extracted layers into a parent folder called `application`. This way, you can create an optimized Docker image while containerizing your Spring Boot application.

Using Cloud-Native Buildpacks

In the previous section, you saw how to create an optimized Docker image by using multi-stage builds.

Spring Boot also provides the option to build the Docker images using buildpacks through a Maven or Gradle plugin. A buildpack is nothing but a set of programs that scans your source code and creates a plan to build and run your application. Cloud platforms like Heroku and Cloudfoundry use buildpacks to build and run the applications automatically.

You can use the `build-image` goal of `spring-boot-maven-plugin` to build an OCI-compliant Docker image.

```xml
<build>
    <plugins>
        <plugin>
            <groupId>org.springframework.boot</groupId>
            <artifactId>spring-boot-maven-plugin</artifactId>
            <executions>
                <execution>
                    <goals>
                        <goal>build-image</goal>
                    </goals>
                </execution>
            </executions>
        </plugin>
    </plugins>
</build>
```

After adding the above goal to the plugin, you can create the Docker image by running the command mvn `spring-boot:build-image`.

As an alternative, you can also use a library called Jib, which is a library created by Google to create Docker images without using the `Dockerfile`. You can read more about it at `https://cloud.google.com/java/getting-started/jib`.

Running Multiple Containers Using docker-compose

If your application depends on multiple services and you need to start all of them in Docker containers, it is tedious to start them individually. You can use the `docker-compose` tool to orchestrate the multiple containers required to run your application. You need to create a `docker-compose.yml` file and configure the services that you want to run.

Create `docker-compose.yml` in the root directory of your application, as shown in Listing 16-14.

Listing 16-14. docker-compose.yml

```
demo-postgres:
  image: postgres:latest
  environment:
    - POSTGRES_DB=demodb
    - POSTGRES_USER=postgres
    - POSTGRES_PASSWORD=secret123
springboot-heroku-demo:
  image: sivaprasadreddy/springboot-heroku-demo
  links:
    - demo-postgres:postgres
  ports:
    - 80:8080
```

Now you can simply run the `docker-compose up` command from the directory where you have the `docker-compose.yml` file to start the application and the Postgres containers.

To learn more about Docker, visit `https://docs.docker.com/`.

Summary

This chapter discussed how to run your production applications and deploy a Spring Boot application on the Heroku cloud platform. You also learned about running Spring Boot applications on the Docker container.

## CHAPTER 17

Spring Boot Autoconfiguration

The Spring Boot autoconfiguration mechanism heavily depends on the `@Conditional` feature. This chapter explores how you can conditionally register Spring beans using the `@Conditional` annotation and create various types of `Conditional` implementations meeting certain criteria. Then you will look into how Spring Boot leverages the `@Conditional` feature to configure beans automatically based on certain criteria.

Exploring the Power of @Conditional

While developing Spring-based applications, you may come across a need to register beans conditionally. For example, you may want to register a `DataSource` bean pointing to the `DEV` database when running applications locally and point to a different `PRODUCTION` database while running in production.

You can externalize the database connection parameters into property files and use the appropriate file for the environment. But you must change the configuration whenever you need to point to a different environment and redeploy the application.

To address this issue, Spring 3.1 introduced the concept of *profiles*. You can register multiple beans of the same type and associate them with one or more profiles. You can activate the desired profile(s) when you run the application. This way, Spring Boot will register only the beans associated with the activated profiles.

```
@Configuration
public class AppConfig
{
    @Bean
    @Profile("DEV")
```

© K. Siva Prasad Reddy, Sai Upadhyayula 2023
K. S. P. Reddy and S. Upadhyayula, *Beginning Spring Boot 3*, https://doi.org/10.1007/978-1-4842-8792-7_17

```
    public DataSource devDataSource() {
        ...
    }
    @Bean
    @Profile("PROD")
    public DataSource prodDataSource() {
        ...
    }
}
```

With this configuration, you can specify the active profile using the -Dspring.
profiles.active=DEV system property. This approach works fine for simple cases, such
as when you're enabling or disabling bean registrations based on activated profiles. But
if you want to register beans based on some conditional logic, the profiles approach is
insufficient.

To provide much more flexibility for registering Spring beans conditionally, Spring 4
introduced the concept of the @Conditional. Using the @Conditional approach, you can
register a bean conditionally based on any arbitrary condition.

For example, you may want to register a bean when

- A specific class is present in the classpath

- A Spring bean of a certain type isn't already registered in the
  ApplicationContext

- A specific file exists in a location

- A specific property value is configured in a configuration file

- A specific system property is present or absent

These are just a few examples, and you can set up any condition you want. The next
section looks at how Spring's @Conditional works.

Using @Conditional Based on System Properties

Suppose you have a UserDAO interface with methods to get data from a datastore.
You have two implementations of the UserDAO interface: JdbcUserDAO talks to the
MySQL database and MongoUserDAO talks to MongoDB. You may want to enable only
JdbcUserDAO or MongoUserDAO based on a specific system property, say dbType.

If the application starts using java -jar myapp.jar -DdbType=MySQL, you want to enable JdbcUserDAO; otherwise, if the application starts using java -jar myapp.jar -Ddb Type=MONGO, you want to enable MongoUserDAO.

Suppose you have the UserDAO interface and the JdbcUserDAO and MongoUserDAO implementations, as shown in Listing 17-1.

Listing 17-1. UserDAO Interface and the JdbcUserDAO and MongoUserDAO Implementations

```
public interface UserDAO
{
    List<String> getAllUserNames();
}
public class JdbcUserDAO implements UserDAO
{
    @Override
    public List<String> getAllUserNames()
    {
        System.out.println("**** Getting usernames from RDBMS *****");
        return Arrays.asList("Jim","John","Rob");
    }
}
public class MongoUserDAO implements UserDAO
{
    @Override
    public List<String> getAllUserNames()
    {
        System.out.println("**** Getting usernames from MongoDB *****");
        return Arrays.asList("Bond","James","Bond");
    }
}
```

You can implement the MySQLDatabaseTypeCondition condition to check whether the dbType system property is MYSQL, as shown in Listing 17-2.

Listing 17-2. MySQLDatabaseTypeCondition.java

```java
public class MySQLDatabaseTypeCondition implements Condition
{
    @Override
    public boolean matches(ConditionContext conditionContext,
    AnnotatedTypeMetadata metadata)
    {
        String enabledDBType = System.getProperty("dbType");
        return (enabledDBType != null &&
        enabledDBType.equalsIgnoreCase("MYSQL"));
    }
}
```

You can implement the MongoDBDatabaseTypeCondition condition to check whether the dbType system property is MONGODB, as shown in Listing 17-3.

Listing 17-3. MongoDBDatabaseTypeCondition.java

```java
public class MongoDBDatabaseTypeCondition implements Condition
{
    @Override
    public boolean matches(ConditionContext conditionContext,
    AnnotatedTypeMetadata metadata)
    {
        String enabledDBType = System.getProperty("dbType");
        return (enabledDBType != null && enabledDBType.
        equalsIgnoreCase("MONGODB"));
    }
}
```

Now you can configure both the JdbcUserDAO and MongoUserDAO beans conditionally using @Conditional, as shown in Listing 17-4.

Listing 17-4. AppConfig.java

```java
@Configuration
public class AppConfig
{
```

```
@Bean
@Conditional(MySQLDatabaseTypeCondition.class)
public UserDAO jdbcUserDAO(){
    return new JdbcUserDAO();
}
@Bean
@Conditional(MongoDBDatabaseTypeCondition.class)
public UserDAO mongoUserDAO(){
    return new MongoUserDAO();
}
}
```

If you run the application, such as java -jar myapp.jar -DdbType=MYSQL, only the JdbcUserDAO bean will be registered. But if you set the system property to -DdbType=MONGODB, the MongoUserDAO bean will be registered. This is how you conditionally register a bean based on a system property.

Using @Conditional Based on the Presence or Absence of a Java Class

Suppose you want to register the MongoUserDAO bean only when the MongoDB Java driver class called com.mongodb.Server is available on the classpath. Otherwise, you want to register the JdbcUserDAO bean.

To accomplish this, you can create conditions to check the presence or absence of the MongoDB driver class called com.mongodb.Server, as shown in Listing 17-5.

Listing 17-5. MongoDriverPresentsCondition.java and MongoDriverNotPresentsCondition.java

```
public class MongoDriverPresentsCondition implements Condition
{
    @Override
    public boolean matches(ConditionContext conditionContext,
    AnnotatedTypeMetadata metadata)
    {
```

```
        try {
            Class.forName("com.mongodb.Server");
            return true;
        } catch (ClassNotFoundException e) {
            return false;
        }
    }
}
public class MongoDriverNotPresentsCondition implements Condition
{
    @Override
    public boolean matches(ConditionContext conditionContext,
    AnnotatedTypeMetadata metadata)
    {
        try {
            Class.forName("com.mongodb.Server");
            return false;
        } catch (ClassNotFoundException e) {
            return true;
        }
    }
}
```

This is how you register beans conditionally based on the presence or absence of a class in the classpath.

Using @Conditional Based on the Configured Spring Beans

What if you want to register the MongoUserDAO bean only when no other Spring bean of type UserDAO is already registered? You can create a condition to check if there are any existing beans of a certain type, as shown in Listing 17-6.

Listing 17-6. UserDAOBeanNotPresentsCondition.java

```java
public class UserDAOBeanNotPresentsCondition implements Condition
{
    @Override
    public boolean matches(ConditionContext conditionContext,
    AnnotatedTypeMetadata metadata)
    {
        UserDAO userDAO = conditionContext.getBeanFactory().
        getBean(UserDAO.class);
        return (userDAO == null);
    }
}
```

Using @Conditional Based on a Property's Configuration

What if you want to register the `MongoUserDAO` bean only if the `app.dbType=MONGO` property is set in the property's placeholder configuration file? You can implement that condition as shown in Listing 17-7.

Listing 17-7. MongoDbTypePropertyCondition.java

```java
public class MongoDbTypePropertyCondition implements Condition
{
    @Override
    public boolean matches(ConditionContext conditionContext,
    AnnotatedTypeMetadata metadata)
    {
        String dbType = conditionContext.getEnvironment().getProperty
        ("app.dbType");
        return "MONGO".equalsIgnoreCase(dbType);
    }
}
```

You have seen how to implement various types of conditions. But there is an even more elegant way to implement conditions using annotations.

Instead of creating a condition implementation for MYSQL and MongoDB, you can create a DatabaseType annotation as follows:

```
@Target({ ElementType.TYPE, ElementType.METHOD })
@Retention(RetentionPolicy.RUNTIME)
@Conditional(DatabaseTypeCondition.class)
public @interface DatabaseType
{
    String value();
}
```

Then you implement DatabaseTypeCondition to use the DatabaseType value to determine whether to enable or disable bean registration, as follows:

```
public class DatabaseTypeCondition implements Condition
{
    @Override
    public boolean matches(ConditionContext conditionContext,
    AnnotatedTypeMetadata metadata)
    {
        Map<String, Object> attributes = metadata.getAnnotationAttributes(D
        atabaseType.class.getName());
        String type = (String) attributes.get("value");
        String enabledDBType = System.getProperty("dbType","MYSQL");
        return (enabledDBType != null && type != null && enabledDBType.
        equalsIgnoreCase(type));
    }
}
```

Now you can use the @DatabaseType annotation on the bean definitions, as follows:

```
@Configuration
@ComponentScan
public class AppConfig
{
    @DatabaseType("MYSQL")
    public UserDAO jdbcUserDAO(){
```

```
        return new JdbcUserDAO();
    }
    @Bean
    @DatabaseType("MONGO")
    public UserDAO mongoUserDAO(){
        return new MongoUserDAO();
    }
}
```

Here, you get the metadata from the DatabaseType annotation and check against the dbType system property value to determine whether to enable or disable the bean registration.

You have seen many examples of registering beans conditionally using the @Conditional annotation. Spring Boot extensively uses the @Conditional feature to register beans conditionally based on various criteria.

Spring Boot's Built-In @Conditional Annotations

Spring Boot provides many custom @Conditional annotations to meet developers' autoconfiguration needs based on various criteria. Table 17-1 lists the @Conditional annotations provided by Spring Boot out of the box.

Table 17-1. *Spring Boot @Conditional Annotations*

Annotation	Description
@ConditionalOnBean	Matches when the specified bean classes and/or names are already registered
@ConditionalOnMissingBean	Matches when the specified bean classes and/or names are not already registered
@ConditionalOnClass	Matches when the specified classes are on the classpath
@ConditionalOnMissingClass	Matches when the specified classes are not on the classpath
@ConditionalOnProperty	Matches when the specified properties have a specific value
@ConditionalOnResource	Matches when the specified resources are on the classpath
@ConditionalOnWebApplication	Matches when the application context is a web application context
@ConditionalOnNotWebApplication	Matches when the application context is not a web application context
@ConditionalOnWarDeployment	Matches when the application to be deployed is of packaging type WAR
@ConditionalOnExpression	Matches based on the result of the provided SpEL (Spring Expression Language) expression

Spring Boot provides implementations for these annotations to verify whether the condition is matching or not. For example, look at the source code of the @ConditionalOnClass annotation and OnClassCondition.java in the Spring Boot source code:

```
@Target({ ElementType.TYPE, ElementType.METHOD })
@Retention(RetentionPolicy.RUNTIME)
@Documented
@Conditional(OnClassCondition.class)
```

```
public @interface ConditionalOnClass {
    /**
     * The classes that must be present. Since this annotation parsed by
       loading class
     * bytecode it is safe to specify classes here that may ultimately not
       be on the
     * classpath.
     * @return the classes that must be present
     */
    Class<?>[] value() default {};
    /**
     * The classes names that must be present.
     * @return the class names that must be present.
     */
    String[] name() default {};
}
@Order(Ordered.HIGHEST_PRECEDENCE)
class OnClassCondition extends SpringBootCondition
        implements AutoConfigurationImportFilter, BeanFactoryAware,
        BeanClassLoaderAware {
    private BeanFactory beanFactory;
    private ClassLoader beanClassLoader;
    @Override
    public boolean[] match(String[] autoConfigurationClasses,
            AutoConfigurationMetadata autoConfigurationMetadata) {
        ConditionEvaluationReport report = getConditionEvaluationReport();
        ConditionOutcome[] outcomes = getOutcomes(autoConfigurationClasses,
                autoConfigurationMetadata);
        boolean[] match = new boolean[outcomes.length];
        for (int i = 0; i < outcomes.length; i++) {
            match[i] = (outcomes[i] == null || outcomes[i].isMatch());
            if (!match[i] && outcomes[i] != null) {
                logOutcome(autoConfigurationClasses[i], outcomes[i]);
                if (report != null) {
```

```
                    report.recordConditionEvaluation(autoConfigurationClass
                    es[i], this,
                            outcomes[i]);
            }
        }
    }
    return match;
}
...
...
...
}
```

You can see how Spring Boot is using the @ConditionalOnClass annotation and OnClassCondition.class to check whether a given class is present or not. Similarly, you can find various conditional annotations from Spring Boot, such as @ConditionalOnBean, @ConditionalOnMissingBean, @ConditionalOnResource, @ConditionalOnProperty, and more.

Note   You can find various condition implementations that Spring Boot uses in the org.springframework.boot.autoconfigure.condition package of spring-boot-autoconfigure-{version}.jar.

Now that you know how Spring Boot uses the @Conditional feature to check whether to register a bean conditionally, you might wonder what exactly triggers the autoconfiguration mechanism. This is what the next section covers.

How Spring Boot Autoconfiguration Works

The key to Spring Boot's autoconfiguration is its @EnableAutoConfiguration annotation. Typically, you annotate the application entry point class with @SpringBootApplication or, if you want to customize the defaults, you can use the following annotations:

```
@Configuration
@EnableAutoConfiguration
@ComponentScan
public class Application
{
}
```

The @EnableAutoConfiguration annotation enables the autoconfiguration of Spring ApplicationContext by scanning the classpath components and registering the beans that match various conditions. Spring Boot provides various autoconfiguration classes in spring-boot-autoconfigure-{version}.jar and they are responsible for registering various components.

Autoconfiguration classes are typically annotated with @Configuration to mark it as a Spring configuration class and annotated with @EnableConfigurationProperties to bind the customization properties and one or more conditional bean registration methods.

For example, consider the org.springframework.boot.autoconfigure.jdbc. DataSourceAutoConfiguration class:

```
@Configuration
@ConditionalOnClass({ DataSource.class, EmbeddedDatabaseType.class })
@EnableConfigurationProperties(DataSourceProperties.class)
@Import({ Registrar.class, DataSourcePoolMetadataProvidersConfiguration.
class })
public class DataSourceAutoConfiguration {
    ...
    ...
    @Bean
    @ConditionalOnMissingBean
    public DataSourceInitializer dataSourceInitializer(DataSourceProperties
    properties,
            ApplicationContext applicationContext) {
        return new DataSourceInitializer(properties, applicationContext);
    }
    ...
    ...
    @Conditional(EmbeddedDatabaseCondition.class)
```

```
@ConditionalOnMissingBean({ DataSource.class, XADataSource.class })
@Import(EmbeddedDataSourceConfiguration.class)
protected static class EmbeddedDatabaseConfiguration {
}
@Configuration
@Conditional(PooledDataSourceCondition.class)
@ConditionalOnMissingBean({ DataSource.class, XADataSource.class })
@Import({ DataSourceConfiguration.Tomcat.class,
DataSourceConfiguration.Hikari.class,
        DataSourceConfiguration.Dbcp2.class, DataSourceConfiguration.
        Generic.class })
protected static class PooledDataSourceConfiguration {
}
...
...
@Configuration
@ConditionalOnProperty(prefix = "spring.datasource", name = "jmx-
enabled")
@ConditionalOnClass(name = "org.apache.tomcat.jdbc.pool.
DataSourceProxy")
@Conditional(DataSourceAutoConfiguration.
DataSourceAvailableCondition.class)
@ConditionalOnMissingBean(name = "dataSourceMBean")
protected static class TomcatDataSourceJmxConfiguration {
    ...
    ...
}
...
...
}
```

Here, DataSourceAutoConfiguration is annotated with @ConditionalOnClass({ DataSource.class, EmbeddedDatabaseType.class }), which means that the autoconfiguration of beans defined in DataSourceAutoConfiguration will be considered only if the DataSource.class and EmbeddedDatabaseType.class classes are available on the classpath.

The class is also annotated with @EnableConfigurationProperties(DataSourcePr operties.class), which enables binding the properties in application.properties to the properties of the DataSourceProperties class automatically.

```
@ConfigurationProperties(prefix = DataSourceProperties.PREFIX)
public class DataSourceProperties implements BeanClassLoaderAware,
EnvironmentAware, InitializingBean {
    public static final String PREFIX = "spring.datasource";
    ...
    ...
    private String driverClassName;
    private String url;
    private String username;
    private String password;
    ...
    //setters and getters
}
```

With this configuration, all the properties that start with spring.datasource.* will be automatically bound to the DataSourceProperties object.

```
spring.datasource.url=jdbc:mysql://localhost:3306/test
spring.datasource.username=root
spring.datasource.password=secret
spring.datasource.driver-class-name=com.mysql.jdbc.Driver
```

You can also see some inner classes and bean definition methods that are annotated with Spring Boot's conditional annotations, such as @ConditionalOnMissingBean, @ConditionalOnClass, and @ConditionalOnProperty. These bean definitions will be registered in ApplicationContext only if those conditions match.

You can also explore many other AutoConfiguration classes in spring-boot-autoconfigure-{version}.jar, such as

- org.springframework.boot.autoconfigure.web.servlet. DispatcherServletAutoConfiguration

- org.springframework.boot.autoconfigure.orm.jpa. HibernateJpaAutoConfiguration

- `org.springframework.boot.autoconfigure.data.jpa.`
  `JpaRepositoriesAutoConfiguration`

- `org.springframework.boot.autoconfigure.jackson.`
  `JacksonAutoConfiguration`

You should now have a basic understanding of how Spring Boot autoconfiguration works by using various autoconfiguration classes along with `@Conditional` features.

Summary

This chapter explained how to register Spring beans conditionally using the `@Conditional` annotation and how Spring Boot leverages `@Conditional` and `@EnableAutoConfiguration` annotations to autoconfigure beans based on various criteria.

## CHAPTER 18

Creating a Custom Spring Boot Starter

The main purpose of Spring Boot is to increase developer productivity by taking an opinionated view of the application and autoconfiguring the Spring ApplicationContext. Spring Boot provides starters for many commonly used frameworks and libraries. Spring Boot's autoconfiguration mechanism configures Spring Beans on your behalf based on various criteria.

In addition to the Spring Boot Starters that come out of the box, you can create your own starter modules. You may have some reusable modules developed in your organization that are used in many applications. You can create your own custom Spring Boot Starter to utilize those reusable modules in a much simpler way in Spring Boot applications.

This chapter looks into how to create a custom Spring Boot Starter. To demonstrate it, you will create `twitter4j-spring-boot-starter`, which will autoconfigure Twitter4j, a Java library that interacts with the Twitter API.

Introducing Twitter4j

Twitter4j provides Java bindings for the Twitter REST API. In order to use Twitter4j, you need to add the following Maven dependency:

```
<dependency>
    <groupId>org.twitter4j</groupId>
    <artifactId>twitter4j-core</artifactId>
    <version>4.0.7</version>
</dependency>
```

© K. Siva Prasad Reddy, Sai Upadhyayula 2023
K. S. P. Reddy and S. Upadhyayula, *Beginning Spring Boot 3*, https://doi.org/10.1007/978-1-4842-8792-7_18

The Twitter4j API main entry point is the Twitter class and you can create an instance of Twitter, as shown in Listing 18-1.

Listing 18-1. Using the Twitter4j API

```
ConfigurationBuilder cb = new ConfigurationBuilder();
cb.setDebugEnabled(true)
  .setOAuthConsumerKey("your-consumer-key-here")
  .setOAuthConsumerSecret("your-consumer-secret-here")
  .setOAuthAccessToken("your-access-token-here")
  .setOAuthAccessTokenSecret("your-access-token-secret-here");
TwitterFactory tf = new TwitterFactory(cb.build());
Twitter twitter = tf.getInstance();
```

Now you can use Twitter instance to get the latest tweets, as follows:

```
List<Status> statuses = twitter.getHomeTimeline();
for (Status status : statuses)
{
    System.out.println(status.getUser().getName() + ":" + status.getText());
}
```

You are going to create a Spring Boot Starter for Twitter4j so that you can autowire Twitter instances without having to register them explicitly.

Custom Spring Boot Starter

In Chapter 3, you learned how Spring Boot autoconfiguration works using the @Conditional feature.

Spring Boot Starter is typically aimed at autoconfiguring some library or framework based on the presence of a class or a configuration property or depends on whether a bean of a particular type is already registered or not.

Creating a custom Spring Boot Starter generally involves

- Creating an autoconfigure module that autoconfigures Spring Beans based on some criteria

- Creating a starter module that provides a dependency to the autoconfigure module along with the dependent libraries

So, you are going to create

- The `twitter4j-spring-boot-autoconfigure` module that contains Twitter4j autoconfiguration bean definitions

- The `twitter4j-spring-boot-starter` module that pulls in the `twitter4j-spring-boot-autoconfigure` and `twitter4j-core` dependencies

After creating the custom Twitter4j starter, you will build a Spring Boot application using `twitter4j-spring-boot-starter`.

Creating the twitter4j-spring-boot-autoconfigure Module

Now you will create a module called `twitter4j-spring-boot-autoconfigure` and add the Maven dependencies such as `spring-boot-autoconfigure`, `twitter4j-core`, and `spring-boot-starter-test`. See Listing 18-2.

Listing 18-2. twitter4j-spring-boot-autoconfigure/pom.xml

```xml
<?xml version="1.0" encoding="UTF-8"?>
<project xmlns="http://maven.apache.org/POM/4.0.0"
  xmlns:xsi="http://www.w3.org/2001/XMLSchema-instance"
  xsi:schemaLocation="http://maven.apache.org/POM/4.0.0
          http://maven.apache.org/maven-v4_0_0.xsd">
<modelVersion>4.0.0</modelVersion>
<groupId>com.apress</groupId>
<artifactId>twitter4j-spring-boot-autoconfigure</artifactId>
<packaging>jar</packaging>
<version>1.0-SNAPSHOT</version>
<properties>
  <project.build.sourceEncoding>UTF-8</project.build.sourceEncoding>
  <maven.compiler.source>17</maven.compiler.source>
  <maven.compiler.target>17</maven.compiler.target>
  <twitter4j.version>4.0.7</twitter4j.version>
  <spring-boot.version>3.0.0-SNAPSHOT</spring-boot.version>
</properties>
```

```xml
  <dependencyManagement>
    <dependencies>
      <dependency>
        <groupId>org.springframework.boot</groupId>
        <artifactId>spring-boot-dependencies</artifactId>
        <version>${spring-boot.version}</version>
        <type>pom</type>
        <scope>import</scope>
      </dependency>
    </dependencies>
  </dependencyManagement>
<dependencies>
  <dependency>
    <groupId>org.springframework.boot</groupId>
    <artifactId>spring-boot-autoconfigure</artifactId>
  </dependency>
  <dependency>
     <groupId>org.springframework.boot</groupId>
     <artifactId>spring-boot-configuration-processor</artifactId>
     <optional>true</optional>
  </dependency>
  <dependency>
    <groupId>org.springframework.boot</groupId>
    <artifactId>spring-boot-starter-test</artifactId>
    <scope>test</scope>
  </dependency>
  <dependency>
    <groupId>org.twitter4j</groupId>
    <artifactId>twitter4j-core</artifactId>
    <version>${twitter4j.version}</version>
    <optional>true</optional>
   </dependency>
  </dependencies>
</project>
```

Note that this example specifies `twitter4j-core` as an optional dependency because `twitter4j-core` should be added to the project only when `twitter4j-spring-boot-starter` is added to the project.

Twitter4j Properties to Hold the Twitter4j Config Parameters

Now you'll create `Twitter4jProperties.java` to bind the Twitter4j OAuth config parameters that start with `twitter4j.*` using `@ConfigurationProperties`. See Listing 18-3.

Listing 18-3. Twitter4jProperties.java

```
package com.apress.spring.boot.autoconfigure;
import org.springframework.boot.context.properties.ConfigurationProperties;
@ConfigurationProperties(prefix= Twitter4jProperties.TWITTER4J_PREFIX)
public class Twitter4jProperties
{
  public static final String TWITTER4J_PREFIX = "twitter4j";
  private Boolean debug = false;
  private OAuth oauth = new OAuth();
  public Boolean getDebug() {
    return debug;
  }
  public void setDebug(Boolean debug) {
    this.debug = debug;
  }
  public OAuth getOauth() {
    return oauth;
  }
  public static class OAuth {
    private String consumerKey;
    private String consumerSecret;
    private String accessToken;
    private String accessTokenSecret;
    public String getConsumerKey() {
```

```java
      return consumerKey;
    }
    public void setConsumerKey(String consumerKey) {
      this.consumerKey = consumerKey;
    }
    public String getConsumerSecret() {
      return consumerSecret;
    }
    public void setConsumerSecret(String consumerSecret) {
      this.consumerSecret = consumerSecret;
    }
    public String getAccessToken() {
      return accessToken;
    }
    public void setAccessToken(String accessToken) {
      this.accessToken = accessToken;
    }
    public String getAccessTokenSecret() {
      return accessTokenSecret;
    }
    public void setAccessTokenSecret(String accessTokenSecret) {
      this.accessTokenSecret = accessTokenSecret;
    }
  }
}
```

The @ConfigurationProperties annotation allows you to bind a set of properties
with a common prefix to Java bean properties. With this configuration object, you can
configure the Twitter4j properties in application.properties, as shown in Listing 18-4.

Listing 18-4. application.properties

```
twitter4j.debug=true
twitter4j.oauth.consumer-key=your-consumer-key-here
twitter4j.oauth.consumer-secret=your-consumer-secret-here
twitter4j.oauth.access-token=your-access-token-here
twitter4j.oauth.access-token-secret=your-access-token-secret-here
```

Twitter4j Autoconfiguration to Autoconfigure Twitter4j

Now you create an autoconfiguration class called `Twitter4jAutoConfiguration`, which contains the bean definitions that will be automatically configured based on some criteria.

What are those criteria?

- If `twitter4j.TwitterFactory.class` is on the classpath
- If the `TwitterFactory` bean is not already defined explicitly

So, you will autoconfigure `TwitterFactory` and the Twitter beans if there is a `TwitterFactory` class in the classpath and if the `TwitterFactory` bean is not already registered.

Create the `Twitter4jAutoConfiguration` class, as shown in Listing 18-5.

Listing 18-5. Twitter4jAutoConfiguration.java

```
package com.apress.spring.boot.autoconfigure;

import org.apache.commons.logging.Log;
import org.apache.commons.logging.LogFactory;
import org.springframework.beans.factory.annotation.Autowired;
import org.springframework.boot.autoconfigure.condition.ConditionalOnClass;
import org.springframework.boot.autoconfigure.condition.
ConditionalOnMissingBean; import org.springframework.boot.context.
properties.EnableConfigurationProperties; import org.springframework.
context.annotation.Bean;
import org.springframework.context.annotation.Configuration;

import twitter4j.Twitter;
import twitter4j.TwitterFactory;
import twitter4j.conf.ConfigurationBuilder;

@Configuration
@ConditionalOnClass({ TwitterFactory.class })
@EnableConfigurationProperties(Twitter4jProperties.class)
public class Twitter4jAutoConfiguration {
```

```java
private static Log log = LogFactory.getLog(Twitter4jAutoConfigurati
on.class);
@Autowired
private Twitter4jProperties properties;
@Bean
@ConditionalOnMissingBean
public TwitterFactory twitterFactory(){
  if (this.properties.getOauth().getConsumerKey() == null
    || this.properties.getOauth().getConsumerSecret() == null
    || this.properties.getOauth().getAccessToken() == null
    || this.properties.getOauth().getAccessTokenSecret() == null)
  {
    log.error("Twitter4j properties not configured properly. Please check
    twitter4j.* properties settings in configuration file.");
    throw new RuntimeException("Twitter4j properties not configured
    properly. Please check twitter4j.* properties settings in
    configuration file.");
  }
  ConfigurationBuilder cb = new ConfigurationBuilder();
  cb.setDebugEnabled(properties.getDebug())
    .setOAuthConsumerKey(properties.getOauth().getConsumerKey())
    .setOAuthConsumerSecret(properties.getOauth().getConsumerSecret())
    .setOAuthAccessToken(properties.getOauth().getAccessToken())
    .setOAuthAccessTokenSecret(properties.getOauth().
    getAccessTokenSecret());
  TwitterFactory tf = new TwitterFactory(cb.build());
  return tf;
}
@Bean
@ConditionalOnMissingBean
public Twitter twitter(TwitterFactory twitterFactory){
  return twitterFactory.getInstance();
}
}
```

This example uses @ConditionalOnClass({ TwitterFactory.class}) to specify that this autoconfiguration should take place only when TwitterFactory.class is present.

It also uses @ConditionalOnMissingBean on bean definition methods to consider this bean definition only if the TwitterFactory bean is not already defined explicitly.

Also, note that the example is annotated with @EnableConfigurationProperties (Twitter4jProperties.class) to enable support for ConfigurationProperties and injected the Twitter4jProperties bean.

Now you need to configure the custom Twitter4jAutoConfiguration in the src/main/resources/METAINF/spring.factories file as follows:

```
org.springframework.boot.autoconfigure.EnableAutoConfiguration=\
com.apress.spring.boot.autoconfigure.Twitter4jAutoConfiguration
```

Next, you are going to create the starter module called twitter4j-spring-boot-starter.

Creating the twitter4j-spring-boot-starter Module

Now you'll create a module called twitter4j-spring-boot-starter and configure its dependencies, as shown in Listing 18-6.

Listing 18-6.   twitter4j-spring-boot-starter/pom.xml

```xml
<?xml version="1.0" encoding="UTF-8"?>
<project xmlns="http://maven.apache.org/POM/4.0.0"
  xmlns:xsi="http://www.w3.org/2001/XMLSchema-instance"
  xsi:schemaLocation="http://maven.apache.org/POM/4.0.0
      http://maven.apache.org/maven-v4_0_0.xsd">
<modelVersion>4.0.0</modelVersion>
<groupId>com.apress</groupId>
<artifactId>twitter4j-spring-boot-starter</artifactId>
<packaging>jar</packaging>
<version>1.0-SNAPSHOT</version>
<properties>
    <project.build.sourceEncoding>UTF-8</project.build.sourceEncoding>
    <maven.compiler.source>17</maven.compiler.source
```

```xml
    <maven.compiler.target>17</maven.compiler.target>
    <spring-boot.version>3.0.0-SNAPSHOT</spring-boot.version>
  <twitter4j.version>4.0.7</twitter4j.version>
</properties>
<dependencyManagement>
  <dependencies>
    <dependency>
        <groupId>org.springframework.boot</groupId>
        <artifactId>spring-boot-dependencies</artifactId>
        <version>${spring-boot.version}</version>
        <type>pom</type>
        <scope>import</scope>
      </dependency>
  </dependencies>
</dependencyManagement>
<dependencies>
  <dependency>
    <groupId>org.springframework.boot</groupId>
    <artifactId>spring-boot-starter</artifactId>
  </dependency>
  <dependency>
    <groupId>com.apress</groupId>
    <artifactId>twitter4j-spring-boot-autoconfigure</artifactId>
    <version>${project.version}</version>
  </dependency>
  <dependency>
    <groupId>org.twitter4j</groupId>
    <artifactId>twitter4j-core</artifactId>
    <version>${twitter4j.version}</version>
  </dependency>
</dependencies>
</project>
```

Note that you are pulling in the twitter4j-core dependency in this Maven module.

You don't need to add any code to this module, but you can optionally specify the dependencies you are going to provide through this starter in the `src/main/resources/METAINF/spring.provides` file as follows:

```
provides: twitter4j-core
```

That's all for this starter. Next, let's see how to create a sample using `twitter4j-spring-boot-starter`.

Application Using twitter4j-spring-boot-starter

You will create a simple Maven-based Spring Boot application and use `twitter4j-spring-boot-starter` to fetch the latest tweets. First, you create a simple Spring Boot application and add the `twitter4j-spring-boot-starter` dependency, as shown in Listing 18-7.

Listing 18-7. twitter4j-spring-boot-sample/pom.xml

```xml
<?xml version="1.0" encoding="UTF-8"?>
<project xmlns="http://maven.apache.org/POM/4.0.0"
    xmlns:xsi="http://www.w3.org/2001/XMLSchema-instance"
    xsi:schemaLocation="http://maven.apache.org/POM/4.0.0
        http://maven.apache.org/maven-v4_0_0.xsd">
  <modelVersion>4.0.0</modelVersion>
  <groupId>com.apress</groupId>
  <artifactId>twitter4j-spring-boot-sample</artifactId>
  <packaging>jar</packaging>
  <version>1.0-SNAPSHOT</version>
  <parent>
    <groupId>org.springframework.boot</groupId>
    <artifactId>spring-boot-starter-parent</artifactId>
    <version>3.0.0-SNAPSHOT</version>
  </parent>
  <properties>
    <project.build.sourceEncoding>UTF-8</project.build.sourceEncoding>
    <java.version>17</java.version>
  </properties>
```

```xml
  <build>
    <plugins>
      <plugin>
        <groupId>org.springframework.boot</groupId>
        <artifactId>spring-boot-maven-plugin</artifactId>
      </plugin>
    </plugins>
  </build>
  <dependencies>
    <dependency>
      <groupId>com.apress</groupId>
      <artifactId>twitter4j-spring-boot-starter</artifactId>
      <version>1.0-SNAPSHOT</version>
    </dependency>
    <dependency>
      <groupId>org.springframework.boot</groupId>
      <artifactId>spring-boot-starter-test</artifactId>
      <scope>test</scope>
    </dependency>
  </dependencies>
</project>
```

Create the entry point class SpringbootTwitter4jDemoApplication, as shown in Listing 18-8.

Listing 18-8. SpringbootTwitter4jDemoApplication.java

```java
package com.apress.demo;
import org.springframework.boot.SpringApplication;
import org.springframework.boot.autoconfigure.SpringBootApplication;

@SpringBootApplication
public class SpringbootTwitter4jDemoApplication
{
  public static void main(String[] args)
  {
```

```
SpringApplication.run(SpringbootTwitter4jDemoApplication.class,
args); }
}
```

Next, create TweetService, as shown in Listing 18-9.

Listing 18-9. TweetService.java

```java
package com.apress.demo;

import java.util.ArrayList;
import java.util.List;
import org.springframework.beans.factory.annotation.Autowired; import org.springframework.stereotype.Service;
import twitter4j.ResponseList;

import twitter4j.Status;
import twitter4j.Twitter;
import twitter4j.TwitterException;

@Service
public class TweetService
{
  private final Twitter twitter;
  public TweetService(Twitter twitter) {
    this.twitter = twitter;
  }
  public List<String> getLatestTweets()
  {
    List<String> tweets = new ArrayList<>();
    try {
      ResponseList<Status> homeTimeline = twitter.getHomeTimeline();
      for (Status status : homeTimeline)
      {
        tweets.add(status.getText());
      }
    }
```

```
    catch (TwitterException e) {
        throw new RuntimeException(e);
    }
    return tweets;
  }
}
```

Now create a test to verify the Twitter4j autoconfiguration (see Listing 18-10). Before that, ensure you set your Twitter4j OAuth configuration parameter to your actual values. You can get them from https://developer.twitter.com/en/apps.

Listing 18-10. SpringbootTwitter4jDemoApplicationTest.java

```java
package com.apress.demo;
import java.util.List;
import org.junit.jupiter.api.Test;
import org.springframework.beans.factory.annotation.Autowired;
import org.springframework.boot.test.context.SpringBootTest;
import org.springframework.test.context.junit4.SpringRunner;
import twitter4j.TwitterException;
@SpringBootTest
public class SpringbootTwitter4jDemoApplicationTest
{
  @Autowired
  private TweetService tweetService;
  @Test
  public void testGetTweets() throws TwitterException
  {
    List<String> tweets = tweetService.getLatestTweets();
    for (String tweet : tweets)
    {
      System.err.println(tweet);
    }
  }
}
```

When you run this JUnit test, you should be able to see the latest tweets on your console output.

Summary

In this chapter, you learned how to create your autoconfiguration classes and your Spring Boot Starter. In the next chapter, you will learn how to develop Spring Boot applications using JVM languages like Groovy, Scala, and Kotlin.

## CHAPTER 19

Spring Boot with Kotlin, Scala, and Groovy

Java is the most widely used programming language on Java Virtual Machine (JVM). There are many other JVM-based languages, such as Groovy, Scala, JRuby, Jython, and Kotlin. Among them, Kotlin is widely adopted and very popular among the Java community.

Spring Boot is a Java-based framework that can also be used with other JVM-based languages. This chapter looks at how to use Spring Boot with the Groovy, Scala, and Kotlin programming languages.

Using Spring Boot with Groovy

Groovy is a dynamically typed language that runs on JVM. Since Groovy's syntax is very close to Java's, it is easy for Java developers to get started with Groovy. Spring Boot applications can be developed using the Groovy programming language.

Introducing Groovy

Groovy is a JVM-based programming language with a Java-like syntax. But Groovy supports dynamic typing, closures, meta-programming, operator overloading, and more. In addition, Groovy provides many cool features such as multi-line strings, string interpolation, elegant looping structures, easy property access, and optional semicolons.

© K. Siva Prasad Reddy, Sai Upadhyayula 2023
K. S. P. Reddy and S. Upadhyayula, *Beginning Spring Boot 3*, https://doi.org/10.1007/978-1-4842-8792-7_19

Groovy Strings

You can create strings in Groovy using either single quotes or double quotes. When using single quotes, the string is treated as an instance of java.lang.String, whereas when using double quotes, it is treated as an instance of groovy.lang.Gstring, which supports string interpolation.

```
def name = "John"
def amount = 125
println('My name is ${name}')
println("My name is ${name}")
println("He paid \$${amount}")
```

When you run this code, it will print the following output:

```
My name is ${name}
My name is John
He paid $125
```

Since single quotes are used in the first println() statement, ${name} is printed as it is, whereas it is interpolated in the second println() statement because double quotes are used there. This code uses the escape character \$ to print the $ symbol.

Groovy supports multi-line strings using triple quotes (""" or ''') as follows:

```
//using single quotes
def content = '''My Name is John.
               I live in London.
               I am a software developer'''
def name = 'John'
def address = 'London'
def occupation = 'software developer'
//using double quotes
def bio = """My name is ${name}.
            I live in ${address}.
            I am a ${occupation}."""
```

Groovy's multi-line supports come in handy while creating strings that span multiple lines like table creation scripts, HTML templates with placeholders, and more.

JavaBean Properties

In Java, you usually create Java beans by creating private properties and setters and getters for those properties. Although you can generate the setters and getters using IDE support, it is lengthy and unnecessary noise.

In Groovy, you can create beans by declaring the properties and then accessing them using the `object.propertyName` syntax without having to create setters and getters.

```groovy
class Person
{
    def id
    def name
    def email
}
def p = new Person()
p.id = 1
p.name = 'Jon'
p.email = 'john@mail.com'
println("Id: ${p.id}, Name: ${p.name}, Email: ${p.email}")
```

Here, you can see that the values are directly assigned to the bean properties, like `p.id=1`, without creating a setter for `id`. Similarly, you can read the property `id` using `p.id`, without requiring a getter for `id`. Behind the scenes, Groovy will generate setters and getters for the properties.

Looping

Groovy supports various looping structures in addition to the regular `while` and `for` loops.

Iterate using the range operator (`..`):

```groovy
for(i in 0..5) { print "${i} " }
```

The output is as follows:

```
0 1 2 3 4 5
```

Iterate using `upto()` with the lower and upper limits inclusive:

```groovy
0.upto(3) { print "$it " }
```

The output is as follows:

```
0 1 2 3
```

Iterate using `times()`, starting from 0:

```
5.times { print "$it " }
```

The output is as follows:

```
0 1 2 3 4
```

Iterate using `step()` with the lower and upper limits and a step value:

```
0.step(10, 2) { print "$it "}
```

The output is as follows:

```
0 2 4 6 8
```

There are many other features provided by Groovy that help you build an application faster:

- Working with collections: http://docs.groovy-lang.org/latest/html/documentation/#_working_with_collections

- Closures: http://groovy-lang.org/closures.html

- Regular expressions: http://docs.groovy-lang.org/latest/html/documentation/#_regular_expression_operators

- Traits: http://docs.groovy-lang.org/latest/html/documentation/#_traits

- Groovy truth: http://docs.groovy-lang.org/latest/html/documentation/#the-groovy-truth

- Typing: http://docs.groovy-lang.org/latest/html/documentation/#_typing

- Parsing and producing JSON: http://groovy-lang.org/json.html

- Processing XML: http://docs.groovy-lang.org/latest/html/documentation/#processing-xml

- Meta programming: http://docs.groovy-lang.org/latest/html/documentation/#_metaprogramming

To learn more about Groovy, refer to the official documentation at `http://groovy-lang.org/documentation.html`.

Creating a Spring Boot Application Using Groovy

You can create a Spring Boot application using Groovy either from the IDE or the online Spring Boot application generator at `http://start.spring.io`.

If you are using the Maven build tool, `gmavenplus-plugin` is configured to compile Groovy code. You can put the Groovy main source code in the `src/main/groovy` folder and then test the Groovy code in the `src/test/groovy` folder. See Listing 19-1.

Listing 19-1. pom.xml

```xml
<?xml version="1.0" encoding="UTF-8"?>
<project xmlns="http://maven.apache.org/POM/4.0.0"
    xmlns:xsi="http://www.w3.org/2001/XMLSchema-instance"
    xsi:schemaLocation="http://maven.apache.org/POM/4.0.0
    http://maven.apache.org/xsd/maven-4.0.0.xsd">
    <modelVersion>4.0.0</modelVersion>
    <groupId>com.apress</groupId>
    <artifactId>springboot-groovy-demo</artifactId>
    <version>0.0.1-SNAPSHOT</version>
    <packaging>jar</packaging>
    <name>springboot-groovy-demo</name>
    <parent>
        <groupId>org.springframework.boot</groupId>
        <artifactId>spring-boot-starter-parent</artifactId>
        <version>3.0.0-SNAPSHOT</version>
        <relativePath/>
    </parent>
    <properties>
        <project.build.sourceEncoding>UTF-8</project.build.sourceEncoding>
        <project.reporting.outputEncoding>UTF-8</project.reporting.outputEncoding>
        <java.version>17</java.version>
    </properties>
```

```
<dependencies>
    <dependency>
        <groupId>org.springframework.boot</groupId>
        <artifactId>spring-boot-starter-web</artifactId>
    </dependency>
    <dependency>
         <groupId>org.apache.groovy</groupId>
        <artifactId>groovy</artifactId>
     </dependency>
    <dependency>
        <groupId>org.springframework.boot</groupId>
        <artifactId>spring-boot-starter-test</artifactId>
        <scope>test</scope>
    </dependency>
</dependencies>
<build>
    <plugins>
        <plugin>
            <groupId>org.springframework.boot</groupId>
            <artifactId>spring-boot-maven-plugin</artifactId>
        </plugin>
        <plugin>
            <groupId>org.codehaus.gmavenplus</groupId>
            <artifactId>gmavenplus-plugin</artifactId>
            <version>1.13.1</version>
            <executions>
                <execution>
                    <goals>
                        <goal>addSources</goal>
                        <goal>addTestSources</goal>
                        <goal>generateStubs</goal>
                        <goal>compile</goal>
                        <goal>generateTestStubs</goal>
                        <goal>compileTests</goal>
                        <goal>removeStubs</goal>
                        <goal>removeTestStubs</goal>
```

```
                </goals>
              </execution>
            </executions>
          </plugin>
      </plugins>
  </build>
  <repositories>
      ...
      ...
  </repositories>
  <pluginRepositories>
      ...
      ...
  </pluginRepositories>
</project>
```

If you selected Gradle as the build tool, the groovy plugin is configured as shown in Listing 19-2.

Listing 19-2. build.gradle

```
...
...
apply plugin: 'groovy'
apply plugin: 'org.springframework.boot'
apply plugin: 'io.spring.dependency-management'
...
...
dependencies {
    compile('org.springframework.boot:spring-boot-starter-web')
    compile('org.apache.groovy:groovy')
    testCompile('org.springframework.boot:spring-boot-starter-test')
}
```

You'll now see how to develop a simple Spring Boot web application using Groovy, Spring Data JPA, and Thymeleaf. Add the Web, Thymeleaf, JPA, and H2 starters dependencies to your application.

Create a JPA entity called User.groovy, as shown in Listing 19-3.

Listing 19-3. User.groovy

```
import jakarta.persistence.*
@Entity
@Table(name="users")
class User {
    @Id @GeneratedValue(strategy = GenerationType.AUTO)
    Long id
    String name
    String email
}
```

Since you are using Groovy, you don't need to create setters and getters for your entity properties.

Create a Spring Data JPA repository for the User entity, as shown in Listing 19-4.

Listing 19-4. UserRepository.groovy

```
interface UserRepository extends JpaRepository<User, Long>
{
    User findByEmail(String email);
}
```

Create a SpringMVC controller to show the list of users, as shown in Listing 19-5.

Listing 19-5. HomeController.groovy

```
import org.springframework.beans.factory.annotation.Autowired
import org.springframework.stereotype.Controller
import org.springframework.ui.Model
import org.springframework.web.bind.annotation.GetMapping

@Controller
class HomeController
{
    @Autowired
    UserRepository repo;
```

```
@GetMapping("/")
String home(Model model) {
    model.addAttribute("users", repo.findAll())
    "home"
}
}
```

In Groovy, the last statement in the method is treated as a returned value, so you can just mention "home" instead of return "home".

Create the Thymeleaf view home.html to render users, as shown in Listing 19-6.

Listing 19-6. src/main/resources/templates/home.html

```
<!DOCTYPE HTML>
<html xmlns:th="http://www.thymeleaf.org">
<head>
    <title>Users List</title>
    <meta http-equiv="Content-Type" content="text/html; charset=UTF-8" />
</head>
<body>
<table>
    <thead>
    <tr>
        <th>Id</th>
        <th>Name</th>
    </tr>
    </thead>
    <tbody>
    <tr th:each="user : ${users}">
        <td th:text="${user.id}">Id</td>
        <td th:text="${user.name}">Name</td>
    </tr>
    </tbody>
</table>
</body>
</html>
```

The main entry point class is created when you generate the application, as shown in Listing 19-7.

Listing 19-7. SpringbootGroovyDemoApplication.groovy

```groovy
import org.springframework.boot.SpringApplication
import org.springframework.boot.autoconfigure.SpringBootApplication

@SpringBootApplication
class SpringbootGroovyDemoApplication {

    static void main(String[] args) {
        SpringApplication.run SpringbootGroovyDemoApplication, args
    }
}
```

Initialize the database with sample data using a SQL script, as shown in Listing 19-8.

Listing 19-8. src/main/resources/data.sql

```sql
insert into users(id, name, email) values
(1,'admin','admin@gmail.com'),
(2,'john','john@gmail.com'),
(3,'test','test@gmail.com');
```

Now you can run the application by executing the SpringbootGroovyDemoApplication.main() method or using the mvn spring-boot:run or gradle bootRun commands. If you point your browser to http://localhost:8080/, you should be able to see user details.

Using Spring Boot with Scala

Scala is one of the most popular JVM-based programming languages. It mixes functional programming and object-oriented programming idioms into a single language.

Spring Initializer (http://start.spring.io) doesn't provide support for Scala yet. Still, you can create Spring Boot applications using the Scala programming language by configuring appropriate plugins based on the build tool.

Introducing Scala

Scala is a JVM-based statically typed programming language that supports functional and object-oriented programming paradigms. You can write programs in Scala concisely and expressively instead of using the verbose and imperative coding style.

The following sections look at a few Scala features that are slightly different from Java.

Type Inference

In Scala, a variable declaration syntax looks like `var variable_name : data_type = value`. But Scala can infer the data type of the variable based on the assigned value. This means you can omit the `:data_type` part in the declaration.

```
var n : Int = 5 //with explicit type declaration
var n = 5 //with type inference
```

Classes and Objects

The classes in Scala are similar to Java and can contain variables, methods, and more. But Scala's class can contain one primary constructor and zero or more auxiliary constructors. The auxiliary constructors should invoke primary constructors directly or through another auxiliary constructor.

```
class Person (val firstName: String, val lastName: String){
  def this(firstName: String) { this(firstName, "")}
}
object Main extends App {
  val p1 = new Person("Siva","Prasad")
  val p2 = new Person("Siva")
}
```

In Scala, there is no concept of `static`. If you want to mimic the static behavior in Scala, you create a *companion object* with the same name as the class and put all the members, including properties and methods, in there. The object in Scala is a singleton, and you can access members without creating an instance.

```scala
class StringUtils {}

object StringUtils {

  def toUpper(str : String): String = {
    return str.toUpperCase()
  }
}
val str = "john"
println(StringUtils.toUpper(str))
```

Traits

Traits in Scala are similar to Java 8 interfaces, which encapsulate fields, methods, and abstract methods. Classes can extend any number of traits.

```scala
trait ReportSender {
  def sendReport(report: String): Unit = {
    //send email with report content
  }
  def generateReport() : String
}
class HTMLReportSender extends ReportSender {
  override def generateReport(): String = "<html><body>ReportData</
body></html>"
}
```

To learn more about Scala, refer to Scala's official documentation at http://docs. scala-lang.org/index.html.

Creating a Spring Boot Application Using Scala

You can develop Spring Boot applications using the Scala programming language. You can use scala-maven-plugin to compile your Scala code while using Maven as the build tool. You can place the main Scala code in src/main/scala and the test Scala code in the src/test/scala folder. See Listing 19-9.

Listing 19-9.   pom.xml

```xml
<?xml version="1.0" encoding="UTF-8"?>
<project xmlns="http://maven.apache.org/POM/4.0.0"
    xmlns:xsi="http://www.w3.org/2001/XMLSchema-instance"
    xsi:schemaLocation="http://maven.apache.org/POM/4.0.0
    http://maven.apache.org/xsd/maven-4.0.0.xsd">
    <modelVersion>4.0.0</modelVersion>
    <groupId>com.apress</groupId>
    <artifactId>springboot-scala-demo</artifactId>
    <version>0.0.1-SNAPSHOT</version>
    <packaging>jar</packaging>
    <name>springboot-scala-demo</name>
    <parent>
        <groupId>org.springframework.boot</groupId>
        <artifactId>spring-boot-starter-parent</artifactId>
        <version>3.0.0-SNAPSHOT</version>
        <relativePath/>
    </parent>
    <properties>
        <project.build.sourceEncoding>UTF-8</project.build.sourceEncoding>
        <project.reporting.outputEncoding>UTF-8</project.reporting.
        outputEncoding>
        <java.version>17</java.version>
        <scala.version>3.1.3</scala.version>
    </properties>
    <dependencies>
        <dependency>
            <groupId>org.scala-lang</groupId>
            <artifactId>scala3-library_3</artifactId>
            <version>${scala.version}</version>
        </dependency>
        <dependency>
            <groupId>org.springframework.boot</groupId>
            <artifactId>spring-boot-starter-test</artifactId>
            <scope>test</scope>
```

```xml
            </dependency>
        </dependencies>
        <build>
            <sourceDirectory>src/main/scala</sourceDirectory>
            <testSourceDirectory>src/test/scala</testSourceDirectory>
            <plugins>
                <plugin>
                    <groupId>org.springframework.boot</groupId>
                    <artifactId>spring-boot-maven-plugin</artifactId>
                </plugin>
                <plugin>
                    <groupId>net.alchim31.maven</groupId>
                    <artifactId>scala-maven-plugin</artifactId>
                    <version>4.6.2</version>
                    <executions>
                      <execution>
                        <goals>
                          <goal>compile</goal>
                          <goal>testCompile</goal>
                        </goals>
                      </execution>
                    </executions>
                    <configuration>
                      <jvmArgs>
                        <jvmArg>-Xms64m</jvmArg>
                        <jvmArg>-Xmx1024m</jvmArg>
                      </jvmArgs>
                    </configuration>
                </plugin>
            </plugins>
        </build>
        <repositories>
            ...
            ...
        </repositories>
```

```
<pluginRepositories>
    ...
    ...
</pluginRepositories>
</project>
```

Note that this code adds `src/main/scala` and `src/test/scala` folders as source folders using the `<sourceDirectory>` and `<testSourceDirectory>` configurations. It also adds the `scala-library` dependency to use Scala.

If you want to use the Gradle build tool, you can use the `scala` plugin, which automatically uses the `src/main/scala` and `src/test/scala` folders as Scala source code directories. See Listing 19-10.

Listing 19-10. build.gradle

```
apply plugin: 'java'
apply plugin: 'scala'
apply plugin: 'application'
apply plugin: 'org.springframework.boot'
apply plugin: 'io.spring.dependency-management'
mainClassName = 'com.apress.demo.Application'
...
...
dependencies {
    ...
    ...
    compile('org.scala-lang:scala3-library_3:3.1.3')
    ...
    ...
}
```

Now you'll see how to develop a simple web application using Spring Boot and Scala. Add the Web, Spring Data JPA, Thymeleaf, and H2 starter dependencies.

Create a JPA entity called `User.scala`, as shown in Listing 19-11.

Listing 19-11. User.scala

```scala
import jakarta.persistence._

import scala.beans.BeanProperty

@Entity
@Table(name="users")
class User {

  @Id
  @GeneratedValue(strategy = GenerationType.AUTO)
  @BeanProperty
  var id: Long = _

  @BeanProperty
  var name: String = _

  @BeanProperty
  var email: String = _
}
```

You use the @BeanProperty to generate setters and getters for fields based on the JavaBean naming conventions.

Now you'll see how to create the Spring Data JPA repository for the User entity. Since Scala doesn't have interfaces, you create UserRepository as a trait, as shown in Listing 19-12.

Listing 19-12. UserRepository.scala

```scala
import org.springframework.data.jpa.repository.JpaRepository
import org.springframework.data.repository.query.Param
trait UserRepository extends JpaRepository[User, java.lang.Long] {
  def findByEmail(@Param("email") name: String): List[User]
}
```

You create a Spring MVC controller to show the list of users, as shown in Listing 19-13.

Listing 19-13. HomeController.scala

```scala
import org.springframework.beans.factory.annotation.Autowired
import org.springframework.stereotype.Controller
import org.springframework.ui.Model
import org.springframework.web.bind.annotation.{GetMapping}
@Controller
class HomeController
{
  @Autowired
  var repo: UserRepository = _
  @GetMapping(path=Array("/"))
  def home(model: Model) : String = {
    model.addAttribute("users", repo.findAll())
    "home"
  }
}
```

You can use the same home.html Thymeleaf template you created for the Groovy sample application. Next, you will develop the application's main entry point class. Since Scala doesn't support static methods, you must create a companion object and write the main() method, as shown in Listing 19-14.

Listing 19-14. Application.scala

```scala
import org.springframework.boot.SpringApplication
import org.springframework.boot.autoconfigure.SpringBootApplication
@SpringBootApplication
class Application{
@main
def main(): Unit = SpringApplication.run(classOf[Application])
}
```

Now you can run Application.main(), which starts your Spring Boot application and accesses it at http://localhost:8080/, which shows a list of users.

Using Spring Boot with Kotlin

Spring Boot officially supports the Kotlin programming language, and you can create Spring Boot applications using Kotlin from Spring Initializer at `http://start.spring.io` or from your IDE. Kotlin support is introduced in the Spring Framework 5 release. You can read more about it at `https://spring.io/blog/2017/01/04/introducing-kotlin-support-in-spring-framework-5-0`.

Introducing Kotlin

Kotlin (`https://kotlinlang.org/`) is a JVM-based statically typed programming language created by JetBrains. One of the key goals of Kotlin is to be interoperable with Java so that you can use Java and Kotlin together in the same project.

Here's how you write a simple Hello World program in Kotlin:

```
package demo
fun main(args: Array<String>){
    println("Hello World");
}
```

In Kotlin, there are no static methods like in Java, so you can write those methods that you want to be static as top-level functions.

Classes

Classes in Kotlin are similar to Scala classes in that they have a class name with one primary constructor and one or more secondary constructors.

```
class Person(val firstname: String,val lastname: String) {
    constructor(name: String) : this(name, "")
    fun printDetails() = println("FirstName: ${firstname}, LastName:
    ${lastname}")
}
```

Interfaces

Interfaces in Kotlin are similar to Java 8 interfaces in that they can have abstract method declarations and implemented methods.

```kotlin
interface ReportSender
{
    fun generateReport() : String
    fun sendReport() {
        val report = generateReport()
        println("Report: "+ report)
        //send email with report content
    }
}
class HTMLReportSender : ReportSender
{
    override fun generateReport(): String = "<html><body>ReportData</body>
    </html>"
}
fun main(args: Array<String>)
{
    val rs = HTMLReportSender()
    rs.sendReport()
}
```

Data Classes

In Java, you usually create data holder classes as POJOs (plain old Java objects) with just private properties and setters and getters. Then you implement the equals(), hashCode(), and toStirng() methods. Kotlin makes creating such classes very easy by using *data classes*.

```kotlin
data class Person(val name: String, val email: String)
```

Just by declaring a class as a data class, the Kotlin compiler will automatically generate the equals(), hashCode(), and equals() methods.

You can learn more about Kotlin at https://kotlinlang.org/docs/home.html.

Creating a Spring Boot Application Using Kotlin

You can create Spring Boot applications using Kotlin from the IDE or http://start.spring.io by selecting Kotlin as the language of choice.

411

If you are using the Maven build tool, kotlin-maven-plugin will be configured to use src/main/kotlin and src/test/kotlin as the main and test source code folders, respectively. See Listing 19-15.

Listing 19-15. pom.xml

```
<?xml version="1.0" encoding="UTF-8"?>
<project xmlns="http://maven.apache.org/POM/4.0.0"
    xmlns:xsi="http://www.w3.org/2001/XMLSchema-instance"
    xsi:schemaLocation="http://maven.apache.org/POM/4.0.0
    http://maven.apache.org/xsd/maven-4.0.0.xsd">
    <modelVersion>4.0.0</modelVersion>
    <groupId>com.apress</groupId>
    <artifactId>springboot-kotlin-demo</artifactId>
    <version>0.0.1-SNAPSHOT</version>
    <packaging>jar</packaging>
    <name>springboot-kotlin-demo</name>
    <parent>
        <groupId>org.springframework.boot</groupId>
        <artifactId>spring-boot-starter-parent</artifactId>
        <version>3.0.0-SNAPSHOT</version>
        <relativePath/>
    </parent>
    <properties>
        <kotlin.compiler.incremental>true</kotlin.compiler.incremental>
        <project.build.sourceEncoding>UTF-8</project.build.sourceEncoding>
        <project.reporting.outputEncoding>UTF-8</project.reporting.
        outputEncoding>
        <java.version>17</java.version>
        <kotlin.version>1.6.21</kotlin.version>
    </properties>
    <dependencies>
        ...
        ...
        <dependency>
            <groupId>org.jetbrains.kotlin</groupId>
```

```xml
            <artifactId>kotlin-stdlib</artifactId>
        </dependency>
        <dependency>
            <groupId>org.jetbrains.kotlin</groupId>
            <artifactId>kotlin-reflect</artifactId>
        </dependency>
        ...
        ...
    </dependencies>
    <build>
        <sourceDirectory>${project.basedir}/src/main/kotlin</sourceDirectory>
        <testSourceDirectory>${project.basedir}/src/test/kotlin
        </testSourceDirectory>
        <plugins>
            <plugin>
                <groupId>org.springframework.boot</groupId>
                <artifactId>spring-boot-maven-plugin</artifactId>
            </plugin>
            <plugin>
                <artifactId>kotlin-maven-plugin</artifactId>
                <groupId>org.jetbrains.kotlin</groupId>
                <configuration>
                    <args>
                        <arg>-Xjsr305=strict</arg>
                    </args>
                     <compilerPlugins>
                        <plugin>spring</plugin>
                    </compilerPlugins>
                </configuration>

                <dependencies>
                    <dependency>
                        <groupId>org.jetbrains.kotlin</groupId>
                        <artifactId>kotlin-maven-allopen</artifactId>
                        <version>${kotlin.version}</version>
                    </dependency>
```

```
            </dependencies>
        </plugin>
    </plugins>
</build>
<repositories>

    ...

</repositories>
<pluginRepositories>

    ...

</pluginRepositories>
</project>
```

Note that the Kotlin library dependencies `kotlin-stdlib` and `kotlin-reflect` are also added. With this configuration, you can place your Kotlin source code in `src/main/kotlin`, which will be automatically compiled using the Kotlin compiler.

If you are using the Gradle build tool, the `build.gradle.kts` file will be generated, as shown in Listing 19-16. Gradle provides out-of-the-box support for Kotlin Script (.kts) files to write the build scripts. Kotlin Scripts enable executing Kotlin code as scripts without prior compilation or packaging the code into executables.

Listing 19-16. build.gradle.kts

```
import org.jetbrains.kotlin.gradle.tasks.KotlinCompile
plugins {
    id("org.springframework.boot") version "3.0.0-SNAPSHOT"
    id("io.spring.dependency-management") version "1.0.11.RELEASE"
    kotlin("jvm") version "1.6.21"
    kotlin("plugin.spring") version "1.6.21"
}
group = "com.example"
version = "0.0.1-SNAPSHOT"
java.sourceCompatibility = JavaVersion.VERSION_17
repositories {
    mavenCentral()
    maven { url = uri("https://repo.spring.io/milestone") }
    maven { url = uri("https://repo.spring.io/snapshot") }
}
```

```
dependencies {
    implementation("org.springframework.boot:spring-boot-starter")
    implementation("org.jetbrains.kotlin:kotlin-reflect")
    implementation("org.jetbrains.kotlin:kotlin-stdlib")
    testImplementation("org.springframework.boot:spring-boot-
    starter-test")
}
tasks.withType<KotlinCompile> {
        kotlinOptions {
          freeCompilerArgs = listOf("-Xjsr305=strict")
          jvmTarget = "17"
        }
}
tasks.withType<Test> {
    useJUnitPlatform()
}
```

The Spring Framework needs configuration classes (classes annotated with @Configuration, @Service, @Component, @Repository, etc.) to be non-final so that it can create CGLIB proxies. But Kotlin classes are final by default. If you want to make a class non-final in Kotlin, you need to add the open modifier to the class.

```
open class Application {
}
```

Since this is a common requirement to be interoperable with many Java-based frameworks, Kotlin provides the all-open compiler plugin, which allows you to specify a list of annotations and make the classes with those annotations open by default. Then you don't have to add the open modifier manually.

The spring plugin opens classes annotated with Spring annotations, such as @Component, @Async, @Transactional, and @Cacheable, automatically. Since other Spring annotations, such as @Configuration, @Controller, @RestController, @Service, and @Repository, are meta-annotated with the @Component annotation, these classes will also be opened automatically. When you generate a Spring Boot application with Kotlin from the Spring Initializer, the kotlin-spring plugin is configured by default.

Now you'll see how to develop a simple web application with Spring Boot and Kotlin. Add the Web, Spring Data JPA, and Thymeleaf starter dependencies.

Create a JPA entity called User, as shown in Listing 19-17.

Listing 19-17. User.kt

```kotlin
import jakarta.persistence.*
@Entity
@Table(name="users")
class User(
        @Id @GeneratedValue(strategy = GenerationType.AUTO)
        var id: Long = -1,
        var name: String = "",
        var email: String = ""
        ) {
    override fun toString(): String {
        return "User(id=$id, name='$name', email='$email')"
    }
}
```

JPA entities should have a default constructor. One option is to have a User entity with a primary constructor using the var type properties with their default values. Another option is to create a no-arg default constructor as a secondary constructor and pass default values to the primary constructor.

Note   You can also use kotlin-jpa plugin to generate a no-arg constructor for JPA entities. Refer to https://kotlinlang.org/docs/no-arg-plugin. html#jpa-support for more information.

Listing 19-18 shows how to create a Spring Data JPA repository for the User entity.

Listing 19-18. UserRepository.kt

```kotlin
import org.springframework.data.jpa.repository.JpaRepository
interface UserRepository : JpaRepository<User, Long> {
    fun findByEmail(email: String): Iterable<User>
}
```

Create a SpringMVC controller to display the list of users, as shown in Listing 19-19.

Listing 19-19. HomeController.kt

```kotlin
import org.springframework.stereotype.Controller
import org.springframework.ui.Model
import org.springframework.web.bind.annotation.GetMapping

@Controller
class HomeController(val repository:UserRepository) {
    @GetMapping("/")
    fun home(model: Model): String {
        model.addAttribute("users", repository.findAll())
        return "home"
    }
}
```

You can reuse the `home.html` Thymeleaf template and `data.sql` script to populate sample users that you created in the previous section.

Finally, create the main entry point class, as shown in Listing 19-20.

Listing 19-20. SpringbootKotlinDemoApplication.kt

```kotlin
import org.springframework.boot.SpringApplication
import org.springframework.boot.autoconfigure.SpringBootApplication
@SpringBootApplication
open class SpringbootKotlinDemoApplication
fun main(args: Array<String>) {
    SpringApplication.run(SpringbootKotlinDemoApplication::class.java, *args)
}
```

This code creates the `main()` method as a top-level function. Now, running the `main()` method will start the application. You can then access `http://localhost:8080/`, which shows the list of users.

Summary

This chapter discussed creating a Spring Boot application using the JVM-based languages Groovy, Scala, and Kotlin. In the next chapter, you will learn about JHipster, a Yeoman-based Spring Boot application generator.

## CHAPTER 20

Introducing JHipster

JHipster is a Yeoman-based generator that creates Spring Boot-based web applications. JHipster configures a wide variety of tools and frameworks commonly used in Spring Boot applications, improving developer productivity.

This chapter covers how to install JHipster and create a monolithic application. It also explores the generated application features and looks at how to create entities using the sub-generator and JDL Studio.

Introducing JHipster

Technology is evolving rapidly and new tools, frameworks, and libraries are created daily. In recent years, there has been a lot of innovation in the JavaScript ecosystem and many high-quality, modern web development tools have been born. There are build tools like Webpack and Gulp. There are single page application (SPA) frameworks like React, Angular, and VueJS. And there are many JavaScript testing libraries like Mocha, Jasmine, and Jest. Integrating all of these tools manually is tedious and repetitive.

Yeoman (`http://yeoman.io/`) is a scaffolding tool that generates web projects following best practices. Yeoman provides various generators to scaffold web projects using various technologies. For example, if you want to create a React-based project, you can use `generator-react`, which will generate a ReactJS project with the Gulp build tool, with karma-based testing support.

JHipster (`www.jhipster.tech/`) is a Yeoman-based generator that generates Spring Boot-based web projects with a wide variety of options for building tools, front-end frameworks, relational databases, NoSQL databases, Spring security strategies, caching options, and more.

© K. Siva Prasad Reddy, Sai Upadhyayula 2023
K. S. P. Reddy and S. Upadhyayula, *Beginning Spring Boot 3*, https://doi.org/10.1007/978-1-4842-8792-7_20

With JHipster, you can generate Spring Boot applications with most configurations appropriately configured and then start implementing the business use cases. JHipster also provides sub-generators to generate JPA entities and a scaffolding UI for typical CRUD operations, making development faster.

Installing JHipster

JHipster is a Yeoman-based generator that depends on the NPM (Node Package Manager). The following section covers the prerequisites for using JHipster.

Prerequisites

Follow these steps to install JHipster:

1. Install JDK 17.

2. Install Git from `https://git-scm.com/`.

3. Install Node.js from `https://nodejs.org/`.

4. Run `npm install -g generator-jhipster`.

You should be able to run `jhipster --help` and see the various commands that JHipster supports.

Creating a JHipster Application

Creating a JHipster application is easy; you simply run the `jhipster` command and answer the questions based on your technology's preferences and application's needs. JHipster can generate a monolithic application or a microservices-based application.

In this chapter, you will create a simple monolithic blog application and then use the relational database `H2` for development and `MySQL` for production.

```
> mkdir jhipster-blog
> cd jhipster-blog
> jhipster
```

The jhipster command will ask you a series of questions. Select the options shown here:

? Which *type* of application would you like to create? Monolithic application (recommended for simple projects)
? What is the base name of your application? jhipsterblog
? Do you want to make it reactive with Spring Webflux? No
? What is your default Java package name? com.apress.jhblog
? Which *type* of authentication would you like to use? JWT authentication (stateless, with a token)
? Which *type* of database would you like to use? SQL (H2, PostgreSQL, MySQL, MariaDB, Oracle, MSSQL)
? Which *production* database would you like to use? MySQL
? Which *development* database would you like to use? H2 with in-memory persistence
? Which cache do you want to use? (Spring cache abstraction) Ehcache (local cache, for a single node)
? Do you want to use Hibernate 2nd level cache? Yes
? Would you like to use Maven or Gradle for building the backend? Maven
? Do you want to use the JHipster Registry to configure, monitor and scale your
application? No
? Which other technologies would you like to use?
? Which *Framework* would you like to use for the client? Angular
? Do you want to generate the admin UI? No
? Would you like to use a Bootswatch theme (https://bootswatch.com/)? Journal
? Choose a Bootswatch variant navbar theme (https://bootswatch.com/)? Primary
? Would you like to enable internationalization support? No
? Please choose the native language of the application English
? Besides JUnit and Jest, which testing frameworks would you like to use?
? Would you like to install other generators from the JHipster Marketplace? No

Based on the options selected here, JHipster will generate a Spring Boot application with the following features:

- Angular-based front end with Webpack configuration

- H2 in-memory database used in development and MySQL used for production

- Liquibase migration support for database migrations

- Spring Data JPA configured for database interaction

- Caching support configured using EHCache

- Spring Security JWT token-based authentication

- An administration dashboard showing application metrics using the Spring Boot Actuator

- Ability to change log levels at runtime through UI

- Open API-based Rest API documentation

- User accounts out of the box with login, change password, and new user registration functionality

You can run the application by running ./mvnw on Linux/MacOS or mvnw.cmd on Windows. This command will start the application dev profile and is accessible at http://localhost:8080/. Next, you'll explore the generated application.

As shown on the home page, you can log in with admin/admin, which has both the ROLE_USER and ROLE_ADMIN roles, or with user/user, which has only the ROLE_USER role.

Log in as the admin user using admin/admin. After a successful login, you will be redirected to the home page. The top navigation bar includes the Entities, Administration, and Account menus. As you haven't created any entities yet, there won't be any entities listed in the Entities menu.

For gateway and microservice-based applications, JHipster provides a default monitoring UI to view the application metrics, such as memory consumption, thread states, garbage collection details, and HTTP request statistics, which are provided using Micrometer (Figure 20-1).

Figure 20-1. *JHipster metrics dashboard*

Click Administration ➤ Database to open the H2 in-memory database console, where you can explore the current state of the database.

You can also manage the application's users by clicking Administration ➤ User Management, where you can perform CRUD operations on users. See Figure 20-2.

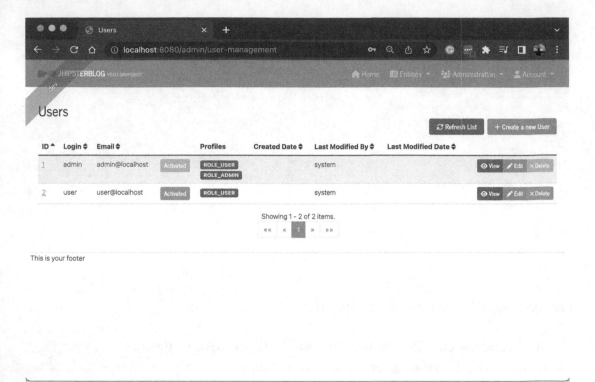

Figure 20-2. JHipster user management

You can view the Swagger documentation for the REST API by choosing Administration ➤ API. You can also view the Request and Response formats for each endpoint and trigger REST API calls by providing inputs if needed.

Creating Entities

Once the application is created, you may want to create entities and a scaffold UI for that entity to perform CRUD operations on it. JHipster provides ways to create entities and perform the following tasks:

- Create a JPA entity

- Create a database table based on the property information provided

- Create a Liquibase changeset for database migration

- Create a Spring Data JPA repository for the entity

- Create a Spring MVC REST controller with basic CRUD operations

- Create an Angular router, component, and service

- Create HTML views

- Generate integration and performance tests

You can generate entities using the `jhipster entity` sub-generator, the JHipster Domain Language (JDL) Studio, or the JHipster UML (`www.jhipster.tech/jhipster-uml/`). The following section uses the JHipster entity sub-generator and JDL Studio to generate entities.

Using the JHipster Entity Sub-Generator

You can generate entities using the `jhipster entity` sub-generator by providing a table name and column details, as follows:

```
jhipster entity Post --table-name posts
```

This command will ask whether you want to add a field to your entity. In this example, you'll add three fields named `title`, `content`, and `createdOn` and specify type and validation rules as follows:

- Name: `title`, Type: `String`, Validation: Required

- Name: `content`, Type: `String`, Validation: Required

- Name: `createdOn`, Type: `LocalDate`

Next, it will ask if you want to add a relationship to another entity. Answer no. You will learn how to manage relationships in the next section.

The following questions will be asked; answer them as follows:

```
? Do you want to use separate service class for your business logic?
? Is this entity read-only? No
? Do you want pagination and sorting on your entity? No
```

You can choose to create data transfer objects (DTOs), which will be used to create a response for the REST API, but for now, you can choose to return entities. You can also choose to create a service layer to perform any business logic, but you are choosing to directly use the Spring Data JPA repositories because there is no business logic involved. Lastly, you can choose whether you need pagination support or not.

After successfully running the JHipster entity sub-generator command, you can run the application and see the `Post` menu item in the Entities menu. You can perform the CRUD operations on the `Post` entity.

Instead of running the entity sub-generator and answering all these questions, you can use JDL Studio to create entities.

Using JDL Studio

JDL Studio is an online utility that creates entities and configures relationships among entities using the JHipster Domain Language (JDL). You can read about JDL at `www.jhipster.tech/jdl/intro`.

If you go to `https://start.jhipster.tech/jdl-studio/`, a sample domain model is configured with various entity definitions and relationships among those entities. Remove all of that and add the `Post` entity definition as follows:

```
entity Post {
        title String required
    content String required
    createdOn LocalDate
}
```

Click the "Download Text File of This JDL" link in the top-right corner. The jhipster-jdl.jdl file will download. Now you can run the `jhipster import-jdl` command to create the entities from the JDL file.

```
> jhipster import-jdl jhipster-jdl.jdl
```

After running this command, the `Post` entity, Spring Data JPA repository, Spring MVC controller, Angular front-end components, and more will be generated. If you already have a `Post` entity, it will update the entity.

Managing Relationships

You can use the JHipster `entity` command not only for creating entities but also to specify relationships among entities. For example, you can create a `Comment` entity, then establish a *one-to-many* relationship from `Post` to `Comment` and a *many-to-one* entity from `Comment` to `Post`.

While creating the Post entity using the `jhipster` entity sub-generator, you can specify the relationship to the Comment entity as follows:

```
> jhipster entity Post --table-name posts
```

As you already have a Post entity, it will display options to regenerate, add, and remove fields and relationships. Choose the following:

```
Yes, add more fields and relationships.
```

```
? Do you want to add a field to your entity? No
? Do you want to add a relationship to another entity? Yes
? What is the name of the other entity? Comment
? What is the name of the relationship? comments
? What is the type of the relationship? one-to-many
? What is the name of this relationship in the other entity? post
```

Now you can generate a Comment entity with the `name`, `email`, `content`, and `createdOn` fields. When prompted to add a relationship to another entity, you can add a many-to-one relationship from Comment to the Post entity as follows:

```
? What is the name of the other entity? Post
? What is the name of the relationship? post
? What is the type of the relationship? many-to-one
? When you display this relationship with Angular, which field from 'Post'
do you want to use? id
? Do you want to add any validation rules to this relationship? No
```

You can use JDL Studio to create entities and specify relationships among them as well. Configure the Post and Comment entities and the OneToMany relationship as follows:

```
entity Post {
        title String required
    content String required
    createdOn LocalDate
}
entity Comment {
        name String required
    email String required
```

```
    content String required
    createdOn LocalDate
}
relationship OneToMany {
  Post{comments} to Comment{post}
}
```

You can download this JDL file and import it as you did earlier. This will create JPA entities and establish JPA relationship as follows:

```
@Entity
@Table(name = "post")
@Cache(usage = CacheConcurrencyStrategy.READ_WRITE)
public class Post implements Serializable {
    ...
    ...
    @OneToMany(mappedBy = "post")
    @JsonIgnore
    @Cache(usage = CacheConcurrencyStrategy.READ_WRITE)
    private Set<Comment> comments = new HashSet<>();
    ...
    ...
}
@Entity
@Table(name = "comment")
@Cache(usage = CacheConcurrencyStrategy.READ_WRITE)
public class Comment implements Serializable {
    ...
    ...
    @ManyToOne
    private Post post;
}
```

JHipster scaffolding will generate a dropdown with posts to select while creating a comment.

You can read more about managing relationships at www.jhipster.tech/managing-relationships/.

By default, when you run `./mvnw`, the application will start in development mode using the dev profile. If you want to run the application in production mode, you can run it using the prod profile, as in `./mvnw -Pprod`.

You can also generate a runnable WAR file using the `./mvnw -Pprod package` command and run the application as follows:

```
java -jar jhipsterblog-0.0.1-SNAPSHOT.war
```

Various optimizations will be performed when you run the application in the production profile. For example, static assets like HTML, JS, and CSS files will be optimized and GZip compression will be configured.

Note   You can also use JHipster to generate Spring Boot-based microservices. To learn how to create microservices using JHipster, refer to `www.jhipster.tech/ microservices-architecture/`.

Summary

In this chapter, you learned how to use JHipster to generate Spring Boot-based web applications with the Angular front end. In the next chapter, you will look at how to run production applications and deploy a Spring Boot application on the Heroku cloud platform.

CHAPTER 21

Spring Native

Recently, serverless computing has gained much traction. Serverless computing is a cloud computing model where the cloud provider provisions the required resources for running an application on demand. With this model, you only provide resources for the application when it's actually in use. In traditional cloud computing models, when you allocate resources to a machine on any cloud provider, you must pay for the machine, even though the application is sitting idle. Serverless computing solves this issue because the resources are allocated only when the application is in use. No resources are allocated to an application if it's not in use.

For this reason, there is a need for your applications to start up and execute requests quickly and gracefully shut down within a matter of seconds. Spring Boot applications usually take longer to start up because they heavily use reflection to scan the classes and interfaces at runtime. The Spring Team came out with the Spring Native project, which supports compiling Spring applications to native executables using the GraalVM native-image compiler. You can read more about GraalVM at `www.oracle.com/java/graalvm/what-is-graalvm/`.

By using Spring Native, you can compile your applications to native images, drastically reducing the application's startup time. In this chapter, you will learn how to use Spring Native. Please note that at the time of writing this book, Spring Native is in the experimental stage. You can refer to the official documentation to see the latest changes at `https://docs.spring.io/spring-native/docs/current/reference/htmlsingle/#overview`.

Let's see how to improve the startup time of your Spring blog application using Spring Native.

431

© K. Siva Prasad Reddy, Sai Upadhyayula 2023
K. S. P. Reddy and S. Upadhyayula, *Beginning Spring Boot 3*, https://doi.org/10.1007/978-1-4842-8792-7_21

Getting Started

To get started, ensure you have the following software installed on your machine:

- Docker

- Java 17 (or) the latest LTS version

- GraalVM

Once you have the necessary software, open the Spring blog application and add the following dependencies to the pom.xml file. You can refer to the GitHub repository to find the starter code.

```
<dependency>
    <groupId>org.springframework.experimental</groupId>
    <artifactId>spring-native</artifactId>
    <version>${spring-native.version}</version>
</dependency>
```

The spring-native.version property is tightly coupled with the Spring Boot version. Make sure you check the compatible versions. At the time of writing, Spring Native version 0.12.1 is compatible with Spring Boot version 2.7.2, and Spring Boot version 3 is not yet supported.

Building a Native Image Using Buildpacks

Now, let's add the native image support using Spring Boot's Cloud Native Build pack support, as discussed in Chapter 16. Replace the spring-boot-maven-plugin with the following plugin configuration:

```
<plugin>
    <groupId>org.springframework.boot</groupId>
    <artifactId>spring-boot-maven-plugin</artifactId>
    <configuration>
        <image>
            <builder>paketobuildpacks/builder:tiny</builder>
            <env>
```

```
        <BP_NATIVE_IMAGE>true</BP_NATIVE_IMAGE>
      </env>
    </image>
  </configuration>
</plugin>
```

Notice that here you are passing environment variable `BP_NATIVE_IMAGE` as true for the `spring-boot-maven-plugin` for the Build pack to create a native image of your application.

Next, you need to add the Spring AOT plugin, which performs the ahead-of-time transformation required to improve native image compatibility and footprint.

To build your Spring Boot application as a native image, run the following command:

```
mvn spring-boot:build-image -DskipTests
```

This command creates a Docker container to build a native application image using the GraalVM native image compiler. Make sure you have enough memory allocated to your Docker instance, at least 8GB, or you may have problems building the image.

After the build is done, you can check for the docker image by running this command:

```
docker images –filter reference=<name-of-your-springboot-app>
```

Now you can run the image to create a native application container by running this command:

```
docker run -p 8080:8080 <name-of-app>:0.0.1-SNAPSHOT
```

If you didn't change the `<version>` tag value inside `pom.xml`, you can leave the snapshot version as 0.0.1-SNAPSHOT.

Now your Spring Boot application starts within <1 second. Of course, the startup varies based on the system configuration, but it should be significantly faster compared to the normal Spring Boot application.

```
c.a.d.springblog.SpringblogApplication   : Started SpringblogApplication in
0.274 seconds (JVM running for 0.276)
```

If you run the `SpringblogApplication.java` class in the starter code of the GitHub repository, you can observe that the application takes approximately 2-3 seconds. The startup time usually depends on the system configuration. On my system, at the time of writing, it took 2.356 seconds.

```
INFO 92136 --- [              main] c.a.d.springblog.SpringblogApplication    :
Started SpringblogApplication in 2.356 seconds (process running for 3.018)
```

You can view the difference in the startup time in Figure 21-1.

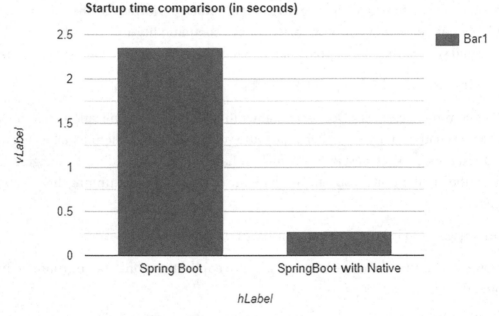

Figure 21-1. *Spring Boot and Spring Boot Native startup time comparison*

By using Spring Native, you will spend more time building the application compared to the start-up time. This is a fair trade-off since you mainly want to improve the application startup time. Figure 21-2 shows the build time comparison between Spring Boot and Spring Boot Native apps. The Spring Boot application `mvn clean package` took 13 seconds to complete on my machine, whereas the Spring Native build command `mvn spring-boot:build-image` took 319 seconds.

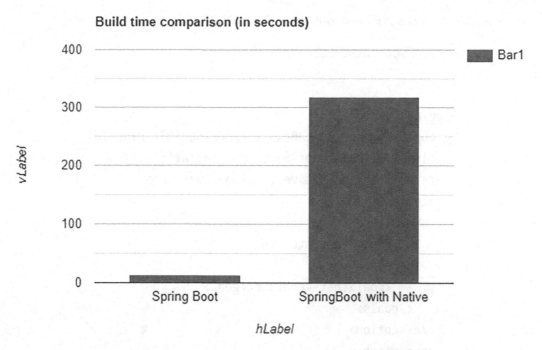

Figure 21-2. *Spring Boot and Spring Native build time comparison*

Building Native Images Using GraalVM Native Build Tools

In the previous section, you saw how to create a native image using Buildpacks backed by Docker. Now let's see how to use the GraalVM compiler to build a native executable file of your application.

In addition to the above setup, add the GraalVM-enabled native Maven plugin (`spring-aot-maven-plugin`) to your `pom.xml` file. This plugin will invoke the GraalVM native image compiler from the build.

To call the native image compiler, even when running the build outside an IDE, use the `junit-platform-launcher` dependency. To control the execution of this plugin and activate the necessary dependencies, set this configuration in a separate Maven profile called `native`.

This is how your pom.xml will look after all the configurations are added:

```xml
<?xml version="1.0" encoding="UTF-8"?>
..
...
            <plugin>
            <groupId>org.springframework.experimental</groupId>
            <artifactId>spring-aot-maven-plugin</artifactId>
            <version>${spring-native.version}</version>
            <executions>
                <execution>
                    <id>test-generate</id>
                    <goals>
                        <goal>test-generate</goal>
                    </goals>
                </execution>
                <execution>
                    <id>generate</id>
                    <goals>
                        <goal>generate</goal>
                    </goals>
                </execution>
            </executions>
        </plugin>

    <profiles>
        <profile>
            <id>native</id>
            <properties>
                <repackage.classifier>exec</repackage.classifier>
            </properties>
            <dependencies>
                <dependency>
                    <groupId>org.junit.platform</groupId>
                    <artifactId>junit-platform-launcher</artifactId>
                    <scope>test</scope>
```

```
            </dependency>
        </dependencies>
        <build>
            <plugins>
                <plugin>
                    <groupId>org.graalvm.buildtools</groupId>
                    <artifactId>native-maven-plugin</artifactId>
                    <version>0.9.13</version>
                    <extensions>true</extensions>
                    <executions>
                        <execution>
                            <id>test-native</id>
                            <phase>test</phase>
                            <goals>
                                <goal>test</goal>
                            </goals>
                        </execution>
                        <execution>
                            <id>build-native</id>
                            <phase>package</phase>
                            <goals>
                                <goal>build</goal>
                            </goals>
                        </execution>
                    </executions>
                </plugin>
            </plugins>
        </build>
    </profile>
</profiles>

</project>
```

To build the native application, you can run the following command:

```
mvn -Pnative clean package
```

After running this command, based on the operating system, an executable file will be generated under the target directory of your project. Just launch the executable file to start the application.

Lastly, if you are facing any issues while building the application, have a look at the "Troubleshooting" section of the Spring Native documentation at `https://docs.` `spring.io/spring-native/docs/current/reference/htmlsingle/#troubleshooting`.

Limitations of Spring Native

As mentioned, Spring Native is still in the experimental stage, so it's not so straightforward to use it directly in your production application because you need to do some configuration changes for some libraries to work with Spring Native.

As of now, with Spring Native version 0.12.1, the following libraries require some special build configuration:

- `spring-boot-starter-web`
  - Only Tomcat is supported as the webserver.
  - If you want to enable HTTPS support, you must add the –enable-https flag.
- `spring-boot-starter-actuator`
- `spring-boot-starter-test`
  - Mockito is not yet supported.

You can keep track of the changes by referring to the official documentation section at `https://docs.spring.io/spring-native/docs/current/reference/htmlsingle/#_` `starters_requiring_special_build_configuration`.

You can find other limitations at `https://docs.spring.io/spring-native/docs/` `current/reference/htmlsingle/#limitations`.

Summary

In this chapter, you learned how to compile your Spring Boot applications as native images and executables using Spring Native.

Index

A

Access token, 241–245, 255, 258–260, 262

Akka Streams, 186

allPosts method, 326

Annotation-based programming model, 190–196

antMatchers() method, 229

Application.java, 26, 43, 298

application-prod.properties file, 49, 342, 343

application-qa.properties file, 49, 342, 343

@Argument annotation, 332

AssertJ, 298

Authentication, 215, 218, 220–222, 231, 233

Authorization, 215, 240–242, 255

Authorization code flow, 243, 244, 262–266

Authorization Server, 241–256

AuthServerConfiguration.java, 251

Autoconfiguration, 1, 27, 30, 88, 111, 163, 361, 372–376, 383–385

@AutoConfigureHttpGraphQlTester annotation, 338

B

BaseTest, 323

BCrypt, 230

BCryptPasswordEncoder, 230

@BeanProperty, 408

Blog post, 60, 61, 65, 72, 74, 82, 162

C

Client Credentials grant flow, 244, 245, 256

Cloud computing models, 431

Comment entity, 426, 427

@Conditional annotations, 369, 370, 372

Configuration properties
    application.properties file, 49
    @PropertySource annotation, 49
    relaxed binding, 51
    type-safe, 50, 51
    validation, 52

@ConfigurationProperties, 51, 276, 381

Containerization technologies, 341

@Controller annotation, 64, 164, 190

createPost() method, 164, 194

Create, Read, Update, Delete (CRUD), 140, 153

Cross-Origin Resource Sharing (CORS)
    API consumers, 173
    class-and method-level, 174, 175
    global configuration, 175
    REST API, 173

Cross-Site Request Forgery (CSRF), 215, 216, 236, 237

CrudRepository, 140, 192

CSRF token, 236, 237

Custom user authentication, 218–221

CustomUserDetailsService, 220

© K. Siva Prasad Reddy, Sai Upadhyayula 2023
K. S. P. Reddy and S. Upadhyayula, *Beginning Spring Boot 3*, https://doi.org/10.1007/978-1-4842-8792-7

Printed in the United States
by Baker & Taylor Publisher Services